John H. Egar

The Threefold Grace of the Holy Trinity

John H. Egar

The Threefold Grace of the Holy Trinity

ISBN/EAN: 9783337286583

Printed in Europe, USA, Canada, Australia, Japan

Cover: Foto ©Lupo / pixelio.de

More available books at **www.hansebooks.com**

THE

THREEFOLD GRACE

OF

THE HOLY TRINITY.

BY

JOHN H. EGAR, B.D.,

RECTOR OF ST. PETER'S CHURCH, PITTSBURG, PA.

PHILADELPHIA:
J. B. LIPPINCOTT & CO.
1870.

PREFACE.

THE sole ambition of this book is to restate in the simplest manner, and with such illustration and reasoning as may show their systematic coherence, those practical truths relating to Divine grace which the author believes the Holy Scriptures teach and the Church has always held. Ever since he became familiar with theological studies he has felt that the two extremes of thought allowed in the communion to which he belongs have, in a manner, divided these truths between them, and that the antagonism developed by their divergence arises from overlooking the fact that the principles of the opposite schools are but the other halves, respectively, of the doctrine which each holds. The one side insists, not a whit too strongly, upon the practical bearings of the Incarnation, and its relation to the Christian Sacraments; but it does seem to give too little place in its system to the extra-sacramental grace of the Holy Spirit, and so to obscure "the witness of the Spirit with our spirit that we are the children of God." The other side, dwelling with equal truth on the extra-sacramental grace of the Holy Spirit, given to every man and indwelling in the true believer, does not sufficiently insist upon the grace of the Incarnate Son, and His personal presence with His Redeemed; and so learns to depreciate the Sacraments, which are the Divinely-appointed instruments of sealing and exhibiting that presence to the faithful soul; and so, further, overlooks the blessedness of the Church as a body separate from the world, in sacramental communion with its Divine, incarnate Head.

The author does not flatter himself that his effort will be immediately successful in reconciling the differences which have sprung up from these one-sided views; but he believes that the system of the Church Catholic not only includes the positive teaching of both parties, but combines them in the unity of Truth; and he has endeavored to point the way in which abler minds than his will labor successfully to bring harmony out of the apparent discord.

Another object which he has had in view, has been to show the relation of the doctrine of the Trinity not only to speculative belief, but to the Christian life. He has felt that the argument for the doctrine, however powerfully and logically put, has failed in energetic influence upon many minds, because it has not been carried forward so as to unfold the experimental communion of the faithful soul with the Divine Persons of the Holy Trinity. Many sincerely religious people do not feel the necessity of faith in Christ as the eternal Son of God, because their apprehension of Christian doctrine does not assign Him a part in the work of grace commensurate with His Divinity. The view given them is something like this: that the Father, being angry with the human race on account of sin, the Son came to earth and made an atonement by dying on the cross; after which He went to heaven, and the Holy Spirit was sent to exert a Divine influence upon their hearts for their conversion. True as every word of this statement is, it does not impress them with an adequate sense of the magnitude of Christ's work, because it is only partial truth. They are able to persuade themselves that God, being a loving Father, can forgive sin without an atonement; and in this way, having eliminated the work of the Son from the scheme of Redemption, they can remove His Person from the Trinity, and then, assuming Divine grace to be the Father's influence upon the hearts of His children, the result is either avowed Unitarianism, or the feeling that the doctrine of the Trinity is only of speculative importance, and not at all of practical value, and therefore not a necessary article of Christian faith.

The remedy for this error consists in demonstrating the personal presence of our Lord with His people, bringing, by sacramental union, the saving virtue of the Atonement into personal contact with their experience,—the Holy Spirit, as the agent of the union, first preparing the heart by conversion and sanctification, and then grafting the Christian into Christ, as the branch into the vine. If Christian doctrine is presented in this way, the omnipresence, and therefore the Divinity of our blessed Lord, is brought home to the apprehension of Christian faith; the Atonement is given its true value, as a propitiation offered to the Father; the three Persons are shown in intimate relation to the soul; and the doctrine of the Trinity is demonstrated as it never can be by mere argument upon texts of Holy Scripture.

This book is but a mere outline of the great subject of which it treats. It is sent forth with the earnest prayer that the Head of the Church will bless it to the furtherance of the Truth.

St. Peter's Church,
  Pittsburg, Whitsuntide, 1870.

CONTENTS.

CHAPTER I.
The Mystery of the Holy Trinity 9

CHAPTER II.
The Grace of God the Father 43

CHAPTER III.
The Grace of the Son 82

CHAPTER IV.
The Grace of the Holy Spirit 184

CHAPTER V.
The Place of the Sacraments in the System of Grace . . 238

THE THREEFOLD GRACE

OF

THE HOLY TRINITY

CHAPTER I.

THE MYSTERY OF THE HOLY TRINITY.

WE are baptized, by the command of our Lord, "in the name of the Father, and of the Son, and of the Holy Ghost;"[a] and therefore every one who is admitted by baptism into the Church of Christ is bound to belief in the Most Holy Trinity. For a minister to baptize a reflecting convert upon any other understanding—to act in the name—that is, by the power and authority—of a Being in whom that convert was not understood to profess belief, would be to sap his authority at the foundation, and to degrade the most solemn function of his office to be considered a fiction. For the convert to be met, at his entrance into the Church, with a ceremony which he is at liberty to con-

---

[a] Matt. xxviii. 19.

sider unmeaning, would be fatal to the strength of any of his religious convictions, and would lead him to disregard all his religious obligations. Neither the minister nor the convert could thus tamper with the Sacrament. So long, therefore, as baptism is administered according to the form prescribed by our Lord Jesus Christ, it will pledge the administrator to require and the convert to hold the faith in the divine name then pronounced, whether in the baptismal office the Apostles' creed have been formally recited or not. The bowing of the head to receive the water administered in that name is full and sufficient confession.

It cannot be otherwise than that such an initiation into the Church was prescribed in order to make the confession of faith in the Holy Trinity essential to her existence, and necessary to the salvation of her members. The truth contained in the baptismal formula is, by the appointment of that formula, separated from other truths which are not contained therein; it is laid at the foundation, and declared to be the chief truth of all. The formula itself, by being pronounced at the beginning of the professedly Christian life, must be recognized as intended by the founder of the Church to assert that faith in the Holy Trinity lies at the foundation of all our religious beliefs. The following pages are written to show that this faith is also the foundation of all practical knowledge of the Gospel; for the Father, the Son, and the Holy Ghost, of whom it teaches, are each personally in the closest relation with us, if we be true Christians, each operative in the work of our salvation through the threefold grace of the Triune God.

The mystery of the Being of God, to faith in which

we are thus pledged, is revealed in the Holy Scriptures. Their authority is the ground of its reception. Their doctrine is clearly, that the Lord our God is One; but that in the Divine Unity there are three Persons—the Father, the Son, and the Holy Ghost. The mystery of this doctrine consists in this, that God is not only *essentially*, but *numerically*, One, and yet the Persons in the Godhead are three. In the language of the Athanasian Creed, "The Father is God; and the Son, God; and the Holy Ghost, God; and yet there are not three Gods, but one God." Nevertheless, the Father is not the Son; nor the Son, the Father; neither the Father, nor the Son, is the Holy Ghost. That this Triune existence is incomprehensible to our understandings, there is no need to confess; but it would be easy to show that it is no more incomprehensible than some proposition in any possible doctrine of the Infinite and Eternal; and therefore it is not to be objected to on this ground.

The connection of the doctrine of the Trinity with our religious duty and experience is that which originates the necessity of our receiving it. The Father enters into relation with us, through the Gospel, as God the Father; the Son, in like manner, enters into relation with us as God the Son; the Holy Ghost the same, as God the Holy Ghost. We must know this relation and act according to it, to do our duty aright, and to have a well-grounded hope of salvation.

Our first labor, then, is a collation of those passages of Scripture in which the truth of the Holy Trinity is taught.

1. God is One. There would be little need to offer

scriptural proof of the Unity of God, since all who believe in the existence of a God acknowledge a supreme unity, were there not a possible misconception of the doctrine of the Trinity which would degrade it into Tritheism.[a] Indeed, there would be no need at all of this chapter, were it not that this book will fall into the hands of some who have not access to the theological treasures of past ages of the Church, nor leisure to read more voluminous writers. For their sakes are here presented the outlines of the arguments by which the Catholic faith is proved to be the truth of the Divine Revelation.

The first commandment of the Decalogue, proclaimed amidst the clouds and thunderings of Mount Sinai, is so peremptory as to shut out all thoughts that there are other Gods than One, were there no other passage of the same tenor in Scripture: "I am the Lord thy God; thou shalt have none other Gods but me."[b] The Decalogue is of universal authority; its mandates are as binding upon all mankind as upon the Israelites.

At the second giving of the Law, Moses relates as follows, the reason for all the wonders which God had displayed before His people, during their forty years in the wilderness: "Unto thee it was showed, that thou mightest know that the Lord He is God; there is none else beside Him."[c] For which reason he counsels the

---

[a] This is a misconception which even so learned a man as Adam Clarke fell into—a proof of the uselessness of learning without judgment, in theology.

[b] Exodus, xx. 2, 3.   [c] Deut. iv. 35.

people thus: "Know therefore this day, and consider it in thy heart, that the Lord He is God in Heaven above, and upon the earth beneath: there is none else."[a] In another place his language is: "Hear, O Israel: the Lord our God is one Lord; and thou shalt love the Lord thy God with all thy heart, and with all thy soul, and with all thy might."[b] And in the close of that sublime song which he sang under divine inspiration, just before he went into Mount Nebo to die, the mortal instrument disappears, and the Divine Inspirer, in His own person, utters the words: "See, now, that I, even I, am He, and there is no God with me: I kill and I make alive; I wound and I heal; neither is there any that can deliver out of my hand."[c]

In Solomon's prayer, at the dedication of the Temple, he ascribes to the one God alone the Divine attribute of Omniscience: "Thou only knowest the hearts of the children of men."

The writer of the eighteenth Psalm, in the fervor of his inspired song, throws his denial of any other Deity besides the Lord into that form which, above all others, gives it force and energy—an interrogation: "Who is God, but the Lord? or who is a rock [*i.e.* of safety], save our God?"[d] And in the sixty-second Psalm the Psalmist confesses his trust in one only God: "He only is my Rock and my salvation."[e]

The evangelical prophet, Isaiah, rises to the most sublime heights, when he is brought into contact with heathen idolatry and Persian dualism, in emphatic re-

---

[a] Deut. iv. 39.   [b] Deut. vi. 4, 5.   [c] Deut. xxxii. 39.
[d] Ps. xviii. 31.   [e] Ps. lxii. 6.

pudiation of all partners in God's glory. Between the fortieth and fiftieth chapters, especially, the passages are very numerous, as thus:

"I am the Lord, that is my name, and my glory will I not give to another."[a] "Thus saith the Lord, the King of Israel, and his Redeemer, the Lord of Hosts, I am the first, and I am the last, and beside Me there is no God."[b] "Is there a God beside Me? yea, there is no God, I know not any."[c] "I am the Lord, and there is none else, there is no God beside Me, that they may know from the rising of the sun, and from the West, that there is none beside Me. I am the Lord, and there is none else."[d] "Thus saith the Lord that created the Heavens; God Himself that formed the earth and made it. He hath established it, He hath created it not in vain, He formed it to be inhabited; I am the Lord, and there is none else."[e] "Tell ye, and bring them near; yea, let them [*i.e.* idolaters] take counsel together. Who hath declared this from ancient times? Who hath told it from that time? Have not I, the Lord? and there is no God else beside Me; a just God and a Saviour; there is none beside Me. Look unto me and be ye saved, all the ends of the earth; for I am God, and there is none else."[f] "Hearken unto Me, O Jacob and Israel, my called; I am He, I am the first, I also am the last."[g]

The New Testament, of course, has the same doctrine. When the devil tempted the Saviour, and

---

[a] Is. xlii. 8. [c] Ch. xliv. 8. [e] Ch. xlv. 18.
[b] Ch. xliv. 6. [d] Ch. xlv. 5, 6. [f] Ch. xlv. 21, 22.
[g] Ch. xlviii. 12.

sought to allure Him to sin against the first commandment, the Lord rebuked him by a quotation from the Old Testament: "It is written, Thou shalt worship the Lord thy God, and Him only shalt thou serve."[a] In His sacrificial prayer, the Saviour thus worships the Father: "This is life eternal, that they might know Thee, the only True God."[b] "We know," says St. Paul, "that an idol is nothing in the world, and that there is none other God but one."[c] And, "To us there is but one God, the Father."[d]

These passages abundantly declare that no teaching supposed to be derived from Holy Scripture may be accepted as militating against the truth of the absolute and simple unity of the Divine Being. They show that the doctrine of the Trinity cannot be that of "three persons in one Godhead," as if the three were one merely in council and association; but that it is the doctrine of the Litany: "Holy, blessed, and glorious Trinity, three persons and one God."

The last text cited introduces the second point in the Christian knowledge of God—that He is a Father. The one God, of whom alone the Scriptures speak as the true and living God, and whom alone we worship, is everlastingly a Father. It is the assertion of our faith that God's relation as a Father is coeternal with His existence as God. He cannot be God and not be a Father. The name does not spring from a merely temporal relationship; it was not assumed by God simply because He has created a universe over which

---

[a] Matt. iv. 10.
[b] John, xvii. 3.
[c] I. Cor. viii. 4.
[d] I. Cor. viii. 6.

He exercises providential care. It has a deeper ground than the creation or preservation of temporal things. God was the Father before the existence of the universe, or anything it contains; as always God, so always Father. Everlastingly existing, He never was when He was not a Father; because he is from everlasting to everlasting the Father of the Son, into whose name we are baptized. The Son of God, by begetting whom He takes to Himself His name of Father, is an eternal Son; and therefore He is an eternal Father. From this paternal relation spring all the acts of God to the temporal creation, as the Father of created beings. Hence we shall best reach the Scripture declarations of the greater truth, through the door and vestibule of the less—tracing, after the manner of our masters in theology, the lower relations of God's temporal paternity, and so ascending, step by step, to the eternal.[a]

The first sense in which God is called the Father arises from His relation to all things as their Creator, through that figurative mode of expression by which the creation of inanimate and irrational matter is called a generation. "These," said Moses, "are the *generations* of the heavens and the earth, when they were created in the day that the Lord God made the heavens and the earth."[b] Hence the book of Job represents God as asking Job, among other questions,

---

[a] The learned reader will see that these pages are but an epitome of Bishop Pearson's statements in his " Exposition of the Creed."

[b] Gen. ii. 1.

"Hath the rain a Father? or who hath begotten the drops of dew?"[a] So St. James calls God "the Father of lights."[b] And St. Paul, though implying the eternal as well as the temporal relation, "To us there is but one God, the Father, of whom are all things."[c]

A nearer approach to a realization of true paternity, and a higher sense in which the name Father is used, is when it is employed to denote God's relation to intelligent and moral beings, who, as possessed of freedom and intelligence, are said to be "made in the image of God."[d] For it is the true notion of paternity that it produces an offspring like the parent. Hence St. Luke, tracing back the genealogy of our Lord, carries it up to "Adam, who was the Son of God."[e] This was a truth of which the heathen were conscious, as St. Paul argued at Athens, quoting, from the Greek poet, the line, "For we are also His offspring." Hence, with the greatest propriety, in the Epistle to the Hebrews, God is called "The Father of Spirits;"[f] for He is a Spirit, and in creating finite Spirits, He has produced an offspring like Himself. So, by the prophet Malachi, we are taught just dealing one towards another, on the motive of a common brotherhood, enforced by this argument: "Have we not all one Father? Hath not one God created us?"[g]

God is also called a Father, because of His paternal care in the preservation of the beings He has created: "A Father of the fatherless, and a Judge of the widows,

---

[a] Job, xxxviii. 28. [c] I. Cor. viii. 6. [e] Luke, iii. 38.
[b] James, i. 17. [d] Gen. i. 27. [f] Heb. xii. 9.
[g] Mal. ii. 10.

is God in His holy habitation,"[a] says the Psalmist. "Behold the fowls of the air," says the Saviour, "your heavenly Father feedeth them."[b] "Therefore take no thought, saying, What shall we eat, or what shall we drink, or wherewithal shall we be clothed? for your heavenly Father knoweth that ye have need of all these things."[c] "Your Father knoweth what things ye have need of before ye ask Him."[d] And on this ground of likeness to God, in His care for our preservation, notwithstanding ingratitude, our Lord inculcates the return of good for evil, thus: "Love your enemies, . . . that ye may be the children of your Father which is in Heaven; for He maketh His sun to rise on the evil and on the good, and sendeth rain on the just and on the unjust."[e]

The mercy of Redemption, again, is allowed to be a part of the paternal relation; hence Isaiah, in the person of the captives of Israel, addresses God thus: "Doubtless Thou art our Father, though Abraham be ignorant of us, and Israel acknowledge us not; Thou, O Lord, art our Father, our Redeemer, from everlasting is thy name." And the same may be our language; for though the Son be the agent of Redemption, and therefore is called more commonly the Redeemer, yet it was the Fatherly love of God which planned the redemption of the world; for "God so loved the world that He gave His only-begotten Son, that whosoever believeth in Him should not perish, but have everlasting life."

---

[a] Ps. lxviii. 5.   [b] Matt. vi. 26.   [c] Matt. vi. 31, 32.
[d] Matt. vi. 8.   [e] Matt. v. 45.

We have a new claim to the title of Sons, and are enabled to call God our Father, by our Regeneration, —the return back, by new birth, into that state of Sonship, the title to which man had lost through sin. "Except a man be born again, he cannot see the Kingdom of God,"[a] is the word of our Saviour, which He reiterates more solemnly: "Verily, verily, I say unto thee, Except a man be born of water and of the Spirit, he cannot enter into the Kingdom of God." Being regenerate, we are children and offspring of God, by partaking of the Sonship of Christ, who only is the true and eternal Son of God. For, "as many as received Him, to them gave He power to become the Sons of God, even to them that believe on His name. Which were born not of blood, nor of the will of the flesh, nor of the will of man, but of God;"[b] and therefore God is their Father.

Our regeneration is called also by the name of adoption, and therefore our teachers in the faith have observed that God is our Father also, if we be regenerate, by the way of adoption. "Behold," says St. John, "what manner of love the Father hath bestowed upon us, that we should be called the sons of God."[c] That love was shown in this way: "When the fulness of the time was come, God sent forth His Son, made of a woman, made under the law, to redeem them that were under the law, that we might receive the adoption of sons. And because ye are sons, God hath sent forth the Spirit of His Son into your hearts, crying, Abba, Father."[d] "For ye have not received the

---

[a] John, iii. 3.
[b] John, i. 12, 13.
[c] I. John, iii. 1.
[d] Gal. iv. 4-6.

Spirit of bondage again to fear; but ye have received the Spirit of adoption, whereby we cry, Abba, Father."[a]

To crown all, God will make Himself our Father in yet another way, by bringing us again from the dead. "They which shall be accounted worthy to obtain that world, and the Resurrection from the dead, are equal unto the angels, and are the children of God, being the children of the Resurrection."[b]

We thus see that Holy Scripture attributes the title of Father to God, as being our Creator and Preserver in the Kingdom of Nature, the author of our Redemption and Regeneration in the Kingdom of His grace, and the worker of our Resurrection into the Kingdom of His glory. The notion of a Father, therefore, belongs essentially to our knowledge of God; we cannot think of Him truly, except under that notion. This truth appears so clearly from the relation of ourselves as created and dependent beings to the Supreme Governor and Creator, that those who impugn the doctrine of the Trinity produce these grounds of the title as sufficient to justify it in its whole extent; trusting that those who listen to them will accept them without inquiring for a sense beyond; thinking that if they can content the mind with a plausible explanation, it will be apt to rest short of a true one. It is necessary, therefore, to disarm them by enumerating all the grounds for the title acknowledged by Holy Scripture, arising out of temporal relations, and then to show that there is still another and infinitely higher reason for the acknowl-

---

[a] Rom. viii. 15.   [b] Luke, xx. 35, 36.

edgment of God the Father in His begetting His eternal Son. We are brought thus to the consideration of the truth that the being a Father is eternally and essentially an attribute of Deity, because He is the eternal Father of His only-begotten Son. He is the Father of the created, because He is the Father of the uncreated; the earthly sonship is the shadow of the heavenly. He is the Father, because of Himself, not because of us.

I have arranged the argument thus, advisedly. In considering Truth, which is objectively indivisible, we are compelled, by the subjective conditions of thought, to separate one notion from another, and thus make logical, when there are no real divisions. I began for this reason, with the conception of the unity of God—that there is one, self-existent, Supreme Being, the first cause and controller of all things. But the mental notion, "one self-existent Supreme Being," does not necessarily contain the conception of Personality, which we must add to it, to reach the true idea of God. Now the Scripture helps us to the conception of God's Personality, by pronouncing His name, "The Father," in connection with the exercise of all these acts of creation, preservation, and redemption above enumerated. He might be a "first cause," and be impersonal; but not so a "Father." To be a Father He must be a person; for all paternal attributes are personal attributes. And conversely, to be a person He must be a Father; for were God not a Father, He would be inert, without offspring, without affection, without any personal attributes; and therefore impersonal. But God never was nor could have been impersonal. He is, therefore, ever the Father. The Divine essence or Being is ever personal as God the Father. This is what we have next to prove from Holy Scripture,—that God is eternally the Father. We shall show also, with equal conclusiveness from Holy Scripture, that the same Divine Nature is also personal in the persons of the Son and of the Holy Ghost.

To guard, however, against every mistake, the reader is requested to fix in his mind the truth that the Divine Nature is simple and indivisible, and as well as infinite and eternal. When we say, therefore, that God is the Father, we mean that the whole Divine Nature, which is eternally self-existent in simple unity of essence, is ever personal in the person of the Father. The proposition is the precise logical equivalent of its converse, the Father is God. The same is true when we say that God is the Son, or the Son is God. We do not by this assert that there is no other person who is God except the Son; but we do assert that there is naught of the Divine nature which the Son does not possess— that the whole Divine Nature is in the Son, as in the Father. The same nature[a] is in the Son and in the Father; in the Father, originally, in the Son, by eternal[b] derivation from the Father. The Divine Being subsists originally, therefore, and absolutely, as

---

[a] *i.e.* the self-same—numerically identical.

[b] Those who accept Locke's absurd definition of eternity, cannot, of course, accept the doctrine of the Trinity. Hence the rise of Socinianism in England, together with the "philosophy" of Locke.

God the Father; derivatively, as God the Son and God the Holy Ghost. That old scholastic realism which held that the Divine Nature was (as it were) a fountain whence were derived, or a *matrix* in which inhered, the three Personalities of the Trinity, is altogether to be shunned. The Father is the fountain of the Divinity, whence is derived the Son and the Holy Spirit. Hence, in the Holy Scripture, when the name of God is spoken without any adjunct determining it to another person of the Trinity,—it is generally[a] intended to refer to the Father—not to the Divine Nature, or to the threefold personality. The Holy Scripture, dealing with realities, and not with logical conceptions, does not distinguish between the Divine Nature and the Divine Person. In our thought, only, do we thus separate conceptions; in the reality all is one. God is always self-existent, and always personal, that is, always a Father. But to be always a Father, He has always a Son, who, being ever-existent, is God, since there is nothing eternal but God, and who, therefore, is the self-same God with the Father, though not the same Person.

The Second Person of the Holy Trinity, thus being both in essence and in person eternally derived from the Father in a way in which no other being is, is for this reason called "the only-begotten Son of God"[b]—only begotten, that is, in this high sense, as eternally begotten, and so eternally existing. In contradistinction to the temporal and momentary generation by which we receive our being, the act by which the Only-be-

---

[a] *Generally*, but not universally.   [b] John, iii. 18.

gotten Son of God receives His being is an eternal act—an act never begun and never ending, eternally proceeding from the infinite activity of God.[a] And this is the meaning of that well-known theological phrase, the "eternal generation of the Only-begotten Son."

This is the doctrine which we have now to prove; and it will be established from Holy Scripture, by showing, first, that God is called pre-eminently, and most frequently, the Father of our Lord Jesus Christ; and conversely, that our Lord is called the only Son, or only-begotten Son of God. Secondly, that Jesus Christ, the only Son of God, is God as well as man, and therefore the same God with the Father. Thirdly, that, being the same God with the Father, He is not the same Person, but a different and distinct person, subsisting distinctly from the Father. Fourthly, that He subsists by receiving, by eternal generation, the Divine Nature from the Father; which generation is the foundation of the relationship of Father and Son.

---

[a] "'Whose goings forth have been from of old, from everlasting.' Micah, v. 2. So use they also [by the plural number] to note out continuance. And so it sets out to us the continual emanation or proceeding of Him from His Father, ὡς ἀπαυγασμα, the Apostle's word, as a 'beam of brightness,' streaming from Him incessantly. Never past—'His generation'—but, as the schoolmen call it, *actus commensuratus æternitate*. For *hodie genui te* is true of every day; yet, because it hath coexistence with many revolutions of time, though it be indeed in itself but one drawn out along, yet, according to the many ages it lasteth, it seemeth to multiply itself into many, and so is expressed plurally."—*Bishop Andrewes' Sermon on the text.*

I. God is called the Father, many times in Holy Scripture, with more particular relation to one Son, who, by way of eminence, is called the "Son of God,"[a] the "only-begotten Son of God."[b] This relation is evidently implied in the baptismal formula: "In the name of the Father, and of the Son." As we naturally ask, "the Son of whom?" and receive for reply, "the Son of the Father;"[c] so we may as naturally ask, "the Father of whom?" and answer, "the Father of the Son here mentioned." The pre-eminence of this Son above all others is shown by the appellation bestowed upon Him, "the only-begotten Son of God;" by the numerous passages in which the Father and the Son are spoken of, without any more particular designation, as if (in the highest sense) but one Father and one Son could be conceived of; and by the closeness of the relationship intimated in the phrases used, such as that the Son "is in the bosom of the Father,"[d] that "the Father loveth the Son, and hath given all things into His hand,"[e] that it is the Father's will, "that all men should honor the Son, even as they honor the Father,"[f] that by the Saviour's granting the answer to prayer, "the Father is glorified in the Son;"[g] that "no man knoweth the Son, but the Father; neither knoweth any man the Father, save the Son, and he to whomsoever the Son will reveal Him."[h]

---

[a] Luke, i. 35.
[b] John, i. 14; i. 18; iii. 16; iii. 18; I. John, iv. 9.
[c] II. John, 3.   [e] John, iii. 35.   [g] John, xiv. 13.
[d] John, i. 18.   [f] John, v. 23.   [h] Matt. xi. 27.

The pre-eminence of this relation above all others is clearly marked by our Saviour Himself, contrasting it with our relationship, in his address to Mary, when He appeared to her after His resurrection: "Go to my brethren, and say unto them, I ascend unto my Father and your Father, and to my God and your God."[a] "My Father *and* your Father," but not my Father *as* your Father, "My God *and* your God," but not my God *as* your God. So the Apostles, marking the same pre-eminence, expressly attribute the title of Father to God, because of the relation to Christ. "Blessed," says St. Paul, making his ascription of praise, "be God, even the Father of our Lord Jesus Christ, the Father of mercies, and the God of all comfort."[b] "Blessed be the God and Father of our Lord Jesus Christ, who hath blessed us with all spiritual blessings in heavenly places in Christ, according as He hath CHOSEN US IN HIM before the foundation of the world, that we should be holy and without blame before Him in love; having predestinated us *unto the adoption of children by Jesus Christ* to Himself, according to the good pleasure of His will."[c] Mark how His Sonship is in this passage made the foundation of our adoption. And when the Apostle would make his most solemn asseveration of his truthfulness, he declares, "The God and Father of our Lord Jesus Christ knoweth that I lie not."[d] So St. Peter speaks of God by the same title, at the commencement of his first epistle: "Blessed be the God and Father of our Lord Jesus Christ, which,

---

[a] John, xx. 17.
[b] II. Cor. i. 3.
[c] Eph. i. 3, 4, 5.
[d] II. Cor. xi. 31.

according to His abundant mercy, hath begotten us again unto a lively hope, by the resurrection of Jesus Christ from the dead."[a] These passages show conclusively that God is called the Father, principally because He is the Father of our Lord Jesus Christ.

Correlatively, Jesus Christ is called, by way of eminence, the Son of God, and so He is doubly identified, both by the way in which God is called His Father, and in this way with the Son, whose relation to the Father is seen to be, from the baptismal formula, so close and intimate. "These things are written," St. John says of His Gospel, "that ye might believe that Jesus is the Christ, the Son of God; and that believing ye might have life through His name."[b] For, "this is the commandment of God, that we should believe on the name of His Son, Jesus Christ."[c] Hence, the angel, announcing His birth to His mother, promised "that holy thing which shall be born of thee, shall be called the Son of God."[d] John the Baptist, when he saw heaven opened, and the Spirit descending upon Him, "bare record that this was the Son of God."[e] The revilers at the cross tell us what the testimony of Christ to Himself was: "He trusted in God," they said, "let Him deliver Him now, if He will have Him; for He said, I am the Son of God."[f] When the eunuch of Candace, Queen of Ethiopia, was baptized by Philip, he thus confessed his faith: "I believe that Jesus Christ is the Son of God."[g] Saul, the converted

---

[a] I. Peter, i. 3.
[b] John, xx. 31.
[c] I. John, iii. 23.
[d] Luke, i. 35.
[e] John, i. 34.
[f] Matt. xxvii. 43.
[g] Acts, viii. 37.

persecutor, afterwards the great Apostle, "preached Christ in the synagogues, that He is the Son of God."[a] The Epistle to the Hebrews tells us: "We have a great high priest, who is passed into the heavens, Jesus, the Son of God."[b] And "whosoever shall confess that Jesus is the Son of God, God dwelleth in him, and he in God."[c]

II. Now since God is, as we have seen, the Father of so many children in so many ways, there must be a special reason for the confession upon which St. John, as above, predicates the communion with God. The faith that Jesus is the Son of God, to be made the ground of such communion, infers a special kind of Sonship, over and above all the reasons for which our Lord has the same right to the title which we have. It is not to be denied that He is called the Son of God, for several subordinate reasons, and in respect of several relations, inferior to the highest. But, admitting these, there is a reason beyond them all; and that is, that Jesus Christ our Lord is a Divine Son; that He is God, having the same nature with the Father, which is our next point to be proved.

1. Jesus Christ is called the "Son of God," because of His birth into our world, which was supernatural. He was born a man; born of a woman, but by no earthly Father. He was "conceived by the Holy Ghost, born of the Virgin Mary." Such a birth gave not only the title of creation, but was a good ground of the appellation in a distinctive sense. Hence the Angel Gabriel announced to Mary His Mother, "That

---

[a] Acts, ix. 20.   [b] Heb. iv. 14.   [c] I. John, iv. 15.

holy thing which shall be born of thee, shall be called the Son of God."[a]

2. Our Lord assigns His commission and mission of the Father, as, in one respect, a reason for His name. When charged by the Jews with blasphemy, He did not care to insist before scoffers upon His Divinity, but replied, "Is it not written in your law, I said ye are gods? If He called them gods unto whom the word of God came (and the Scripture cannot be broken), say ye of Him whom the Father hath sanctified and sent into the world, thou blasphemest, because I said, I am the Son of God?"[b]

3. As we shall be the "children of God," being the "children of the Resurrection," so God's bringing Christ again from the dead is a reason for His being called "the Son of God." So St. Paul expounded the second Psalm to prophesy of the Resurrection, preaching in the synagogue of Antioch in Pisidia as follows: "We declare unto you glad tidings, how that the promise which was made unto the Fathers, God hath fulfilled the same unto us their children, in that He hath raised up Jesus again; as it is also written in the second Psalm, Thou art my Son, this day have I begotten thee."[c] So in the Epistle to the Colossians, our Saviour is called "the first-born from the dead."[d]

4. He is called the Son of God, also, with respect to His inheritance of the Father's riches and power and glory. "God . . hath spoken unto us by His Son, whom He hath appointed heir of all things; who,

---

[a] St. Luke, i. 35.
[b] John, x. 35, 36.
[c] Acts, xiii. 33.
[d] Col. i. 18.

.. when He had by Himself purged our sins, sat down on the right hand of the Majesty on High; being made so much better than the angels, as He hath by inheritance obtained a more excellent name than they. For unto which of the angels said He at any time, Thou art my Son, this day have I begotten Thee?"[a]

5. Now, to use the language of Bishop Pearson, from whom this argument is taken: "The actual possession of His inheritance, which was our fourth title to His Sonship, presupposes His Resurrection, which was the third; and His commission to His office, which was the second, presupposeth his generation of a virgin, as the first." "But besides these four, we must find yet a more peculiar ground of our Saviour's filiation, totally distinct from any which belongs unto the rest of the Sons of God, that He may be clearly and fully acknowledged the Only-begotten Son." Hence we must show that our Lord Jesus Christ was a person existing before He was born into the world; and that He so existed as God, having the same nature with the Father, and having received it from the Father.

That the Son of God was, before He was born of the Virgin Mary, is proved by His testimony, that when He came into the world, He came down from Heaven: "I am the living bread which came down from Heaven."[b] "I came down from Heaven, not to do mine own will; but the will of Him that sent me."[c] "I came forth from the Father, and am come into the world; again I leave the world, and go unto the

---

[a] Heb. i. 1–5.   [b] John, vi. 33, 51.   [c] John, vi. 38.

Father."[a] So John Baptist assigns the reason for the Saviour's taking precedence of himself. "He that cometh from above is above all: he that is of the earth is earthly, He that cometh from Heaven is above all."[b] "This is He of whom I said, After me cometh a man which is preferred before me; for He was before me."[c] And our Lord, directing the minds of the carnal Jews to heavenly truths of which He had been speaking, alludes to His future ascension thus: "What and if ye shall see the Son of Man ascend up where He was before?"[d] thus again asserting that He was in Heaven before He came to earth.

This being which He had before He became a man, is eternal, without beginning. The creation of the first created thing was "the beginning," and nothing which had beginning existed before it. That therefore which was before the Creation, or which already existed "in the beginning," had itself no beginning, that is to say, is eternal. Such the Scriptures represent to be the being of Christ, the Son of God. He was not only before John the Baptist, as proved above, but before Abraham; "Before Abraham was, I am;"[e] not only before Abraham, but before the world; "The world was made by Him,"[f] says St. John. God "hath spoken unto us by His Son, by whom also He made the worlds,"[g] says the Epistle to the Hebrews, which also interprets of the Son, the well-known passage from the 102d Psalm: "Thou Lord, in the beginning hast

---

[a] John, xvi. 27, 28. [c] John, i. 30. [e] John, viii. 58.
[b] John, iii. 31. [d] John, vi. 62. [f] John, i. 10.
[g] Heb. i. 2.

laid the foundations of the earth, and the heavens are the work of thy hands. They shall perish, but Thou shalt endure; they all shall wax old as doth a garment, and as a vesture shalt thou change them, and they shall be changed; but Thou art the same, and Thy years shall not fail."[a] That He is before all created things, St. Paul expressly asserts in a passage, the full force of which is missed in our translation: "He is the image of the invisible God, first-begotten before all creation.[b] For by Him were all things created, that are in Heaven, and that are in earth, visible and invisible, whether they be thrones or dominions or principalities or powers, all things were created by Him and for Him. And He is before all things, and by Him all things consist."[c] And St. John, to the same effect, in the opening of His Gospel: "In the beginning was the Word, and the Word was with God, and the Word was God. The same was in the beginning with God. All things were made by Him, and without Him was not anything made that was made."[d] "And the Word," it is farther stated, to identify this Divine eternal Being with our Lord Jesus Christ, "was made flesh and dwelt among us."

The existence of our Lord before His birth as a man, being, as thus proved, before all time and all worlds, and therefore eternal, cannot be any other than Divine. He is eternal, and therefore He is God; for there is no other eternal being except God. Moreover, it is said that He made the world and all things; therefore He

---

[a] Heb. i. 10.
[b] πρωτοτοκος πασης κτισεως.
[c] Col. i. 15–17.
[d] John, i. 1–3.

is God: for there is no Creator except God. Besides, in the last text cited, He is expressly called God; and thus the question is set at rest without further argument. Nor is this the only passage in which it is unequivocally asserted that Christ is God. God declared by the prophet Isaiah, as we have seen, against idolatry and Persian philosophy: "I am the first and I am the last, and beside me there is no God." But the Saviour declared Himself to be the first and the last when He appeared to St. John, in the Revelations: "These things saith the first and the last, which was dead and is alive."[a] "I am Alpha and Omega, the beginning and the ending, saith the Lord,[b] which is, and which was, and which is to come, the Almighty."[c] So the Epistle to the Hebrews quotes the forty-fifth Psalm as addressed to the Son: "But unto the Son he saith, Thy throne, O God, is for ever and ever."[d] And so the Apostle Paul preaches: "Being in the form of God, He thought it not robbery to be equal with God."[e] Nor could it be robbery of God for Him to take this honor unto Himself, for "in Him dwelleth all the fulness of the Godhead bodily."[f] He is "God manifest in the flesh,"[g] and His name is "Immanuel, which is, being interpreted, God with us."[h] St. Thomas, being convinced of the truth of His resurrection, confessed faith in His deity by exclaiming, "My Lord and my God."[i] And his adversaries, the Jews, understanding rightly His claim to be the Son of

---

[a] Rev. ii. 8.
[b] *i.e.* the Lord Jesus Christ.
[c] Rev. i. 8.
[d] Heb. i. 8.
[e] Phil. ii. 6.
[f] Col. ii. 9.
[g] I. Tim. iii. 16.
[h] Matt. i. 23.
[i] John, xx. 28.

God as including the assumption of Divinity, but refusing to admit that claim, objected it against Him as blasphemy, "because that Thou, being a man, makest Thyself God."[a] St. John, who is called "the Divine," because he discoursed so much of the deity of the Lord, ends his first Epistle with the declaration: "We know that the Son of God is come, and hath given us understanding, that we may know Him that is true, and we are in Him that is true, even in His Son Jesus Christ. This is the true God, and eternal life."[b] Finally, St. Paul enumerates among the glories of his kinsmen according to the flesh, that "of them, as concerning the flesh, Christ came, who is over all, God blessed forever. Amen."[c]

This abundant proof that Christ is God is proof also that He is the same God with the Father; for since, as was proved in the first place, there is no God but one, Christ must be that God, or not God at all. But that God is shown to be God the Father; therefore Christ, the Son, is the same God with the Father.

III. But, being the same God, He is nevertheless a different Person from the Father. He has the same Divine Nature with the Father and the Holy Spirit, but a different personal subsistence[d] from both. The very names, Father and Son, testify this so clearly that there would be no need to insist upon it, were it not that "the thing that hath been, that is it that shall be," and therefore the old Sabellian heresy may arise again. Hence it is to be noted that the difference of Persons

---

[a] John, x. 33.
[b] I. John, v. 20.
[c] Rom. ix. 5.
[d] Gr. ὑπόστασις.

in the Divine Trinity was manifested at the baptism of Jesus: "The Heavens were opened unto Him," it is said, "and He saw the Spirit of God descending like a dove, and lighting upon Him; and lo, a voice from Heaven, saying, This is my beloved Son, in whom I am well pleased."[a] Here the voice was the voice of the Father; He upon whom the Spirit descended was the Son; and the descending Spirit was the Holy Ghost. He who gave, and He who received, and He who was given, are clearly distinguished. The personal distinction thus demonstrated was carefully preserved by our Saviour, when speaking of Himself and His Father: "My Father is greater than I." "I came forth from the Father and am come unto the world, again I leave the world, and go unto the Father." "As the Father gave me commandment, even so I do." "Ye believe in God [*i.e.* the Father], believe also in Me." "I am the true vine, and my Father is the husbandman." "Father, the hour is come, glorify Thy Son, that Thy Son may also glorify Thee." So in numberless passages the personal distinction is clearly implied, proving that while the nature is the same the personal subsistence is other.

IV. It is as clear also, from Holy Scripture, that the Son, who is God eternally with the Father, receives His Divine Being from the Father, which is the last point to be proved. It is evident from the mutual relations of the terms Father and Son; for the name "the Son," in its proper acceptation, rests upon derivation of being from the parent; and that name be-

---

[a] Matt. iii. 16, 17.

longed to our Lord Jesus Christ before He was born into the world; and therefore it infers the derivation of His Divine Being from His Father. Thus, applying the name to His Divinity, the Epistle to the Hebrews informs us that "God hath spoken unto us by His Son, by whom [that is, by which Son] He made the worlds;"[a] whence it is to be concluded that the Person spoken of as a Son, was a Son before "the worlds were made," and therefore *a fortiori* before he was born as a human Son. It has been before noticed that He is called "the only-begotten Son," because of His Divine Being which He alone has of all the Sons of God. He is therefore a "begotten Son," that is, a Son who derives His being from His Father—an "only-begotten Son," as He alone derives by His generation a Divine Being from His Father. "No man hath seen God at any time," says St. John, "the only-begotten Son, which is in the bosom of the Father, He hath declared Him;"[b] which passage can only be interpreted of the Divine Nature of our Lord. And reason, of itself, might conclude this generation; for, as there is but one Divine Nature, which is infinite, and at the same time one and indivisible, and as that Divine Nature is originally in the Father, the Son could not have being at all unless He had received that being from the Father. The Divine Essence could not subsist in two persons were not one derived from the other. Hence our Saviour testifies that what He is He has received from the Father: "All things whatsoever the Father hath are mine."[c] "As the Father hath life in Himself, so

---

[a] Heb. i. 2. [b] John, iii. 18. [c] John, xiv. 15.

hath He given to the Son, to have life in Himself."[a] "Verily, verily, I say unto you, the Son can do nothing of Himself but what He seeth the Father do."[b] "I know Him, for I am from Him."[c] "I and the Father are one."[d] "If I do not the works of my Father, believe me not. But if I do, though ye believe not me, believe the works; that ye may know and believe that the Father is in Me, and I in Him."[e] The derivation asserted in these passages the Epistle to the Hebrews represents by a happy figure, "Who being the brightness of the Father's glory, and the express image of His person," etc.—coming forth from the Father, that is, as the ray from the sun, and answering to the Father's likeness as the wax to the seal by which it is impressed.

We thus at length arrive at the proposition laid down at the beginning of this somewhat complicated argument, having proved fully by it that God is always a Father—the Eternal Father of an Eternal Son. Collaterally the doctrine respecting the Son has also been brought out, part by part, and clearly shown by Scripture teaching.

III. The truth concerning the Holy Spirit, the third Person of the blessed Trinity, is easy of reception when we believe in the Son. All that we need is Scripture testimony to the facts; and the teaching of the sacred volume will be clear if we show that the Holy Spirit is God,—that the attributes which are peculiar to God alone are assigned to Him,—whence

---

[a] John, v. 26. [b] John, v. 19. [c] John, vii. 29.
[d] John, x. 30. [e] John, x. 37, 38.

we infer that He is God; that He is a person distinct from the Father and the Son; and that He receives His being by proceeding from the Father and the Son.

1. The Holy Scriptures, understood in their plain and natural sense, call the Holy Spirit God, and assign to Him attributes which belong to God alone. As we infer the Son to be God, because "by Him God [the Father] made the worlds," so we understand the Holy Spirit to be God, because the same operation of Creation is attributed to Him in the words, "By His Spirit He hath garnished the Heavens." For if the Son were existent before the world, as He must have been if God made the world by Him, so also the Spirit must have been pre-existent, and co-operative in the Creation, and therefore uncreated, and therefore God. So the Angel Gabriel promised that the Son of Mary should be called the Son of God, because He was conceived by the Holy Ghost. "The Holy Ghost shall come upon thee, and the power of the Highest shall overshadow thee; therefore that holy thing which shall be born of thee shall be called the Son of God." Not as if the Holy Ghost were the Father of our Lord according to the flesh, but that, according to the mystery of the Triune activity, the Holy Spirit is the immediate agent of all operations of the Father. It is to be concluded, also, that He is God, because the bodies of those to whom He is given as the Indwelling Spirit are said to be "temples," since temples are exclusively the habitations of Deity: "What! know ye not that your body is the temple of the Holy Ghost, which dwelleth in you?" Omniscience is one of His attributes: "The Spirit searcheth all things, yea, the deep things of God.

For what man knoweth the things of a man, save the spirit of man which is in him? even so the things of God knoweth no one,[a] but the Spirit of God."[b] Were He not God, no sin could be committed against Him so fearful as to preclude forgiveness; yet our Saviour says: "All manner of sin and blasphemy shall be forgiven unto men, but the blasphemy against the Holy Ghost shall not be forgiven unto men. And whosoever speaketh a word against the Son of Man, it shall be forgiven him; but whosoever speaketh a word against the Holy Ghost, it shall not be forgiven him, neither in this world, neither in the world to come."[c]

The baptismal formula is an incontrovertible argument for the Divinity of the Holy Ghost. For as we are baptized in the name of the Father, who is God, and in the name of the Son, because He is God, so we are baptized in the name of the Holy Ghost, because He also is God. In the benediction, also, the union of His name with that of the Father and that of the Son is an argument of the same force: "The grace of our Lord Jesus Christ, and the love of God, and the fellowship of the Holy Ghost, be with you all. Amen."[d]

The Holy Ghost, moreover, is expressly called Lord and God: "Now the Lord is that Spirit, and where the Spirit of the Lord is, there is liberty."[e] When Ananias kept back part of the price of his land, falsely pretending that he had brought the whole as a donation to the church, St. Peter rebuked him with the words:

---

[a] οὐδείς.   [b] I. Cor. ii. 10, 11.   [c] Matt. xii. 31, 32.
[d] II. Cor. xiii. 14.   [e] II. Cor. iii. 17.

"Why hath Satan filled thine heart to lie to the Holy Ghost? . . . Thou hast not lied unto men, but unto God."[a]

Now, since the Holy Ghost is, according to Holy Scripture, possessed of the attributes which belong only to God, is joined in the baptismal formula with the Father and the Son, each of whom has been proved to be God, and moreover is in the Scripture expressly called Lord and God, it is therefore to be concluded that that Blessed Spirit is God—the same God with the Father and the Son.

2. But the Holy Ghost is a Person distinct from the Father and the Son. He performs actions towards the Father and the Son which fully distinguish Him from them. He is distinguished from the Father, because "He maketh intercession for the saints, according to the will of God."[b] That is, He makes intercession to the Father; but the Father, it would never be said, makes intercession to Himself; as it must be said if the Father and the Holy Ghost were the same person. He comes in obedience to the mission of the Son: "It is expedient for you that I go away: for if I go not away, the Comforter will not come unto you; but if I depart, I will send Him unto you."[c] But the Scripture would not represent our Lord as saying that He would send Himself, as it must if the Spirit and the Son were the same person; much less when He had just declared that He was about to depart, and that He who was to be sent would come in His stead. "Through the Son," says St. Paul, distinguishing the Persons,

---

[a] Acts, v. 3, 4.   [b] Rom. viii. 27.   [c] John, xvi. 7.

"we have access by one Spirit to the Father." And so in the benediction, "The grace of our Lord Jesus Christ, and the love of God [the Father], and the fellowship of the Holy Ghost, be with you all. Amen."

3. The Holy Spirit receives His Divine Being from the Father and the Son. For, as the Son receives the Divine Nature from the Father, or He could not be at all, so the Holy Spirit could not be, unless He received it from the Father and the Son. This truth is intimated by His being named, "the Spirit of God," "the Spirit of the Father," "the Spirit of the Son," "the Spirit of Christ." Of His being called the Spirit of God, examples are so numerous that it will not need to cite them; it is sufficient to open the Bible at the first chapter of Genesis, where we read, "The Spirit of God moved upon the face of the waters." He is called the "Spirit of the Father" by our Lord, encouraging the disciples to bear witness boldly before governors and kings: "It is not ye that speak, but the Spirit of your Father which speaketh in you."[a] "Because we are sons," says St. Paul, "God hath sent forth the Spirit of His Son into our hearts."[b] "Now if any man have not the Spirit of Christ, he is none of His." The procession of the Spirit from the Father is asserted in express terms: "He proceedeth from the Father."[c] And in equivalent words from the Son, "He shall receive of mine, and shall show it unto you."[d]

The Scripture teaching respecting the Holy Trinity

---

[a] Matt. x. 20.
[b] Gal. iv. 6.
[c] John, xvi. 26.
[d] John, xvi. 14.

is thus shown to be full and clear. The doctrine taught is thus concisely summed up in the Athanasian creed: "The Father is God, the Son is God, and the Holy Ghost is God. And yet there are not three Gods but one God." The object of the present volume is to inquire into the practical relation of this doctrine with our religious life, through the grace given by each Person to the Christian, in applying to him, the Redemption and salvation of the Gospel.

CHAPTER II.

THE GRACE OF GOD THE FATHER.

THE truth which God has revealed respecting Himself is not a *speculative*, but a *regulative* truth. We have not faculties for speculation upon the nature of God. The proper exercise of thought in religion is to purify our understanding of the revealed Word from errors of misapprehension, to accept the truth in its transcendent mystery, and to carry it into our lives, by making it the source of all our comfort and the sanction of all our duty. We miss of the value of the Revelation altogether, unless we receive it as intended to govern our religious life. Our knowledge of God is not knowledge of Him in Himself, apart from us; but knowledge of Him in relation to us. Our faith in the Holy Trinity is the highest reach of thought, above which it cannot ascend into a philosophy of the Absolute, such as has been vainly imagined possible; it is rather the starting-point from which reason may descend to the world and to ourselves. When, therefore, we attempt to comprehend the mystery of God's being as he is in Himself, we fail; but when we set ourselves at our proper business—to understand the relation of the Ever-blessed Trinity to the world and to mankind—the truth will be found to arrange itself in intelligible conceptions, to be coherent, systematic, and, to careful reflection, easily understood.

A merely speculative truth, unnecessary to Christian practice, would be devoid of influence in life, and therefore useless. Much as has been written concerning the pursuit of knowledge for its own sake only, the practical sense of the world has continually demanded that the result of science should be the perfection of art. The spirit of inquiry may be supreme, as such, in individuals, in order that they may devote themselves untiringly to investigations of which the practical value is not foreseen; but the world has no honor for the inquirer, until it sees that something can be *done* by means of his discoveries. All science seeks an application; even the most abstract metaphysical inquirers aim at an ultimate influence upon conduct, either by laying down principles of morals or by guiding intellectual activity. Hence, in a matter which concerns every one as closely as religion, truth is altogether regulative; the faith is given to enter immediately into the life of man and become the supreme governing principle of his conduct, without which he cannot shun evil and attain good.

What we want to know and understand is, what God is to us, what He does to us, and what He requires from us; and this, of course, implies some knowledge of what God is in Himself; but it also implies that that knowledge, so far as comprehensible by us, is sufficiently comprehended in the relations to us, of which it is the foundation. The unity of God is sufficiently revealed in the unity of His Law, which is the same law, whether viewed as given by the Father, or published by the Son, or written in our hearts by the Holy Spirit. The difference of Persons is sufficiently revealed in the difference of operations of the Three in our Redemption—the Father justifying and adopting, the Son redeeming, the Holy Spirit sanctifying.

Conversely, without the knowledge of God thus given, we cannot understand our position, or our hopes, or our duty in the world; but with it we have all that is practical, and, therefore, all that is necessary. Hence the Apostles' and the Nicene Creeds, the Church's concise but systematic expositions of the truth which it has learned from God's revelation of Himself, have been, the one for eighteen hundred, the other for fifteen hundred years, allowed to be the sum of the fundamental truths of Christianity, have been found by experience sufficient to regulate conduct and to preserve from deadly error, and are rightly required to be believed, on pain of exclusion from her body and from participation in her hopes.

The absolute necessity of Christian faith in God the Father, the Son, and the Holy Ghost consists in this, that God requires it; and though we can give no other certain reason (since we cannot affirm that God could not save us without the exercise of faith on our part), yet there are reasons which show us the fitness and, to a certain extent, the necessity of this dispensation. One such reason is thus stated in the Epistle to the Hebrews: "Without faith it is impossible to please God; for he that cometh to God must believe that He is, and that He is a rewarder of them that diligently seek Him!"[a]

---

[a] Heb. xi. 6.

Following the example of the Apostle, we may assign such others as present themselves—as thus: There is a relation of each Person to us, and an operation of each Person towards us, which it is every way expedient we should know, that we may willingly respond to it; and there is a duty required from us towards each Person, which it is certainly necessary we should understand in order to be able to perform it; and the knowledge and understanding of these relations, operations, and required duties implies, as a condition, faith in the Persons who are their source and object. The work of Redemption is a complex operation of the Three Divine Persons, in which each bears His own distinctive part. There is an operation of the Father, an operation of the Son distinct from that of the Father, and an operation of the Holy Ghost distinct from those of the Father and the Son. The knowledge that these operations are effectually performed in us to our salvation gives us the only well-grounded comfort and Christian joy; since it only can relieve us from the danger of self-deception and false security, and put to flight the doubts of an unsettled heart.

Were this all it were surely enough to make the believer "contend earnestly for the faith once delivered to the saints;" but it becomes vastly more important to have a right faith, when duties are based upon it, without the due performance of which we are not in the state of salvation, and without which God will not give us the full benefits of His grace. A living, justifying faith, the Apostle teaches us, is a "faith which worketh by love;" it is a faith manifested in obedience. And therefore faith in the Holy Trinity stands in the closest connection with our spiritual life. For the influences of Divine grace are partly given before, and partly follow after, our doing what is required of us. Moulding us beforehand to the will of God, they yet depend on our faithful obedience to become complete in effect,—prevenient grace not availing towards final salvation, unless we believe and obey. Faith and obedience are the outward branching and fructifying of the spiritual life of the Christian of which the root is grace—itself a principle not perceivable, but becoming visible and conscious to the possessor by projecting itself in thought and action; the form of thought being faith, and the form of action, obedience. In their root, therefore, faith and obedience are the same, —the answer of the soul to the Divine operations, and the measure of the degree in which we have profited by the grace given us; besides, they exert a reflex action upon the life from which they spring, strengthening and perfecting it. Now, though true obedience is that which is rendered unhesitatingly to the positive commands and teachings of God, because they are His commands and teachings, without any questionings as to the reasonings for them, yet it needs to be assured that the commands of the Father, Son, and Holy Ghost are all alike the commands of God, and that the duty which springs from our relation to each of those three persons is alike our duty towards God. Hence the faith is necessary to this end, and we are helped to obey more cheerfully and with greater satisfaction when we can discover in the truths it delivers the reasons and grounds of command and duty.

And lastly, the necessity of this faith must be still

more apparent in the fact that it is made the condition of our receiving the chief benefits of the Gospel by opening our souls to them, in conscious understanding of what we are to receive, of the manner of obtaining, and of the meritorious cause whose virtue we must plead with the Father; thus throwing out other and contrary thoughts, and the feelings and intentions which would make grace useless if it were given. For all these reasons—right acceptance of, and co-operation with, the gift of salvation, true comfort and hope in the gospel, and right obedience to the commands of God —the faith in the Holy Trinity may be seen to be the foundation upon which all who profess and call themselves Christians must build the edifice of their religious life.

The purpose of this volume is to inquire into the operations of the Blessed Trinity towards and upon man, in regenerating and sanctifying him. For these operations, manifold and varied as they are, a name has been found comprehensive enough to include them all—the word *grace*. The grace of God is the whole work of God in redeeming the world. In the present chapter we consider the grace of God the Father Almighty.

The word *grace* in Holy Scripture has three general significations: first, it means the favor, love, mercy, kindness, or benevolence of God, the Divine affection of God towards us;[a] secondly, the spiritual gifts, whatsoever they be, imparted to our souls by God through

---

[a] Rom. iii. 24, etc.

His favor and love;[a] and thirdly, in a sense admitting the plural number, the effect produced in us by the gift of Divine grace,[b] as the grace of humility, the grace of charity, etc.

In order to understand what is the grace of God the Father towards us, some consideration is necessary of the relation in which He stands to the whole creation at large, to mankind as originally created upright, and, lastly, to mankind as fallen and redeemed. And since the Church's understanding of Scripture teaching respecting the Creation is (according to the formula of Hooker),[c] that "all things are from the Father, by the Son, through the Spirit," something more must be said, in order to understand this concerning the attributes exercised in the Creation of the world, and the Redemption of mankind, as related to the action of the three persons.

The Church, looking upon the Creed as a regulative truth, teaches us, in her catechism, this answer to the question, "What dost thou chiefly learn in these articles of thy belief?" "First, I learn to believe in God the Father, who hath made me and all the world; secondly, in God the Son, who hath redeemed me and all mankind; thirdly, in God the Holy Ghost, who sanctifieth me, and all the people of God." The three titles, then, which the Church gives to the three persons of the Holy Trinity are, God the Father, the Creator; God the Son, the Redeemer; God the Holy Ghost, the Sanctifier. These titles represent to us, as the subordination of persons, so also the subordination

---

[a] Eph. iv. 7.   [b] II. Cor. viii. 7.   [c] B. i. c. 2.

of attributes in the Godhead. They tell us that the attribute specially exercised in the act of Creation, is first in order; that the special attribute which governs the work of redemption is second; and that that which carries on the work of sanctification is third. These are, Power, the creative attribute; Wisdom, the redeeming attribute; Love, the sanctifying attribute. All these attributes belong to each of the three persons of the Blessed Trinity; for it is of the essence of a person (so far as we are able to conceive; and God, so far as revealed, is revealed according to our conceptions, and is unrevealed, so far as He transcends them) that He should possess power or will, and also wisdom or intelligence, and also love or affection. The distinction of persons to us in the unity of essence, consists in the manifestation of each attribute in a different person. The characteristic attribute of God the Father, and the source of both the others, is His glorious and infinite power, which, by its own self-determinations, is the origin of all that Wisdom beholds or Love delights in. The Son is distinguished from the Father because His power, though infinite and eternal as the Father's, is not self-determinant, but subordinant to that Wisdom which is the full beholding of the glory and mind of the Father. "The Son can do nothing of Himself, but what He seeth the Father do."[a] Hence the name given by St. John is, "the Word" or "Wisdom" of God; for the first eternal energy of the Father's power has for its result eternal, infinite Wisdom. The Holy Spirit, so we are taught by our Fathers in the faith, as

---

[a] John, v. 19.

the third Person of the Blessed Trinity, has for His chief attribute, infinite, eternal Love—for what can be the further outflow of that infinite essence, which is self-developed into infinite power and infinite wisdom, but infinite goodness—that is, infinite love?

These, then, in the Catholic theology, are the distinguishing attributes of the three Persons, as standing respectively first in the order of their perfections. But each Person, by reason of their co-essential equality, has all the attributes in common with the other two, only in a different order; which difference of order guides them in their operations. The Father, as the source of all being, has Power first, and, from that, Wisdom, which is in Him self-derived, and Love, which is complete in Himself. The Son has first, Wisdom, from the Father, and from Him also Power and also Love. The Holy Spirit, proceeding from the Father and the Son, has Love, first, and also Wisdom and also Power; for all these attributes are essential to each Person, as personally subsisting. Thus, obtaining their doctrine from Holy Scripture and a sanctified philosophy, the Fathers of the Church, describing the Persons of the Trinity by their chief attributes, represent the Father as the Supreme Power, the Almighty; the Son as the Divine Word or Wisdom (for the Greek word[a] used by St. John means both); and the Holy Ghost as the Divine Love. Hence, bringing these attributes into operation, God the Father is, by His Power, the Creator; God the Son is, by His Wisdom, the Redeemer; God the Holy Ghost is, by His Love,

---

[a] ὁ λογος.

the Sanctifier. That is, all those operations of the Godhead in which Power is immediately subordinate to Love, are operations of the Holy Ghost; all those in which Power is immediately subordinate to Wisdom, are operations of the Son; all those in which Power is originant of that which to love, is to be good, and which to know is to be wise, are operations of God the Father. This being true, it may be understood how the Creation is "of the Father, by the Son, through the Spirit." As receiving being it is "of the Father;" as arranged by manifold operations of wisdom, it was so wisely constituted by the power of the Son, working under the wisdom common to the Father and the Son; as made "very good," it was wrought through the Spirit, under that Love, which, with Wisdom and Power, the Spirit is, in common with the Father and the Son.

It may, however, at first sight, seem hard to receive, that Power is the highest attribute of the Godhead. That this is true we have inferred from the first article of the Creed: "I believe in God the Father *Almighty*, Maker of Heaven and Earth." Still, when we look abroad on the world, and ask ourselves, Whence came all its order and beauty and harmony? it is not unnatural, that the further question should arise, Is Power, really, the chief attribute? Must not Wisdom guide and rule Power, and Love guide and rule Wisdom? Are not Love and Wisdom, then, predominant over Power? The true answer to this is, that in the unity of the Divine Nature, Power and Wisdom and Love are co-equal, co-inclusive,[a] and co-eternal, and therefore

---

[a] εμπεριχωρητος.

inseparable. But we are now considering them as coming forth into activity, as relative to the creation of the world;[a] and it is evident that temporal creation depended on the enactment of eternal, unchangeable law. In reply to these questions, then, we ask another: What is there for Wisdom to behold, or Love to delight in until the Infinite Will has determined in its own unity and perfection the harmonies of His own eternal law? The earth and the heavens have their harmonies, and the universe runs round its appointed cycle, in obedience to eternal and immutable laws, of which all our science is the study. In thinking upon the Creation, therefore, we have to consider, not only the being of the world, but the being of the law that governs it. What are these laws which we call eternal and necessary? Do they exist without the enactment of God? Are there other eternally existing beings besides God? for, if eternal laws be eternally self-existent, they must be existences other than God, and independent of Him. Or are they not rather the determinations of His eternal will—the enactments of His Infinite Power? Clearly, there is nothing existing from all eternity but God; and therefore these eternal, immutable, necessary laws, which govern God's works, must be themselves enactments of God's infinite, unchangeable, eternal will. Without the infinite Almighty Power of God there could be no such thing as wisdom, no such thing as love; for wisdom is the knowledge of God's eternal laws, and love is the acceptance of, and delight in, their perfections. Infinite, Almighty, perfect will and

---

[a] προφορικος.

power stand first in the Godhead; and the proper name of God the Father is that in the Creed, "I believe in God the Father Almighty, Maker of heaven and earth."

Nor does the supremacy of this infinite Power of God in any way suggest the idea of capriciousness, as being governed by no law derived from any other attribute. It is governed by God's own essence, which is perfect unity, and therefore cannot but be at unity and harmony with itself. "The Being of God," says Hooker, "is a kind of law to His working." The power of God possesses the perfections of His being; and because it is perfect, one, unchangeable, and eternally active, from it springs eternally, His wisdom and His love; and thus from His Power and Wisdom and Love the Creation receives its being—its law and order and glory.

Here, then, is the scriptural representation of our relation to God the Father. God is the God of law. He ordained the universal law of all things. His oneness makes that law a harmonious, perfect, just, upright, all-holy law. We have no law but that which God has given. We move and breathe, we live and die, under His enactments. Nor is there any other origin of that law which prescribes our duty. God has not only given, but published, the law under which we are to act. He demands obedience. He is our Governor, and we can plead no allowance for disobedience to His commands. As an infinite, eternal, and unchangeable God, He is a just and holy God; and as such He cannot overlook unholiness and disobedience. Our relation to God the Father is that of children and subjects. The debt which we owe to Him—worship, adoration, humility, whatever it be—is all comprehended in the two words, faith and obedience.

This, then, is the first relation of man towards God, partaking of His love, and therefore held to obedience to His law. Man was originally created capable of perfect obedience; and if he had always rendered it, his relation to his Creator would not have been complicated with the dark and awful fact of the Fall, nor with the wonderful mystery of Redemption. It would have been the perfect love of a Father, governing His children, and of children rendering willing obedience to their Father in Heaven. Such will be the relation of the Redeemed to God, in the eternal world, after the Resurrection. The history of fallen man moves between the obedience of Eden and the obedience of Heaven; and the present operation of grace belongs to the period included within these bounds, beginning with the Fall, and ending with the Resurrection. But in man's first estate the grace of God was simply love and favor towards His child; and its result was all the blessings, whatsoever they were, which could be bestowed upon Adam to make him perfect in happiness.

The fact of the Fall, therefore, has a direct bearing upon the doctrine of grace; and its consideration leads us to inquire more particularly into the nature of the law given to Adam, and the nature of the act by which he fell.

The law of God given to the perfect man was threefold, mirroring thereby the threefold personal attributes of the Deity. First, the law of nature, or natural affection; secondly, the law of reason; thirdly, the law of positive command, or conscience,—the first, governing man according to his constitution and being; the second, governing him in his occupations in the world; the third, governing him in his closer relation to God as a responsible and spiritual being.

By the law of nature, I understand the necessary impulses inherent in the original constitution of beings of whatever kind, which urge to physical, involuntary, instinctive, or emotional[a] action. Such is the law by which planets revolve around the sun; that by which the relations of inanimate things are established; by which geological changes take place, by which substances enter into chemical combinations, by which planets grow according to their kinds, by which animals seek their food, and by which their life is developed, preserved, and propagated. In this, its comprehensive sense, the law of nature includes, not only such relations as govern inanimate beings, and animated beings simply as organized bodies, but also such as govern animated beings in those acts which are not purely acts of a proper will, working under reason towards a purpose, or consciously obeying a command,—that is, those acts which animated beings perform by impulse or instinct of nature rather than by rational volition. As man is a natural being, and was so in Paradise, he was there governed as he is now, by a law of nature. He had his place on the earth by the law of gravitation; his organization was subject to the laws and conditions of animal life; the involuntary movements of

---

[a] I use this word to designate action prompted by the natural emotions or passions of animate beings.

the heart and lungs were governed in him as in lower animals by the law of nature. And so, also, his sinless instincts, desires, appetites, and affections furnished him a law of nature to guide his more common and necessary actions.

In the highest generalization, it will not be very far out of the way to define the law of nature as the law of the attraction of beings towards, or their repulsion from each other, according to the natures given them by God. Thus, with respect to man; his place upon the earth is secured by the attraction of gravitation; his growth is effected by the attraction of necessary nutriment from the food digested to the various parts of the body; his food is selected by its attractiveness to the appetite; his likes and dislikes, his passions and desires, are simply attractions and repulsions. The law of attraction rises higher than the control of merely physical movements, and in some degree enters into the moral sphere, into combination with the understanding and the will. Man has appetites, desires, sentiments, emotions, instincts, affections, under which he acts in part involuntarily, in part consciously; and by these, so far as they influence him rightly, the law of nature is proclaimed. His emotional and instinctive faculties were given him for wise and good purposes; and though now (like the nobler faculties) perverted by the fall, they had place in the perfection of Paradise, and were there the expression of laws of action, which were consciously obeyed. Natural law, in this sense, stood between merely physical natural law and the law of reason, differing from the one, in that its obedience is unconscious and altogether involuntary;

and from the other, in that the will is permissive rather than directive. The instincts, in a perfect state, would tend to self-preservation, and the affections and sentiments would govern the relations of society, without the need of being informed by any processes of reasoning or any revealed law, the golden rule being "written on the heart." They would thus be natural teachers of the duties men owe to each other in society, and perhaps of the duties we owe to God. It pleased God not to leave society to the cold impulses of mere rational conclusions in respect of these things; but to implant in our nature those social principles in accordance with which even now, fallen as we are, society shapes itself and coheres together, and which, were we as perfect as Adam was made, would of themselves be a perfect law of social action and human morality.

That system of faculties which proclaims the law of nature is called, in Holy Scripture, *the heart*. The law of the heart, if the heart were perfect, would be, under the present constitution of society, the ten commandments; nor can that be a right heart whose determinations, claiming authority under color of being natural feelings, differ from the commandments. We are, at the present day, too much inclined to take our hearts and feelings for our guides, not reflecting that they are fallen, as they are, and need to be taught by Holy Scripture and cleansed by Divine grace, to give us right impulses and a right obedience to God. But in Paradise, the nature of Adam being perfect, his heart proclaimed truly God's law of nature; and that law being in principle the ten commandments, so far as they applied to a possible society in that perfect state, this is the reason, I suppose, that we do not read of any moral law given to Adam by express revelation.

The law of nature, as the bond of society and the principle of attraction by which all things, animate or inanimate, seek what is best for them, and (so to speak) love each other, is correspondent to the Divine love; and since that is the third in the order of the Divine attributes, this law acknowledges in man, as a spiritual being ordained to the highest knowledge of God, a twofold higher law,—that of wisdom or reason, and that of command or conscience.

Under the law of reason, instead of emotion, or instinct, or appetite, or affection, the will substitutes *purpose* as its principle of action. It sets before itself ends to be attained other than the gratification of present feelings; it governs our calling and occupation in this life; it puts us in the way of discovering means and ways of action; it enables us to decide whether our purposes are wise, and whether our means are adapted to the end in view. For example, legislation in our present state is, or ought to be, an exercise of reason, seeking means to preserve society from disruption, since nature is no longer sufficient. The laws of a state are laws of human reason; and so is every rule which implies a purpose consciously adopted, and the choice of means to carry it into effect. Like the heart, the reason is now fallen, and therefore its determinations are neither the wisest nor the best; but in Paradise it was, in its sphere, a perfect guide, ruling Adam in his occupation. We read that "the Lord God put the man into the garden of Eden to dress it and to keep it." That means, He gave him an occupation to which his mere instincts and emotions did not urge him. Purpose not resting upon impulse is supposed in this, and means inferred. The discovery and adaptation of means to purposes, and the adoption of rules of action, were exercises of reason, leading further to the knowledge of laws and principles, and so to an insight into the works and ways of God. The law of Reason thus represents in man that wisdom which is the second of the attributes of God.

It is true, therefore, that man, in his perfection, was created to be governed by the law of reason as well as by the law of nature; but they have a very false idea of human nature, and of our position under God's government, who suppose that this is all which even the perfect man must obey, or that nothing more is necessary to bring him into full communion with God. Adam obeyed the law of nature almost unconsciously —by instinct, as it were; he obeyed the law of reason by reflection upon the ends to be attained and the means to attain them; but there needed a *positive command*, to which neither instinct pointed nor reason reached, to try his faith, his obedience, and his filial love. The highest spiritual qualities—faith, love, fidelity—could find expression only in obedience to a positive revealed command. Hence, the laws of reason and of nature being presupposed, we are told that God commanded the man, saying, "Of every tree of the garden thou mayest freely eat: but of the tree of the knowledge of good and evil, thou shalt not eat of it: for in the day that thou eatest thereof thou shalt surely die." This law of positive command represented, in the sphere of human activity, that primordial, constitutive will which is the first of the Divine attributes.

We are told that disobedience to the *command* was the cause of the fall. To see, then, how obedience to a law of which we do not see the reason, ennobles, and how disobedience debases a moral being, even while obeying the laws of nature and reason, and so to realize something of a true philosophy of human nature and its obligations, let us contrast this account of the fall with one of the many ways in which the existence of evil is explained.

It is said, for example, that evil is necessary in the world as subordinate to the purposes of good,—that the good finds opportunity to develop itself in the work of restoration only because evil is at work marring all things. Human nature is thought to develop in accordance with the necessity of evil. It is at first unconsciously innocent, ignorant of right and wrong, and, prior to experience, without a rule of judgment. It must, therefore, fall into evil, and thus a twofold effect is obtained,—the evil of one furnishes the opportunity for the good of another; and one's own experience leads him finally to reject the evil altogether and to choose the good. The education of humanity, in this view, consists in setting before it the evil and its consequences, that it may taste their misery and so choose the happiness of the good. Each person must learn by his own experience to make the choice for himself; and therefore the necessity of an experience of evil was inherent in human nature; and there has never been a fall; and no blame attaches on account of sin, since it is only an unavoidable misfortune.

The various propositions of this theory are argued somewhat after the following manner:

Why, it is asked, does God permit the whirling tornado to sweep over, or the rumbling earthquake to tremble beneath a town, and cripple man or bury his home in devastation, or crush in its ruins the partner or the child? We bow in silence at the inscrutable counsels of our Creator, and confess that He has done His will. The afflicted and the bereaved appeal to our sympathies, and afford us opportunity for the exercise of virtue in acknowledgment of the brotherhood of humanity. With this admission, the argument is taken up again, and we are asked, "Is not *moral evil*—man's sin against his fellow—ordained for the purpose of developing otherwise hidden virtue? Is not the aggregate of human action grander and nobler for the virtue of the many developed by the sin of the few? How much of our sympathy is excited, and how many mighty schemes of benevolence are carried on, it is argued, to remove the misery of the world, which has its roots in antecedent sin! Is not the development of this virtue, and the happiness occasioned thereby, more than the evil which called it forth? How nobly, for example, Christian fortitude enables us to bear the ills put upon us by injustice and harsh dealing! How unweariedly reason—that loftiest faculty of man—is exercised in devising wise laws to meet the wants of society which we have learned from our experience of evil! Were all men innocent, it is argued, there would be no need of studying laws and principles, no moral reason and intelligence, no call for benevolence, no active sympathy, no high endurance, no Christian forgiveness, no opportunity of our benefiting one another and of becoming more excellent thereby. Fraud and violence and oppression, it is admitted, reduce to poverty; drunkenness and neglect involve families in misery; evil passions inflict injuries; careless selfishness tramples on hearts without a thought. But these painful effects of evil, it is argued, develop a far greater degree and higher state of virtue than could otherwise be developed, in those who suffer nobly and act charitably and reap a reward infinitely outweighing all mortal sufferings, in the exalted sphere to which the soul is translated after death. Upon the mountain-tops, in a purer but rarer atmosphere, virtue, it is thought, is stripped of its warmth, like the sunlight lying on eternal snow; but in the denser air of lower earth it fills the otherwise dreary void with deeds of benevolence and love, which, without the coexistence of evil, it would have had no power to perform. In a world without sin, it is said, forgiveness could have no place, firmness and constancy no trial; humility shows lovely in contrast with pride, and love itself is noblest when overcoming hate. Hence, it is said, there must be evil, or there could be no good.

To this, our direct answer is short. The theory does not meet the fact,—it does not admit the magnitude of the evil in the world. Is evil really so little that it is but the uncomely handmaid of good? Far from it. What history does not teem with crimes? What nation's record shows virtue persistent on the throne? What star of empire has not set in blood, amid a people weltering in corruption?

Human nature, however, is supposed to be constituted under such a necessity of evil within it and around it. It is further argued that there must be evil in others, for it to be around us; and in us, that it may surround others, in order that mankind, by overcoming it, may attain to the highest good. For this reason, they say, man is not fallen; but was created in a childish unconscious innocence, knowing neither good nor evil. An ignorance of temptation, it is said, and said truly, is less of good than a strong and conscious virtue victorious over it, or which has passed through the flames, and learned to embrace the good through loathing at the evil. Hence, it is argued, we must fall in order to rise. That soul only, it is to be inferred, can gain true intelligence and true virtue which has had a wild and bitter experience. The storms must beat upon it, that it may rise above them, and so attain the calm. Only by passing through the cloud is the sunshine beheld in all its brightness. So, it is thought, must the soul be under the cloud of sin, that it may drink in the brightness of God's goodness. Hence, it is concluded, our moral progress is from unconscious innocence into the deep and the dark of sin, and through that to awakened conscience and resistance and victory, until it stands forth in the uprightness of the moral athlete, able to endure every conflict and secure in abundant strength.

But this theory, to be complete, must add something more. If man have been, not only the victim of evil himself, but also the cause of grief and sorrow to others,—a leader of others into excesses, a bad example, and bad companion,—he has really been a benefit to the world; for his evil is balanced by the good that accrues, when the virtue he has been the means of developing, in those who have suffered heroically from himself and his bad associates, falls upon him in bright contrast to his hateful self, and so brings him back from the pit of sin to the love of good. For it is not unreasonable, in this Utopia, to hope for the universal result, that the man of guilty passions, at war with himself (no account being taken of the slavery in which his passions hold him), will be led, by seeing the goodness around him, to love it and embrace it, and to flee from his guilty self to a better life, under the guidance of that overruling power, to carry out whose educational purposes he has been playing with the fierce and scorching lightnings. Or, if, untouched by the light (as it must be confessed many seem to be all their life through), he die wallowing in the mire, then, seeing that his guilt arises from a defect in his education, it is thought that his career in another world will be, though bereft of much happiness as a lower and debased nature, yet free from actual misery; while those who have been led to virtue by overcoming evil will rise to heights otherwise impossible; so that the sum of happiness in the future will, in any event, have been increased by the evil of the present.

The fallacy from which this speculation starts is transparent enough. It supposes the primal innocence to have been simple unconsciousness of right and wrong. Innocence, it thinks, is thoughtful and confiding, happy and free, childlike and simple, lovable and yet defenceless,—a beautiful flower, but frail, and delicate and exposed. Such an unconsciousness must be at the mercy of the deceiver to be imposed upon, and of the tempter to be led away at the first allurement. If such be the original state of man,—if such were the condition of our first parents,—if they were innocent in the same sense in which we employ the term in speaking of childhood, human nature *must* be led away at the first temptation. Thinking no evil itself, it cannot comprehend the possibility of the tempter's thinking evil, and so *must* fall into the snare. Such innocence, having no knowledge of the law of God as a rule of life, the penalty of which is to be feared, cannot be held back from sin by fear; not knowing wrong to be contrary to God's love, it cannot be held from it by the love of God. It must, therefore, trust to experiment for its enlightenment. The conflict of the soul with itself, in passing through the dark labyrinth of sin, will be necessary, with such a start, to give it reason and reflection and watchfulness and faith. Hence men think they have discovered the true account of the world's mystery of sin and sorrow, when they have supposed the human race exposed innocent and defenceless to every temptation to sin and crime. If its primal innocence were a childish unconsciousness of wrong,—a mere happy, thoughtless life, governed by its own impulses of self-preservation, nothing could elevate it to the dignity of rational, intelligent obedience but the experience of danger through the experience of sin.

But if the evil of humanity in its origin be not necessary, but voluntary,—the consequence of a fall, and not inherent in us at first, though it be now,—then it is evident that the innocence of our first parents was something other than this mere defenceless unconsciousness and unsuspecting confidence. If man were a moral and reasonable being, who was put into a state, not of *education*, but of *probation*, then evil was not necessary to bring him to the highest good, and the guilt of its appearance belonged to him alone; he had all the consciousness of good, all the defence, all the safeguard against evil, all the moral height and grandeur of his nature, when he came from his Maker's hand blessed and pronounced very good, which he could have after the fight had been fought and the victory won; and the trial, even had he not sinned, could have left him nothing more than he was at first,—his only excellence being the persistent preservation of that holiness with which he was originally endowed.

The picture which Holy Scripture shows us of the first man is this: not that, while he remained pure in the garden of Eden, he did good and right unconsciously; but that he did good consciously, knowing it to be good, and forewarned, and therefore forearmed against evil. His innocence was not merely negative, the want of experience of evil; but it was the innocence of self-restraint, of obedience, of faith and love, of truth known as fully and completely as it could ever be. Adam was not created a child, nor a savage; he was made a man. His innocence was not childish and unsuspecting, but manly and reflective; and therefore he had no need of sin and evil for an education into character. When he sinned, whatever may have been the labyrinth in which his soul wandered and bewildered itself so as to choose evil for its portion,—whatever may have been the secret interior moral history of the fall,—whatever the thoughts which passed through his soul, and induced him to yield to temptation,—he lost by the experiment; he could not gain; and nothing in this mortal life, not even the glorious gospel of redemption itself, can restore man, while on earth, to his pristine perfection, or give him the same moral judgment and moral knowledge of good which Adam possessed when first from his Maker's hands, his soul illuminated with the full light of the Holy Spirit. His primal innocence was that of principle, of knowledge, of reflection, of self-restraint, of reason, of obedience, of perfect and complete manhood.

This is proved by two facts in the history of the fall. First, God gave to Adam an occupation and a law; He endowed him with a calling and laid upon him a command, which appealed to his reason and reflection as strongly as any experience of sin could be supposed to do. His life was to be a life of earnest work, without pain, indeed, and without sweat, but still work. "The Lord God took the man, and put him into the garden of Eden to dress it and to keep it." "And the Lord God commanded the man, saying, Of every tree in the garden thou mayest freely eat: but of the tree of knowledge of good and evil, thou mayest not eat of it: for in the day that thou eatest thereof thou shalt surely die." Here was reflection and consciousness of responsibility, developed by the law demanding obedience, and therefore not needing a fall to develop it. The second fact is, that the perfection of Adam was to be retained by *self-restraint*. The tree seemed every way a desirable one; it was "good for food, and pleasant to the eyes, and a tree to be desired to make one wise." It allured him to try his self-restraint, and the devil, in addition, was permitted to tempt him, to try his faith; and this he did by holding out a false idea of the knowledge of good and evil. The tree was called the tree of knowledge of good and evil, not because by it came the knowledge of good as well as of evil; but because by it came the experience of evil in contrast with the good he had lost. To eat of it was, in reality, to obtain the knowledge of good lost and of evil gained, changing the one into the remembrance of a lost glory, and enthroning the other as an ever-present tyrant. But before he ate Adam had the knowledge of good, without the experience of evil, and in this consisted his perfection. The law and the sense of responsibility were the instruments and means of producing that reflective, faithful obedience in which true perfection consists.

Now, the having a law is not sin, nor is it evil; nor is the being subject to temptation for probation. The yielding to temptation and the disobedience to law are the sin and the evil. There was, it is true, the possibility of sin; but the possibility of sin is not actual sin. There was no evil in the world when sin was only possible and not actual. The possibility of evil is the condition of moral freedom itself; but there is no need that moral freedom should lead us into sin. Free obedience is far more moral freedom than actual disobedience. Hence, had Adam obeyed the law and kept from yielding to the temptation, there would have been the highest good without any evil. Here, then, is the true solution of the question respecting perfection of nature in Adam. His moral and spiritual qualities were developed and brought into action by the *law of positive command*, and that law was the condition of his spiritual probation. The *law of nature* was preservative of his existence; the *law of reason* governed him in his worldly occupation; but *the law of command* brought him into the communion of faith and obedience with his God and Father.

The significance of the law of positive command is thus made evident. It is the condition of his becoming a higher being than a mere animal. For if we examine carefully, we shall find that all the difference in action between a spiritual nature and an animal nature is contained in the idea of *moral responsibility*, or *accountability*. And this accountability being analyzed, implies a *mutual trust* of each other on the part of two parties; the superior committing to the inferior a trust, on the faith that he will keep it, without any positive guarantee of the confidence thus reposed; and the inferior accepting the trust, without any guarantee of the reward or punishment, except his faith and confidence in the superior. Now, if the trust be betrayed, responsibility rests, because of the personal offence implied in unfaithfulness. The disobedient subject puts a personal affront upon the superior by doubting his word, or setting at naught his menace, or making light of his proffered rewards. His disobedience and unfaithfulness imply contempt of the person who has put the law upon him; while, on the other hand, obedience and faithfulness imply faith, love, trust, high principle, hope, and confidence. Obedience or disobedience to a positive command is, therefore, a strictly *personal* concern; the imposition of such command brings God and man into personal communion with each other, in a way which could not have been accomplished by the law of nature, or the law of reason. For faith, love, and trust come in when a law is given to us of which we do not see the reason; when we do see it, the reason is sufficient to determine us, without either faith, or love, or hope. But only by positive command can a law be given of which we do not see the reason; and therefore, if there had been no command in Paradise, Adam would not have been in the way of developing those moral and spiritual qualities, nor gifted with that personal communion with God, which made him the chief of the terrestrial creation.

But as it was the law of command which gave Adam his moral being, so it was in disobedience to it that he fell. The possibility of his elevation involved the possibility of his fall. It being God's gracious will, therefore, to give man the loftiest position possible for a created being to attain, He did not shrink (if we may so speak) from any possible consequences which that intention involved, nor did He fail to make such provision for the reparation of the evil as might be necessary in case it occurred. "The Lamb" was "slain from the foundation of the world." Out of the *command* grew the whole moral and spiritual history of mankind. Nor is it conceivable how, were there not the command, any disobedience or sin could have been possible,—how any man could have been *free* to do right because *able* to do wrong. For the impulses, emotions, and instincts which proclaimed the law of nature were themselves the agents in obeying it; in proclaiming it, they were actually at work obeying it; the proclamation and the obedience were in general identical, and the perfect man would never will to do anything which the law of nature prohibited. The same is true with respect to the law of reason. Guided by reason, we always choose that which seems to us to be best; and if reason were perfect, as it was in Adam, it would show us that which is really the best; nor is it agreeable to the nature of reason, seeing the best, to choose a worse. Hence there could be no disobedience to the law of reason in a perfect state. As far as it or the law of nature is concerned, we should stand on the moral level of the brutes, who have no morality, have no personal faith, are conscious of no accountability, because they are subject to no positive command. The moral station which implied the possibility of choice inherent in the nature of freedom is that of subordination to a command; and this station is the highest to which any created being can aspire.

Adam misused his freedom to disobey the command; he sinned, and lost his innocence, his favor with God, his happy Paradise, and his perfection of nature.

Of the fall itself, speculation can give us no clearer knowledge than our possession of the simple fact. Adam was tempted; he had the power of resistance, he was forewarned of the consequence, he did not resist, he was unfaithful, disobeyed, and fell. The effect of the fall upon himself was the guilt of his disobedience fixed upon his soul, the withdrawal of God's favor, the departure of the indwelling Spirit of God, the loss, consequently, of immortality, spiritual death immediately, and temporal death after a short delay; and, besides this, such a corruption of his being, such an indwelling sin, that neither nature nor reason would henceforth proclaim audibly and clearly the law they were intended to teach. The depravation of the spiritual being spread into the rational and the natural being, and depraved them likewise, so that, in every part of his constitution, he was "very far gone from original righteousness," had within himself the seeds of sin, and transmitted this fault, and corruption and unhappy state to all his posterity.

Here, then, is the true explanation of those facts which the false theory noticed above misconstrues and perverts. The primitive state of man is for us only a fixed point of observation,—not a present or attainable state. We are not as Adam was; evil is now a melancholy experience, and sin a dreadful plague. Our present state, with all its moral phenomena, is the consequence of that original sin which brought death into the world, and changed the whole pathway of humanity towards eternal life. The redeemed and regenerate man has a different development of spiritual life from what would have been had he retained his purity. He comes into the world a sinner, as made by Adam; he leaves it a saint, as new-made by Christ. He derives guilt from Adam, and he must arrive at the knowledge of good through Christ. The work of grace is the work of restoration.

It is true that on coming into the world, and for a long time after we have attained some physical and intellectual growth, we are in a state of moral unconsciousness; but it is not the true explanation of the fact that unconsciousness in man is innocence. *Moral unconsciousness is moral guilt,*—the effect of the loss entailed upon us by the fall. To one who watches with an observant eye, it cannot but be evident how easily and how unconsciously the so-called innocence of childhood falls from one wrong into another as years pass on, totally defenceless (if apart from the saving influence of God's grace given to His church) against the assaults and seductions of the tempter. The cycle of life, in too many cases, it is admitted, runs through and because of moral unconsciousness, into actual and open sin; then, by the grace of God, the sin is brought home to the conscience, the man passes through a crisis of the spiritual life, and at length begins to serve God aright, having developed, by the aid of Divine grace, moral consciousness, reflection, repentance, living faith, self-examination, repudiation of sin, and the endeavor to lead a holy life. But why so defenceless against sin at the first, except that he has inherited a fall? That cannot be true innocence which falls naturally, as the powers waken, into first the little sin, then the great sin, then the life of sin. It is *guilt*, needing the atoning blood of the Redeemer to wash out its stain,—needing the alarm of conscience urging it to seek the conscious innocence of justification by grace.

The true account of our actual sin is not that it is our necessary education up to good, but that it is the fruit and manifestation of that original sin in which we were born. We are justly held guilty before the act, because by our birth-sin, our fallen estate, and our want or our neglect of the safeguards of religion, we carry the principle of disobedience or unruliness within and have no defence against it.

"Sin," says St. John, "is the transgression of the law;" and therefore its chief offence is against God the Father, since He is that person of the Holy Trinity who is the giver of the law. This consideration enables us to observe the difference between the grace of the Father, and the grace of the Son and of the Holy Spirit,—the Father's grace accepting the atonement, the Son making it; the Father granting our sanctification, the Spirit working it. The contrast we have just concluded, of the fallen with the unfallen state of man, will show us also what action of the grace of God the Father is directed towards us in our fallen, and what in our regenerate state.

1. In the holy and happy state of Paradise, since there was no need of redemption, there was no need of redeeming grace; still there was grace of God the Father with the man unfallen. Applied to what Adam enjoyed in that state, the word grace is used in its primary sense, to denote the favor and love of God bestowed upon Adam in the perfect bliss of full communion and personal converse with his Maker. We may also apply the word to the indwelling presence of the Holy Spirit which was in Adam until he lost his innocence.[a] Thus the word bears its second sense, a gift actually given,—in Scripture language, "poured out upon" or infused into the mind or soul of man. A clear apprehension of the distinction between these two meanings is most important, for the reason that while the first sense is common to each of the three persons of the Holy Trinity, the second sense is peculiar to the second and third persons, as will be seen further on. In the first sense, grace or favor is not a gift actually given over to man; it is (to speak after

---

[a] See Bp. Bull's Fifth Discourse.

the manner of the schools) an affection of the Divine Mind immanent in Deity; in the second sense, grace is a spiritual gift transferred to man by a Divine act, and remaining with him, unless, in consequence of sin, it be withdrawn. Both kinds of grace were enjoyed by Adam in Paradise,—the presence of the Spirit as a gift, the love and favor of the Father as a disposition or affection; the latter the source of the former, as, indeed, of all other gifts, of whatever kind, which added to the blessedness and happiness of Adam's perfection.

All things, it was said, are of the Father, by the Son, through the Holy Spirit. The Father is the source or origin of all beings; the Son and the Spirit are the immediate agents by whom all operations are carried on. What the Father wrought in the creation of the world, He wrought by the Son, and through the Holy Spirit. So, likewise, in the work of grace, what the Father, who is the source and original of grace as of all other good, communicates to mankind, is given by the Son, through the Holy Spirit. The Father, therefore, enters not *personally* into our souls; but the grace which enters into man as a gift, is given personally by the Son, or by the Holy Spirit, and the Father is present essentially, by His unity with the Son and the Holy Spirit, whom He gives to us.[a] Hence the grace which He personally shows to man is His favor and love, His forgiveness and justification and adoption, the immanent affection which is the foundation of the grace given by the other Persons of

---

[a] St. John, xiv. 23.

the blessed Trinity. And with this fundamental conception of the grace of God the Father, the language of Scripture uniformly agrees.

2. The grace of God the Father towards fallen, unregenerate man, must, of course, differ in its manifestation from that towards him in his first estate. It is developed in showing mercy. Love and favor, as such, are for the perfect; mercy is for the fallen.

By his disobedience, man forfeited the love and favor of God. Instead of continuing a child of God, he became a rebellious and condemned sinner, a child of wrath whose future, by his own act, was the penalty of which he had been warned, temporal and eternal death. The Holy Spirit, who had clothed him with a robe of righteousness, was withdrawn; he was guilty, naked, ashamed, conscience-stricken, already unhappy, self-condemned, and expectant of unhappiness forever. He had offended God, had no more title to Divine grace in any form, had arrayed against himself, on the contrary, every attribute of the Divine nature. The justice of God required satisfaction; His holiness, the condemnation of sin; His truth, that the threatened penalty should be inflicted; His majesty, the vindication of His law; even His love, that the disorder and disturbance of a perverse will should be banished from the harmonies of the Creation. The sin of Adam was no "being overtaken in a fault." The command had been disobeyed with full knowledge of the consequences. No account of the event will meet the truth, but that it was the wilful, conscious disobedience of pride and ambition, by which Adam set himself against God, and sought another place than that which God had assigned him; and of necessity he set God against himself, unless some means were found, by which God and man might be reconciled.

Now, since God the Father, as we have seen, is the giver of the Law, the offence was particularly against Him. He was the offended person. The Son and the Holy Spirit could not but partake in the Father's indignation against and abhorrence of the sin, as being one with Him, as having the same will, and the same holiness; but against the Father, formally and principally was the sin committed. The alienation was a total alienation from God, but specially from God the Father. The Father, therefore, could not, by the necessities of the case, be the person who actively wrought the reconciliation. The grace, which even as an affection was forfeited, could not become a gift immediately from the Father, entering into the soul of man, and so regenerating him. It could only remain (so far as Scripture gives us ground for concluding) as a merciful disposition, and a merciful suspension of judgment until the Atonement was made for the sin, and its effect upon man's nature was blotted out by his regeneration and renewal. If any act or gift of grace could restore the filial relation, it must come into our souls, whether as an object of faith, or as a regenerating power, from the Son, or the Holy Spirit; the deed availing to reconciliation must be acted towards the Father, not by the Father. We have seen that the grace of God could become a gift to the man unfallen, only in the person of the Son and of the Holy Ghost; there must be added the additional reason against its becoming so, in the case of fallen man, that God the Father was the offended person, and so set at an immeasurably greater distance from mankind. In the attitude of hostility (for it was no less) in which man had set God the Father against him by his transgression,—when the primitive love and favor had been forfeited, no further advance or closer approach could be thought of, until the atonement was provided, on the part of that person against whom the sin had been committed, and all whose attributes were pledged to vindicate the broken law.

The *prevenient grace* of God the Father, therefore, is His merciful disposition towards mankind, displayed in several acts preparatory to their forgiveness, regeneration, and readoption into His Kingdom and family. The Holy Scripture shows us the extent of this merciful disposition: "God so loved the world that He gave His only-begotten Son, that whosoever believeth in Him should not perish, but have everlasting life." He suspended the infliction of extreme punishment on Adam; He permitted his posterity to come into the world with a hope of redemption, though born in sin; He sent His Son in due time to make the atonement, and authorized a new covenant, whereby its virtue could be communicated to each particular man for the forgiveness of his sins. For if there were not this prevenient grace and merciful disposition of God the Father towards man, how could the means of regeneration and restoration ever have been provided? Unless God the Father had the merciful will to accept the atonement and permit the regeneration, neither the atonement nor the regeneration would have been possible by the agency of the Son and the Holy Spirit, who are in all things subordinate to the Father, and can do nothing against His will.

Every man, then, who is now born into the world, stands in this relation to God the Father. He is born in sin, with the taint of guilt and the disorder of nature under which Adam remained after the Fall; subject, therefore, to condemnation; called in Holy Scripture a "child of wrath." But, by the mercy of God, the condemnation is suspended, the execution stayed, and an opportunity offered to escape it altogether. Man is not, at birth, in a "state of salvation," but of condemnation suspended by grace; and this suspension of judgment, together with the provision for the atonement, is the *prevenient* grace of the Father. Before we can be truly in a "state of salvation," we must be made actual partakers of the virtue of the atonement, by regeneration through the Son, and sanctification of the Spirit.

3. Then will God the Father accept us again into the fulness of His love and favor as His own children by adoption. This is the third bestowal of the grace of the Father. When regenerate in Christ, God restores us to His love, and adopts us again into his family. The suspended condemnation is now altogether removed; instead of a mere provisional existence, a toleration conditional on a future regeneration, we are now "accepted in the Beloved." The dividing line between this grace of complete acceptance and that of forecasting mercy is, for all who live where the Gospel is known (and of others we have no means of judging), the moment when they are made one with Christ in the waters of regeneration. Before that moment, they

are sinners under sentence of death ; after that, they are children of God, restored, regenerated, accepted, adopted, heirs of the everlasting inheritance of His love and favor as Adam was at first,—nay, better than in Adam's first estate, for they are beloved in Christ, still subject, however, to the "infection of nature, which remains even in them that are regenerated,"[a] and which cannot be wholly eradicated until the death of the body, and its resurrection from the grave.

This final and full grace of God the Father is manifested particularly in the economy of Redemption, by those declarative acts of Divine goodness towards us, which assure us of our estate, conditioned on the effectual operations of the Son and of the Holy Ghost, respecting which we shall treat in the subsequent chapters. They are : 1. Remission, or Forgiveness, by which all our sins are pardoned and blotted out of the book of God's remembrance, no more to appear against us. 2. Justification, by which we are declared or accounted just before God, for the merits of His Son Jesus Christ, in whom we are regenerate and made righteous. 3. Adoption, by which the cloud on our Sonship of the Universal Father is removed, and we can rejoice in the love He dispenses to His children. For which mercy and grace to Him be praise and thanksgiving for ever and ever.

---

[b] Art. IX, of the XXXIX Articles.

CHAPTER III.

THE GRACE OF THE SON.

MAN fell, as we have seen, by a voluntary act of disobedience; and his fall was the death of his spiritual nature, God's favor and the presence of His Spirit being withdrawn; for, "as the soul is the life of the body," says an old author, "so God is the life of the soul." By the fall, his rational nature also became depraved, and his animal nature corrupted; so that he could work righteousness neither by the natural law nor by the law of reason, any more than by the commandment. We fallen men, in our wickedness, act both disobediently, and irrationally, and unnaturally; in every way, therefore, we disobey the law of God, and are amenable to His severest displeasure. But in the midst of His anger God remembered mercy; He provided a way for our restoration; "He so loved the world" that He gave His Son for our Redeemer, a Mediator between God and Man.

The work set before the Mediator was twofold: 1, to satisfy the law of God, by an atonement for the transgression, and thus to blot out the sin (so to speak) from the book of God; and 2, to regenerate, renew, and finally restore man to a state of perfect righteousness, so that no record nor trace of sin remains in the book of human nature. Both these operations are necessary; for whether God read the record of sin in His own book, or in man's book (if it were possible, which it is not, that it could be blotted out from the one while it remained in the other), it must meet with condemnation, wherever it is read, and therefore it must be wiped from both records. The one work is performed by the Atonement which Christ offered to the Father; the other, by the communication of His grace to each person who receives it,—for, unless we be partakers of Christ's grace to blot out our sins from our own hearts, the Atonement does not avail to blot them out from the book of God's remembrance.[a]

The Grace of the Son is His entire work of mediation, undertaken in obedience to the Father, and from love and mercy to us men; but specially, the term is used in this book to designate His influence and work in the nature of man, regenerating and restoring it. Preliminary to the inquiry what that influence and work are, it is important to answer the question, What are the conditions in human nature to be met by the act which restores?

It is evident that the restoration cannot be, like the fall, an act purely voluntary on the part of man, else would no mediator and no grace be required. But since man has still a will (though enfeebled, naturally disposed only to evil, and unable to do good of itself),

---

[a] Misapprehension of the relation of grace imparted and the Atonement offered, is the foundation of the difficulty from which the Calvinists seek to escape by their sad error of "Particular Redemption."

and since one effect of the restoration must be to bring the will back to the freedom it has lost, so that it will be a restored will, obeying freely, the grace of the Redeemer will be made a matter of voluntary acceptance, and the restoration will be so far voluntary on man's part, as that he is willingly, or not at all, a subject of regenerating grace.[a] Man, though he is unable to "turn and prepare himself by his own natural strength and good works to faith and calling upon God,"[b] is able, when his heart has been touched by the Spirit, and the salvation is offered to his personal acceptance, to exercise a choice in respect of it, to accept or to reject it. The means by which he is Divinely enabled to act with freedom in seeking and receiving the regeneration will be seen in the next chapter, in which we treat of the grace of the Holy Spirit; for the present, attention is asked to the fact that we are voluntary subjects of the grace of the Son.

To accept that grace voluntarily, is to accept it by an act; and so to bring it under the conditions of human actions in general.

To perform any voluntary action, man needs, under the laws of his finite nature, (1) the motive, (2) the opportunity, and (3) the power to accomplish what he wills. The Infinite will draws all the conditions of action from itself, unbounded by anything without itself; but a finite will, before it can act, must be stirred by the heart with a *motive* to act, in a desire

---

[a] The case of infants, before they reach the age of consciousness and responsibility, is an exception to be noted hereafter.

[b] Article X, of the XXXIX Articles.

which seeks realization; it must be afforded the *opportunity* for action, which is perceived by the mind, the observing and thinking faculty. Having the motive and the opportunity, the freedom of the will consists in this, that it is not necessarily controlled by them; it has an inherent ability to adopt or resist the motive, to perform or decline the action. This seems to be the law of finite, voluntary action, so far as we are able to conceive it. A perfect finite will, therefore, is that to which the heart always presents the right motives and the mind the right opportunities; and which retains in itself, unimpaired, the power of action with which it was originally endowed by its Creator.

The human will, however, is not perfect. It is corrupt and depraved, partly in its loss of power to do what otherwise it might have done, and partly in its connection with the other faculties of our nature. In fallen man, the heart, the seat of the desires, affections, and other motives, is fallen; by its separation from God it has lost faith, hope, and love, the higher spiritual motives to action; it retains only the lower, disorderly, selfish or sensual passions and emotions. Now, when these are all the motives which the heart presents to the will, the will itself may be free; but, from its very constitution, as depending on motives, it is, in the language of the old theologians, "free only to do evil" apart from Divine grace; free of choice, but having a choice only among diverse modes of evil. In this fallen state, helpless, hopeless, and unholy, if man were forsaken of all influences of Divine grace, none but evil motives could be present in his heart, none but opportunities of evil action could present themselves to his mind; and therefore his will could have neither power, nor motive, nor opportunity to do the thing that is right. For without the Redeemer and the Gospel, and the grace given for the Redeemer's sake, there could be no repentance, and no impulse towards it; no faith as a ground of hope; no opportunity of regeneration, and no motive to seek it. The will could act freely and by choice, up to its power, under the motives presented; but those motives themselves, being all evil, would urge only to the short-lived pleasures of sin, or to hate against God, under whose righteous condemnation we lay. That this is not our state is of the prevenient mercy and grace of God.

The three things, then, which it was necessary to provide for man, to meet the conditions of human action, and enable him to accept as a voluntary agent the grace of regeneration, are—(1) for his heart, a motive to seek and accept it; a "conviction of sin, of righteousness, and of judgment;"[a] (2) for his mind, a knowledge of the Redeemer, by whom, and the means by which, it may be obtained; and (3) for the will itself, an exertion within his ability, by which, under the direction of the heart and the mind, it may take hold of, and receive back again, the life and power, by the loss of which it has been unable to do good, by the restoration of which it will be enabled to serve God more and more perfectly, growing day by day to spiritual manhood.

Correspondingly the act of the man, requisite to

---

[a] John, xvi. 8.

obtain the gift which entitles him to his readoption into God's family, unfolds in a threefold development: (1) obedience to the *motive*, the forsaking of sin, the return to good works, the desire to be cleansed from guilt, the determination to live as becometh the child of God,—*repentance*, the allegiance of the heart to God; (2) recognition of the Redemption wrought, trust in the Redeemer, perception of the opportunity and means offered, or *faith*, which is the allegiance of the mind; and (3) the seeking by the appointed means, and the thankful and joyful receiving the gift by which the will and the whole man is *regenerated*.

Repentance, faith, regeneration, these three acts, or rather, these three developments of the one act, must agree in the man who is restored by the grace of the Son, to the favor and grace of the Father. Repentance without faith will not avail, nor faith without repentance (were either possible separately, which neither is), nor both faith and repentance without the actual gift of regeneration. Salvation is a grace given unto us. Though voluntarily receptive, we are *only receptive* in every stage of our spiritual renewal. Even repentance and faith are the yielding to an influence from above. The act, then, throughout is receptive; it has its virtue in the work of the Mediator; and thus the conditions are harmonized that it is under the conditions of our voluntary action, and yet is entirely the work of the Son of God.

The reader will bear in mind that I am now treating of the Grace of the Son. Many questions will doubtless suggest themselves, and press for an immediate reply, touching the genesis of repentance and faith, which, in order of time, precede the gift of the regenerating grace of the Son; they will be answered in the subsequent chapter on the Grace of the Holy Spirit. Nor is what has been said intended as a complete account of repentance and faith. As viewed thus far, they are rather a preparation for, than a part of, the Christian life, which does not begin until our regeneration; after which both faith and repentance have a new development and office. What it is wished to fix attention upon at this time is, that three operations of the spiritual faculties of man must coincide in one complex act of voluntary return to God, and acceptance of the offered salvation, in order to begin the new life.

It has pleased the Divine Wisdom that these faculties should all find their object in the one person, who is set forth as the Redeemer, in whom are combined all the attributes and offices required as the complement of man's needs and weaknesses, and guilt and dire necessity.

The one testimony of our Saviour to Himself, therefore, which is all-inclusive,—the text in which He has collected all His multifarious revelations of Himself into one focus,—is the declaration: "I am the Way, the Truth, and the Life; no man cometh unto the Father but by Me."[a] Of this text, so full of meaning and so wide in application, comprehending all provision for the necessities of man, regenerate or unregenerate, the meaning doubtless is: "The Way," by which the penitent may return and be accepted; "The

---

[a] John, xiv. 6.

Truth," which the faithful behold; "The Life" communicated to the regenerate. To repent and plead Christ's merits is to enter on the way; to believe in Him is to know the truth; to be made one with Him in His Church is to have the life.

The consideration of the grace of the Son, therefore, divides itself into three heads: (1) as he is the Way; (2) as he is the Truth; (3) as he is the Life.

In each development, however, it has the same relation to its source, which is therefore first to be noted.

The grace of the Son is personal,—given from Himself as distinct from the Father and from the Holy Spirit. The Son is the second Person of the Holy Trinity, and upon this His distinct personality depends His power to help us in our needs. "In Him was life, and that life was the light of men."[a] "As the Father hath life in Himself, so hath He given to the Son to have life in Himself."[b] Hence He takes of His own to give unto us, that "through Him we may have access to the Father."[c]

Now His personal grace is the effluence and act of whatsoever belongs to His personality. His whole Person is at work in the atonement He has made for us, and in the grace He gives to us. But His Person includes both His Deity and His humanity. He is God, and He became man; He is God and man thenceforth, in one person. He became man for the work of Redemption; He is God and man, therefore, in whatsoever appertains to that work.

This truth the Church confessed in the decision of

---

[a] John, i. 4.   [b] John, v. 26.   [c] Eph. ii. 18.

her General Councils of Ephesus and Chalcedon, that the two natures, Divine and human, exist in the one person of Christ. The Divine Person assumed human nature, not a human person, into conjunction with Himself, so that after the conjunction there were no more persons,—there was no other person than before. He took a complete human nature,—a human body and a human soul; but He who assumed it was still the one person and no other,—God the Son. His human nature belonged to His personality; it did not constitute another personality. In the well-known language of our great Hooker, "If the Son of God had taken to Himself a man new-made and already perfected, it would of necessity follow that there are in Christ two persons,—the one assuming and the other assumed; whereas, the Son of God did not assume a man's person into His own, but a man's nature to His own person, and therefore took *semen*, the seed of Abraham, the very first original element of our nature, before it was come to have any personal human subsistence. The flesh and the conjunction of the flesh with God began both at one instant; his making and taking to Himself our flesh was but one act, so that in Christ there is no personal subsistence but one, and that from everlasting. By taking only the nature of man, He still continueth one person, and changeth but the manner of His subsisting, which was before in the mere glory of the Son of God, and is now in the habit of our flesh."[a]

Now, as He became man, that He might accomplish

---

[a] Ec. Pol., b. v. ch. lii. 3.

our Redemption, it follows that His Atonement is the compound effect of His Divine worth and His human action; it follows, also, that His regenerating and restoring grace is a compound influence of His Divine life and His glorified humanity. There is a human part or element in the grace of the Son, as well as a Divine. He is the Way, by being man, as well as by being God; the Truth, as God, and also as man; the Life, both as God and as man. His Divine and human natures are united in His action and influence, as they are united in His person. This truth seems to have been strangely overlooked in our day; but it was universally admitted and dwelt upon by our Fathers in the faith. "Doth any man doubt," asks Hooker, "but that even from the flesh of Christ our very bodies do receive that life which shall make them glorious at the latter day, and for which they are already accounted parts of His blessed body?"[a] The conjoint activity of the two natures in the work of grace was so universally received that that great divine could not conceive the possibility of a negative answer. The grace of the Godhead, filling Christ as man, is diffused from Him, as man, upon those whom "He is not ashamed to call His brethren;"[b] and by vital union with Him, the second Adam, drawing immortality from Him as we drew nature from the first Adam, we who are regenerate are made living members of His body, living branches of Him, the true vine.

His mediatorial work, therefore, in all its parts, depends on His Incarnation,—His being made flesh. He

---

[a] Ec. Pol., b. v. ch. lvi. 9.   [b] Heb. ii. 11.

"was made man;" He lived upon earth thirty-three years and a third; He taught, He suffered, He died; thus accomplishing the first part of His Mediation, the making atonement to the Father for our sins. After this, He rose from the dead, and ascended into heaven, in token that the atonement is sufficient. This was preliminary to the gift of His indwelling grace. Even the salvation of those who died in faith before He came seems to have waited for its completion until His death, according to that passage in the Epistle to the Hebrews: "These all, having obtained a good report, through faith, received not the promise: God having provided some better thing for us, that they, without us, should not be made perfect."[a] As respects us who live after His day, our part in the atonement is conditioned on our participation of His grace.

It does not fall within the plan of this work to discuss at large the logical conceptions under which men have presented to themselves fuller or more partial views of the Atonement; nor to consider the perversions of Scripture language by those who deny it. It has been argued that the Atonement is offered to the justice of God, as the assumption by Christ of our penalty; that it is the means of appeasing the anger of God; that it is directed to the holiness of God; that the actual sufferings of the Saviour were equivalent to the aggregate pains of all who would have been lost without Him. But it is rather, I conceive, to be accepted as a transcendent truth, above all logical statements or analysis, containing within itself a likeness to

---

[a] Heb. xi. 39, 40.

The Grace of the Son.

all the analogies by which it is represented in the Holy Scriptures, both of the Old and New Testaments, but not to be adequately described by any one; a fact, indisputable on the authority of Holy Scripture, but, like the Incarnation, a mystery above our comprehension. It satisfies, and is addressed to all the attributes of God; it is, at once, the mirror of His love, the satisfaction of His justice, the vindication of His holiness, the manifestation of His wisdom, the exhibition of His power, the assertion of His sovereignty, the example of His mercy, the display of His glory, "which angels desire to look into and are not able."[a] Against those, however, who deny the death of Christ to be a proper sacrificial act, an atonement and propitiation for sin, while they profess to receive Holy Scripture, we need urge but one reflection. If His death on Mount Calvary were not a propitiatory and expiatory sacrifice for the sins of the world, to what effect were the multitudinous sacrifices of bulls and goats and lambs offered up, day by day, for so many centuries, by God's appointment, in the tabernacle and the temple, in prophecy and type of that "blood of Jesus Christ which cleanseth from all sin?" It is not that the Sacrifice of Christ is represented of like nature with those others by a Divine accommodation to the partial conception of the human understanding, but that those precedent typical sacrifices themselves were established by Almighty God, for the express purpose of educating the human mind to a right conception of that precious death of Christ. The

---

[a] The student may follow out for himself the train of thought thus suggested.

type took its meaning from the antitype, not the antitype from the type. By the sacrifices of the Mosaic law, God taught the world that the death of Christ was truly an expiation; and if the type—so many thousands of lives sacrificed day by day and year by year—if this type were so great, even counted by money value and mere number—if the principle of sacrifice for expiation and for purification were made to pervade every part of the national and the individual religion—if these millions of stricken victims and seas of blood were but the type, what must be the infinite dignity and awfulness of the antitype?

As a man, "the Christ," the "anointed Man," the Son, became our Prophet, Priest, and King. He combined in His person all the offices to which the anointing oil, which was the type of His Spirit, consecrated men. Elisha was His type, thus consecrated a Prophet; Aaron, thus set apart a Priest; David, thus made a King. As a Priest, Christ atones for, intercedes for, blesses us; as a Prophet, He reveals, teaches, instructs; as a King, He protects, governs, and feeds us. This is the Catholic conception of Christ's office. It is but another way of saying what He Himself said, in the text we have quoted. As Priest, He is the Way; for by His atonement and intercession we can approach the Father, and by His blessing all favor from the Father is given us. As Prophet, He is the Truth, for He is Himself the doctrine He reveals. As King, he is the Life, for from His royal treasure-house of grace we receive our new life of pardon and obedience, and our nourishment with heavenly food.

These offices are inseparable in Him, as are His two

natures, both in themselves and in relation to us. The atonement He made as priest does not avail for us individually, unless we have accepted Him as prophet; nor does He make the revelation of Himself as the Truth, in His full blaze of glory and, of comfort to our souls, until we are subject to His kingly rule, partakers of His kingly bounty, and related to Him as "the first-born among many brethren." He is not the Way for us, unless He is for us the Truth; nor is He the saving Truth for us, unless He is in us the Life. "In Him was life, and *that life* was the *light* of men." His act, though complex, is one; though consisting of many parts, it is a complete whole, of which all must be ours, or not any.

It being laid at the foundation, therefore, that the grace of Christ is a compound effect of His own two natures in the unity of His person, having both a Divine and human element, and reposing upon the fact of the Atonement; and these truths being such as must not be lost sight of for an instant, but are assumed in all which is hereafter said, we proceed to consider each declaration separately. And as our purpose is to state the doctrine of Holy Scripture, we shall chiefly occupy ourselves with ranging under each head such passages as belong there, pointing out their bearing and interpretation when necessary.

I. First, then, Christ is "the Way." The reader will have seen, by this time, from the course of the argument, that the significance of this title which our Lord assumed to Himself is derived from the sad but certain truth, that by sin man is set afar off from God, that the communication has been broken off between the sinful being and his Maker. This necessitated a mediation and a Mediator. It was in respect of the mediation of His Son Jesus Christ, as at a future time to be accomplished, that God gave His prevenient grace to those who lived acceptably before the coming of Christ; and it is with respect to the same mediation that He now gives grace and shows mercy to men, even before they are actually accepted into saving union with the Head of the Church. Whatsoever dealings of God with man, therefore, have been merciful (as what dealings have not?), whether before the Atonement was made or since, whether the recipients of mercy are accepted Christians or not yet regenerate; whatsoever access man has had to God, to ask either for transitory mercies or for everlasting salvation, have been procured for us by the mediation of our Lord Jesus Christ,—by His priestly acts of atonement for our sins, and of intercession on our behalf. He has made "a new and living way, through the veil, that is to say, His flesh."[a] He is thus the Restorer and the means of communication between God and man; and this is His meaning in calling Himself "the Way." "No man cometh to the Father but by Me." And, conversely, no man receiveth from the Father but by Him.

This general truth is expressed in several different parts of Holy Scripture. It is revealed in shadow in the dream of Jacob, in which he saw a ladder set on the earth, and the top of it reached to heaven, and by it the angels of God ascended and descended from earth to heaven and from heaven to earth.[b] That the

---

[a] Heb.   [b] Gen. xxviii. 12.

ladder was a type of Christ, our Lord Himself teaches, interpreting it, as He closed His interview with Nathanael: "Verily, verily, I say unto you, Hereafter ye shall see heaven open, and the angels of God ascending and descending upon the Son of Man."[a] The author of the Epistle to the Hebrews founds his exhortation upon the figure thus: "Having, therefore, brethren, boldness to enter into the holiest by the blood of Jesus, by *a new and living way* which He hath consecrated for us through the veil, that is to say, His flesh, and having an High Priest over the house of God, let us *draw near* with a true heart, in full assurance of faith, having our hearts sprinkled from an evil conscience, and our bodies washed with pure water."[b] So St. Paul, writing to his Ephesian converts, reminds them of the contrast between their former heathen darkness and their present Christian blessedness: "Remember that ye, being in time past Gentiles in the flesh, . . . at that time ye were without Christ, being aliens from the commonwealth of Israel; . . . but now, in Christ Jesus, ye, who sometimes were far off, are *made nigh* by the blood of Christ."[c] A little further on, he refers to the same figure: "Through Him we both [Jew and Gentile] *have access* by one Spirit to the Father."[d] And again: "In whom we have boldness and *access with confidence* by the faith of Him;"[e] which idea is expanded, in the Epistle to the Romans, thus: "Being justified by faith, we have peace with God through our Lord Jesus Christ, by

---

[a] John, i. 51. [b] Heb. x. 19–22. [c] Eph. ii. 11–13.
[d] Eph. ii. 18. [e] Eph. iii. 12.

whom also we have access by faith into this grace wherein we stand, and rejoice in hope of the glory of God."[a] "I am the Door," says our Saviour Himself: "by Me, if any man enter in, he shall be saved, and shall go in and out and find pasture."[b]

The grace of Christ, then, for which He calls Himself "the Way," is the virtue of His sacrificial death and priestly power. This may, indeed, seem to exhaust His work and comprehend all its results. For if He be a way by which we have access to God, and by which blessing is returned from God to us, our salvation is all accomplished,—we are fully restored. But, in truth, the different views of the office of Christ are only different aspects of the same whole, according as it is seen from different points, and in relation with different needs of humanity. Are we viewed as in a state of banishment from God, Christ is "the Way" of return; are we groping in mental and spiritual darkness, He is the "Light" and the "Truth;" are we spiritually dead, He is the "Life." Hence, if we be "brought nigh" in the way, it follows that we shall be "walking in the light," and be made "alive from the dead." We cannot contemplate one view without finding features common to the others. The progress is the same along each line of advancement,—they all converge in the act of our Regeneration.

Not to digress, however, the grace of Christ, "the way," is the virtue of His sacrificial death and priestly power. His priestly mediation, being the condition precedent of all grace whatsoever, having been estab-

---

[a] Rom. v. 1, 2. [b] John, x. 9.

lished in the eternal counsels before any grace was given by Father, Son, or Holy Ghost, and being also, through the intercession He makes in heaven, the means by which all blessings, spiritual and temporal, are obtained for us, day by day into all the future, the priesthood of Christ must be commensurate with our salvation, even to our immortality. Hence we are told, "He abideth a priest continually."[a] "He hath an unchangeable priesthood."[b] He is "a priest forever, after the order of Melchizadek."[c]

The priestly office under the law, which was the pattern of things unseen, had three functions: 1. To offer the sacrifice of atonement for sin, or of thanksgiving for mercies. 2. To make prayer and intercession to God on behalf of the people. 3. To bless the people with authority on behalf of God. By the two former acts, taken together as essentially the same, is represented the mediatorial work of Christ, our great High Priest, directed on our behalf towards God; in the latter act was foreshadowed His mediatorial work towards us,—comprehending together, with all exercise of His Kingly munificence, our absolution from our sins, and the "sprinkling" or cleansing our consciences from their stain, by the actual, but spiritual application of His blood.

There is thus presented to our view a twofold grace of our High Priest: first, His Divine love, leading Him to give Himself for us,—in combination with His human sympathy, by which He ever feels for us; and secondly, His gift or communication to the soul (by

---

[a] Heb.   [b] Heb.   [c] Heb.

which it becomes regenerate) of a grace supernatural, derived from Himself as God and man, which, so far as relates to this division of our subject, is called in Holy Scripture "the sprinkling with His blood." This last is the act which seals the reconciliation. When the conscience is thus cleansed, and God is thereby reconciled to the individual believer by the personal appropriation to him of the atoning blood, then is Christ "the way;" the access to God is free and open, and they "who were far off" are "made nigh by the blood of Christ."

This twofold grace has a fourfold operation,—a final observation, which enables us to understand and harmonize all the Scripture declarations respecting the Priesthood of Christ. 1. He made the Atonement to God for us. 2. He absolves us, for God. 3. He entered into Heaven as our Intercessor. 4. He enters into our souls as our Restorer. These four particulars underlie all the statements of Holy Scripture. In the Epistle to the Hebrews, which is the inspired treatise that expounds systematically the doctrine of the Evangelical Priesthood, they are everywhere assumed, and appear throughout the whole course of the argument, so that for proof we need only refer to that Epistle.

Thus, (1) for the first particular, we read in the very beginning of the first chapter, He "being the brightness of the Father's glory, and the express image of His person, when He had by Himself (that is, by His sacrifice of Himself) purged our sins, sat down on the right hand of the Majesty on high."[a] And

---

[a] Heb. i. 3.

again: "Every high priest taken from among men, is ordained for men, in things pertaining to God, that he may offer both gifts and sacrifices for sins."[a] "Such an high priest became us, who is holy, harmless, undefiled, separate from sinners, and made higher than the heavens; who needeth not daily, as those high priests, to offer up sacrifices, first for his own sins, and then for the people's: for this He did once, when He offered up Himself."[b] "For every high priest is ordained to offer gifts and sacrifices; wherefore it is of necessity that this man have somewhat also to offer."[c] Hence, "Christ being come an High Priest of good things to come, by a greater and more perfect tabernacle, not made with hands, that is to say, not of this building; neither by the blood of goats and calves, but by His own blood, He entereth in once into the Holy Place, having obtained eternal redemption for us."[d] Of such passages as these it is needless to argue an interpretation, so plain are they in teaching the sacrificial atonement made by Christ.

2. For the second particular, His blessing of absolution on the part of God, we have such passages as these: "Verily, He took not on Him the nature of angels; but He took on Him the seed of Abraham. Wherefore, in all things it behoved Him to be made like unto His brethren, that He might be a merciful and faithful High Priest, in things pertaining to God, to make reconciliation for the sins of the people. For in that He Himself hath suffering being tempted, He is able also to succor [that is, to *absolve*, as well as to

---

[a] Heb. v. 1.   [b] Heb. vii. 26, 27.   [c] Heb. viii. 3.
[d] Heb. ix. 11, 12.

succor in other ways] them that are tempted."[a] "Every High Priest is ordained for men . . . who can have compassion on the ignorant [*i.e.* absolving them], and on them that are out of the way, for that He Himself also is compassed with infirmity."[b]

3. For the third particular, His Intercession within the veil, we read more clearly, as follows: "We have an high priest, who is set on the right hand of the throne of the Majesty in the Heavens; a minister of the sanctuary, and of the true[c] tabernacle, which the Lord pitched, and not man."[d] "Christ is not entered unto the Holy Places made with hands, which are the figures of the true; but into Heaven itself: now to appear in the presence of God for us."[e] "This man, because He continueth ever, hath an unchangeable priesthood. Wherefore He is able also to save them to the uttermost that came unto God by Him; seeing He ever liveth to make intercession for them."[f] "This man, after He had offered one sacrifice for sins forever, sat down on the right hand of God; from henceforth expecting until His enemies be made His footstool."[g]

4. The fourth particular, the application of His blood, and His entrance into our souls, with restoring power, is declared with emphasis, thus: "If the blood of bulls and of goats, and the ashes of an heifer, sprinkling the unclean, sanctified to the purifying of the flesh; how much more shall the blood of Christ, who, through the Eternal Spirit offered Himself without spot

---

[a] Heb. i. 17, 18. [b] Heb. v. 2. [c] $\alpha\lambda\eta\theta\iota\nu\sigma\varsigma$. [d] Heb. viii. 1, 2.
[e] Heb. ix. 24. [f] Heb. vii. 24, 25. [g] Heb. x. 12, 13.

to God, purge your consciences from dead works to serve the living God."[a] The point of the passage, it is to be noted, lies in the words, "sprinkling the unclean," compared with "the blood of Christ shall purge your consciences," teaching most certainly that there is a gift of grace from Him, which may and must be so described; to which effect also, the following: "Having, therefore, brethren, boldness to enter into the holiest by the blood of Jesus, by a new and living way which He hath consecrated for us through the veil, that is to say, His flesh, and having an High Priest over the house of God; let us draw near, with a true heart, in full assurance of faith, having our hearts sprinkled from an evil conscience, and our bodies washed with pure water."[b] And still more plainly, that noble doxology of St. John, in the Revelations: "Unto Him that loved us, and washed us from our sins in his own blood, . . . to Him be glory and dominion for ever and ever."[c]

Combine these four operations into one view, as the work of Christ's twofold grace of Divine affection, and actual gift, and include also His continual priesthood, and we have the full interpretation of His figurative expression, "I am the way." The act of man by which he comes to God through Christ, the Way, is, as we have said, Repentance. The priesthood of our Redeemer is the objective fact correlative to Repentance in the soul. Repentance is possible only because Christ has made the atonement for our sins, and intercedes for us by the virtue of His merits; it is only

---

[a] Heb. ix. 13, 14.   [b] Heb. x. 19–23.   [c] Rev. i. 5, 6.

complete when He has blessed us with remission of sins, has sprinkled us with His blood, and infused into us His new life for a continual principle of resistance to and triumph over the old life of sin and rebellion. By making it possible for us to be restored, He furnishes to the heart the motives of hope, if we repent, of fear if we remain in sin; of love, for His love; of thankfulness for the mercy of God. By giving us the power and fruition of repentance, He enables us to bring the motives into act, forsaking our sins, and rendering to God the allegiance of our hearts; and thus, "we who sometimes were far off are made nigh by the blood of Christ."

We are thus able to give a more particular account of Repentance. The reader will recur to what has been said respecting the human conditions of the problem of restoration,—the needs of the heart, the mind, and the will of man, to enable him to return to God. He will remember that we saw the need of a motive for the heart; and he will also observe the distinction that while the conviction of sin, of righteousness and of judgment is the *motive*, repentance itself,—the giving to God the allegiance of the heart was asserted to be an *act*, corresponding to, and predicated upon the motive. This distinction is most important, both scientifically and practically. For to be simply under conviction, to be touched at heart by the preaching of the Gospel, to fear its threatenings and to desire its hopes, is not repentance. It is, indeed, the operation of the prevenient grace of the Holy Spirit urging us *to* repentance; but if the effect is circumscribed in the sphere of the emotions it does not reach to be repentance.

Repentance is more—it calls into operation more faculties—it is *an act;* as such it includes all the parts of an act, and implies all its conditions. While, therefore, we define in few words, repentance to be the allegiance of the heart to God, we must remember that, as a constant *act* of allegiance, it is essentially an exercise of the will, and comprehends also a mental element co-operating in the right direction of the heart, its withdrawal from earthly and sinful desires, and its elevation to heavenly and pure affections. In other words, true and complete repentance is the power of the regenerate will, directed by a right faith, and under the influence of motives derived from the preaching of the Gospel, withdrawing the heart from its evil propensities, and turning it towards the law and will of God. As an act, then, Repentance includes faith and obedience, and issues in Divine love;—for the Christian is an indivisible whole, just as the Redeemer's work is one whole, and therefore the different views of it are mutually inclusive. Repentance is both a constant, all-pervading act of self-renunciation, and a continual series of acts done in obedience to the commands of God. As the one, it revolutionizes the inner life; as the other, it controls and directs anew the outer life, and in doing so, is itself confirmed and made perfect.

True repentance thus pervades the whole nature, and extends over the whole mortal life of man. Its history, therefore, is divided into two great periods, that preceding, and that following, regeneration. It must exist incipiently and progressively before our regeneration, to make us capable subjects of that great gift. So existing, it is wrought by the prevenient grace of the

Holy Spirit, by ways and means which He knows; but which are to us as "the wind that bloweth where it listeth, and we hear the sound thereof, but can not tell whence it cometh and whither it goeth." After regeneration it must exist continuously, still the work of the same Holy Spirit,—its office then to keep us from sin, sorrowful for our lapses, steadfast in our renunciation, untiring in our resistance. In the former state its prevailing character is sorrowful, fearful, burdened with its load, and waiting to receive the gift of remission at its regeneration; in the latter state, it is forgiven, hopeful, loving, humble, ever watchful against a relapse.

The view, therefore, of the grace of Christ as our High Priest (and this remark completes this part of our subject) which is presented to the truly repentant, while yet unregenerate, is His atonement offered up on Calvary, and His present Intercession; after his regeneration, the Christian adds to this, his knowledge of absolution or remission of his sins, his faith in the Divine gift applied at his regeneration to his soul, cleansing it by the sprinkling of the blood of Christ. The mediatorial work thus complete, he is assured of his reconciliation to, and his participation in the grace of, God the Father—he is in a "state of salvation."

II. Complete, however, as this view of the mediatorial office of our Saviour seems to be, He has thought good to add to His revelation of Himself "the Way," the declaration that he is also "the Truth"—thus requiring us to contemplate Him, and our relation to Him, on a different side, viewing His Person and His work as related to the thoughts and mind of man, and our appropriation of the gift of salvation, as an act of faith, as well as of repentance; He being both Prophet and Truth, as well as Priest and Sacrifice.

The reader will observe here also, that we speak of belief as an *act* of faith, in the same way, as we just now spoke of repentance as an act,—meaning thereby, that faith is not merely an impression upon the mind, but a voluntary act of allegiance, in which both the heart and will concur to direct the mind aright. "With the heart, man believeth unto righteousness, and with the mouth, confession is made unto salvation." It is impossible, therefore, to have a true, complete, and perfect faith in Christ without true repentance, or before we have been made partakers of the life through regeneration; since it is this regeneration which gives spiritual power to the will, besides making the Truth a matter personal to, and operative in ourselves, incorporate (as it were) with us, and not an abstract, external, far-off Truth. This needs especially to be borne in mind, since, otherwise, dwelling on the lofty expressions in which Holy Scripture indulges with regard to faith, but forgetting that it includes repentance, men have fallen into the Antinomian heresy; and, forgetting that it includes regeneration, they have denied the necessity of the Holy Sacraments of our Lord's institution. Whereas, the Apostles considering faith to be inclusive, all that they say of justification by faith only is true in its fullest and most absolute sense, and yet is fully reconcilable with all that is attributed to any other parts of the Christian scheme.

Passages of Holy Scripture which reiterate and expand the statement that Christ is the Truth, are such as follow: "In Him was life, and the life was the light of men."ᵃ "That was the true light, which lighteneth every man that cometh into the world."ᵇ "I am the light of the world; he that followeth me shall not walk in darkness, but shall have the light of life."ᶜ "While ye have light [the Saviour is referring to Himself], believe in the light, that ye may be the children of light."ᵈ "God, who commanded the light to shine out of darkness, hath shined in our hearts, to give the light of the knowledge of the glory of God, in the face of Jesus Christ."ᵉ "He is the image of the Invisible God;"ᶠ He is "the brightness of the Father's glory, and the express image of His person,"ᵍ the manifestation of whatever truth may be known of the Father. His name is, "The Word of God."ʰ "In whom are laid up all the treasures of wisdom and knowledge."ⁱ

Other passages sum up the whole of religious knowledge in the term, "believing in the Lord Jesus Christ," and its correlative expressions; thus as fully concentrating the whole of truth in the person of the Saviour, as for example: "Whosoever believeth in Him, should not perish, but have everlasting life."ʲ "He that believeth on the Son hath everlasting life; and he that believeth not the Son shall not see life; but the wrath of God abideth on Him."ᵏ "A man is not justified by the works of the law, but by the faith of Jesus Christ."ˡ "The Holy Scriptures are able to make thee wise unto

---

ᵃ John, i. 4.
ᵇ John, i. 9.
ᶜ John, viii. 12.
ᵈ John, xii. 36.

ᵉ II. Cor. iv. 6.
ᶠ Col. i. 15.
ᵍ Heb. i. 3.
ʰ Rev. xix. 13.

ⁱ Col. ii. 3.
ʲ John, iii. 15.
ᵏ John, iii. 36.
ˡ Gal. ii. 16.

salvation, through faith which is in Christ Jesus."[a] So also all those texts which speak of "preaching Christ," meaning thereby, preaching the whole Gospel.

From the use of such a mode of speech, commonly and familiarly, we may see how this idea filled the minds of the writers of Holy Scripture, so as to underlie it, and be assumed in it everywhere, coming to the surface in these detached passages. Not, however, as though, all truth being "in Christ," it were indifferent what belief we have respecting the other Persons in the Godhead, or the other beings in the Creation; but rather that other persons and other beings are only rightly known by being manifested in, or seen in relation with Him. As He is not identical with other beings who coexist with Him, other things must be known as well as He; but the Truth of them is only known through Him. He is the Keystone of the arch of knowledge, which binds all things in the symmetry, and self-sustaining power of truth,—take Him away, and they drop into the confusion and disorder of falsehood.

The weighty declarations of Holy Scripture cannot be understood as teaching less than two things: (1) that our Lord Jesus Christ is in His own person the principal object of the Christian's knowledge, as being "God manifest in the flesh," and therefore revealing the Father and the Holy Spirit to the world; and (2) that He is the centre from which Truth radiates upon all other things; so that even the beings of the created universe only manifest themselves truly when they re-

---

[a] II. Tim. iii. 15.

flect His light, and are apprehended in their relation to Him, "by whom all things were made," and "by whom all things consist."

Mutually inclusive as are all true views of Christ, and all Christian acts, it is evident that what has been said concerning the priesthood and sacrifice of Christ is a necessary part of that Truth, which is presented to our faith. A knowledge of Him as "the Way," is, so far, a knowledge of Him as the Truth in the most essential particular. What has been said, therefore, on that subject will be understood, without reiteration, to have its place in this division; so also the statements made with respect to His Divine personality, His coexistence with the Father and the Holy Spirit, His incarnation and subsistence forever hereafter in two natures, Divine and human. And so also, what will hereafter be shown to be implied in His declaration that He is "the Life," is a part of that Truth which we receive when we believe in Him.

The Incarnation, indeed, is the centre of the whole body of truth; not only as being the most wonderful mystery upon which thought can dwell, but also as being the fact which makes it possible for us to live. Hence so much of the Creed is taken up with the confession of His Being as God Incarnate, and of the acts He performed while present on earth. We believe in Him as God and man; and thus the incarnation is the well-spring of the grace of faith, as of all other grace.

Into the depths of this mystery it is not for us to penetrate. We may well be content to be ignorant *how* it can be a truth, being satisfied that so it is; and that, therefore, Christ is, so to speak, the point where God takes hold on the Creation, and when the Creation reaches up to God. But it is given us to behold how from this centre truth irradiates upwards to God, and downwards to man. The Incarnation is itself a twofold Revelation : (*a*) of God as made manifest to human conceptions; and (*b*) of human perfection in the sight of God.

(*a*) The Persons of the Holy Trinity being the same in essence and attributes, equal in power, having the same law, the same moral and spiritual qualities, the same character (if we may so say),—differing only in the subordination of one to the other, as already explained; it follows that if one Person be manifested to human conceptions, so far also are the other Persons. In this sense, the Incarnation of the Second Person of the Holy Trinity is a manifestation of the whole Godhead; for His person, being the "express image"[a] of the person of the Father, the Divine character which He manifests is the character of the Father and of the Holy Spirit as well as His own. It is admitted that the Divine nature is in itself incomprehensible. The adequate self-knowledge which the Divine Intelligence possesses needs translation and reduction into human thought to be transferred to human minds. It has pleased God, therefore, that the manifestation of Himself should be made by His Son becoming human, that we may thus see the Divine itself under a human form.

This is what is meant by the scriptural declaration, "God was manifest in the flesh."[b] The Divine

---

[a] Heb. i. 3.   [b] I. Tim. iii. 16.

Essence itself was not made visible at the Incarnation; but the Divine character was, the Divine attributes, the Divine laws, the Divine dealings with man, the Divine mind and Spirit, by the Divine Person becoming man. The substantial, actual union of the Divine and human natures in the person of Christ was an invisible union, and (it is almost needless to remark) the word "manifestation" is not to be taken as asserting that the Divine nature or essence became visible by union with humanity. No one who saw our Lord Jesus Christ after the flesh would see more than the visible part of His manhood; no one could perceive where (if we may so say without irreverence) the Divine nature joined, or how it was united to the human. That is an incomprehensible mystery. We cannot, when the fact is revealed to us, comprehend how such an union could take place—how Divinity could inhabit a human form. With respect to our understanding, or our imagination, such a question is like that respecting the union of soul and body in ourselves; which is a truth, not so stupendous, indeed, as the mystery of the Incarnation, but fully as inexplicable.

When we speak, then, of the manifestation of the Godhead in the face of Jesus Christ, we mean that in Christ, and through Him, we know what otherwise we could not have known of the attributes of God, of His dealings with us, of His will concerning us, of His judgment and mercy towards us. The manifestation of God by the manhood of Jesus Christ is like the manifestation of our souls to one another by means of our bodies. We do not see one another's souls; and yet we know of them, their feelings, tempers, and dispositions towards us, their thoughts and intentions. They are manifested by that incomprehensible action of the soul on the body, which we cannot reach by analysis nor anatomy. The soul manifests itself by giving life to the body; by making it its instrument. So our Lord Jesus Christ is the manifestation of God to us, by being bodily, mentally, morally, humanly, the instrument of the Divine nature, which invisibly inhabited His visible form; by showing in Himself the Divine character, in His acts, the Divine operations, principles, laws, in such manner that man can grasp them, can know God in them, and become Godlike by following Christ.

Christ is thus the Truth, because He is the *Revelation*, as well as the *Revealer*. We speak popularly, and, for practical purposes, correctly, of the Holy Bible as the revelation of God, as the word of God; but it may be well to recall that in strict and proper language, it is not so much the Revelation itself, as the inspired record of that Revelation. Our Lord Jesus Christ is the Revelation of God. The Bible is our spiritual guide because it shows Him to us. He is the exemplar of the Divine Mind. What we know of God, we know clearly and truly and sufficiently, only by knowing His life on earth. The light that streams from Him is the light of God. What is in Heaven above we know, if we have learned what He was on earth.

If we have paid any attention to the speculations of philosophers respecting the nature and being of God, we must have been struck with the unsatisfactory nature of their conclusions, and the difficulty, nay, the impossibility, thus made evident of knowing the infinite and absolute perfection of God. Philosophy has no terms by which to describe infinite or absolute justice and virtue. It has no conceptions by which to contemplate, out of all relation, in the unchangeableness of eternity, those ultimate principles which govern the relations of a transitory and mutable life. It is startling, if it is true, to say that God, the absolute Being, has no human virtue; a philosophy which thus ends in negation is of no practical value in determining what is the character of God. But if we cannot know what God's perfections are in themselves, we must know, as the next possible thing, what human conceptions of virtue, holiness, justice, will stand as correct representatives before our minds of those infinite perfections. Our ideas of God, to be receivable by us, must be translated from the infinite, absolute reality, into the form and likeness of humanity. They must be reduced from the infinite to the finite; they must be presented to us in definite relations, shown in acts with which we have something in common, given in the way of example. We must be able to refer to some acts which are intelligible in their moral relations, and be able to say, "These are the acts of God, under circumstances in which we may be placed; these were the rules of Divine life, when a Divine Person was in our condition; this is the Divine measure of human thought and life." The infinite justice of the Absolute Being must be translated into human justice, infinite love into human love, infinite holiness into human holiness, infinite law into human law, to be intelligible to us. This is done for us in the coming of our Lord Jesus Christ. We cannot make the translation for ourselves. Fallen and erring as we are, we cannot take our own human natures to be for us the correct image of the Divine attributes; we cannot say that our own untutored conceptions of what is just, or holy, or pure, or lawful, are correct representations of God's perfect judgments. We cannot affirm that what we consider just and right action, under the influence of our selfish and sensual passions, is just and right in the sight of God; or that (to speak plainly) God would act as we do,—when we know how often we regret what we have done. Hence we cannot argue, from the fallen moral basis of our own nature, what God's nature is. We must get beyond ourselves. We must have some example by which to rectify our mistakes. We must have God Himself in the likeness of man, since we cannot know God from our own broken image and marred likeness of Him. His glory, therefore, was manifested in the person of our Lord Jesus Christ. He is "the Truth" which we know of God. The Gospels have their inestimable value, because they preserve to us the lineaments of Christ; the whole Bible has its priceless worth, because it is the expansion of the Gospel, the reduplication of His likeness, in which the faithful behold

"Him first, Him last, Him midst, and without end."

And so we have "the light of the knowledge of the glory of God, in the face of Jesus Christ." In Him the likeness of God is reduced to a size which we can receive, and still remains perfect.

And as He is thus the Revelation of the Attributes of God, so is His Incarnation also the evidence or proof to us of that great doctrine of the Holy Trinity, which, with the Incarnation, makes up the very matter and substance of our faith. I do not say that without the Incarnation God could not have made this truth evident to the mind of man; nor do I mean that in logical statements of the doctrine, and its logical proof, stress is laid upon the Incarnation itself as a necessary evidence, except as connected with words spoken by the Incarnate Son. Those great doctors who have stated the logical argument upon Holy Scripture, do not formally support the proposition, that the doctrine of the Holy Trinity must be true, because "God was manifest in the flesh." But the practical and real argument in all minds,—the conviction underlying all the logical arguments, the very centre and essence of them all, drawn, as they all must be, from Holy Scripture, is this: "The doctrine of the Holy Trinity must be true, because the Second Person of the Holy Trinity was Incarnate among men."

(*b*) Our Lord Jesus Christ, again, is the pattern and exemplar of man, as he should be, in the sight of God, and also the evidence what he is in that sight.

"When the fulness of time was come, God sent forth His Son, made of a woman, made *under the law*." "He became *obedient* unto death." That is, He took upon Himself, with the form of a man, the state also and condition of a man, its duties and its obligations, as completely as if He had been none other than the son of man and woman. He fulfilled all the law, both in outward blamelessness of conduct, and with spiritual perfection of submission; and thus He became to us the example what our perfection is in the sight of God.

It differs, in some respects, from the native human idea of perfection. Notice this, for brevity's sake, in only two points.

He was poor and self-denying, a "man of sorrows and acquainted with grief," not having where to lay His head, despising the riches and glory of this world; and all this voluntarily, as an act of humility and self-denial; submitting to indignity, reproach, and persecution without retaliation,—thus showing it to be a part of the perfection of humanity to be humble and self-denying. The native human idea, on the contrary, sees perfection in pomp and self-gratification, so that they who have most means and capacity to indulge themselves are called "the better classes," and "our best society."

He was obedient; and here, again, He contradicted our common ideas. We think it the glorious thing of life to have our own way, to do what we will, to have means to carry out our purposes and designs. But Christ came on earth to do, not His own will, but His Father's. "My meat is to do the will of Him who sent me," is His own word. "He was obedient unto death," says His Apostle. In the mystery of His being, His Divine will must always have concurred with the will of His Father, as being one with it; but His human will shrank oftentimes (and what wonder!) from the bitter cup He was to undergo; yet in all things He surrendered Himself—though He shuddered—freely, unreservedly, to do His Father's will. Now it is not, perhaps, sufficiently noticed by pious readers of Holy Scripture, that the will of God towards Him, after He assumed humanity, was directed by those universal principles by which God governs all mankind; so that, though He stands alone and unapproachable in the magnitude of the benefits He obtained for mankind, and in the righteous purity of His self-sacrifice, yet, in respect of the *principle of obedience*, He was on a level with His brethren in the flesh. All that Christ did for mankind, He did as a duty, as an obligation, which became such when He took human nature. The all-inclusive act of free grace was His willingly becoming man; but when He had done this, He (as it were) put the Divine under human law; so that what obligations lay upon man according to the power of man, He, having superhuman power, met in a superhuman manner, being, nevertheless, "under the law." As, for example, thus: By that law of human sympathy and social communion by which we are held in the bonds of a common brotherhood,—that law which is made objective in the Divine command, "Thou shalt love thy neighbor as thyself,"—the duty of help in difficulty, of comfort in sorrow, of charity in sickness or in want, became as binding upon Him, the man, as upon every one else who partook of that human nature; and therefore, in helping the afflicted, in healing the sick, in comforting the sorrowful, and in providing for the hungry, all by miraculous means, He was acting, though by Divine power, under the law of humanity, giving "what He had," on the principle of obedience, as well as of love, because it was His duty so to do. And that, not as His peculiar, individual duty, under a covenant of obedience singular to Himself, as if isolated by His Divinity from mankind, but as verily and indeed in the "form of a servant," upon the same principle on which His disciple acted when he raised the lame man with the words, "Silver and gold have I none, but such as I have, give I thee," —on the same principle on which any of us must act when met by the calls of the suffering. And if we may penetrate into the mystery of that sublimest act of all, His offering Himself upon the Cross, and apply to it the principle of obedience in illustration of human duty, we may say of that also, that therein He acted on the same principle,—offering up His Divine worth for His brethren, as a duty appertaining to the manhood He had assumed, by its relationship with the fallen creatures who needed that redemption. For if it had been possible that a mere man, one of ourselves, could have redeemed the world by the offering of his life, there can be no question that it would have been his duty under the law of love; and therefore, the same law applying, when the only sinless man who ever lived had that power of atonement, because He was also Divine, He became the Sacrifice, on the principle of duty; "being found in fashion as a man, He became *obedient unto death*, even the death of the Cross."

Christ is then the truth of human nature, so absolutely and so purely, that so far as we can, under the illuminating power of Divine grace, by constant meditation and study, realize the character of His life on earth, as a human life, as well as a divine, we shall have the perfect rule of all human conduct before God. If we were able to answer accurately and infallibly with reference to every important event of life, the question, "How would our Lord Jesus Christ have acted under these circumstances had He been placed in them?" and if we were able to, and did act according to the rule so elicited, we should be perfect. So the Apostle St. John argues in relation to the future world: "We shall be like Him, *for* we shall see Him as He is." His Person, then, it is not too much to say, is the *only* complete and all-sufficient rule of our lives before God. His precepts and teachings are, indeed, a perfect rule; but they need to be informed by a living faith in Him,—they are only a part of the law by which the Christian is governed, only a part of the truth which he must behold. We must live according to them to the minutest letter, since "not a jot or a tittle shall in any wise pass from the law till all be fulfilled,"—since "Heaven and earth shall pass away, but His words shall not pass away." It is idle to speak of following Christ, and yet disregarding any of His spoken commands, as if Christ could be inconsistent with Himself; yet to rest in the letter is not enough. We must have the letter, but we must have the Spirit as well. The letter is but one of the indications of the "mind of Christ," and it is that mind which is the ultimate object of our research. "The words that I speak unto you," said He, "they are Spirit and they are life;" but they are this, by leading us beyond themselves to Him and the true faith in Him, as the exemplar of true obedience, the rule of true life, the law of redeemed humanity.

c. But further: Our Lord Jesus Christ is also the evidence what human nature actually is in the sight of God. We have in Him not only the realization of an ideal of perfect humanity under the conditions of mortal existence in such a world as ours is, but also in His incarnation and death the dominant *fact* according to which we must arrange all our knowledge and observation of ourselves as we actually are. The moral quality of our actions is settled, not by speculations in morals, seeking for abstract grounds of action, not by Platonic, or Aristotelian, or Stoic, or Epicurean theories, but by their agreement or disagreement with His example and teachings, and the principles they disclose. What is and what is not sin; what is the future consequence of sin; what right and duty are; and how far we fall short of our duty,—these questions are to be decided by our knowledge of Christ "the truth." The moral history of man, as a race or as an individual, is comprehensible only by the light of his coming into the world; and his state at any given period is fixed by his relation to the Gospel. What view we understand Revelation to give of the origin of our moral history has been seen in the discussions of a former chapter, which it is not necessary here to repeat. Whether that, or any other account, be the truth, must be decided by the perfect harmony of the system in which it is contained with the revelation of the Redeemer incarnate; just as the truth of our modern account of the solar system is demonstrated by the completeness, the comprehensiveness, and the simplicity with which it harmonizes all the phenomena of the planetary world on the heliocentric theory. As it would be the height of absurdity to attempt to frame a planetary theory without the sun, so no account of human nature and human position can be a true one which does not harmonize with the

Incarnation and Redemption of God the Son. Hence all researches into, all observations and experiences of, human nature, physical, physiological, metaphysical, however accurately registered as separate facts, can only be bound together in a true system by putting this fact at the center, and searching till we find the true relation of the others to our faith in Christ. By the revealed truth, the great and difficult fact of evil in humanity is accounted for and shown to be accordant with the goodness of God, because of the universality of the Remedy offered to man's acceptance; its origin by the fall is declared, its subordination to an end in our probation for another life, the cause and use of the mingled web of joy and sorrow with which we are clothed in this world,—all these are made apparent, and the solutions of the perplexing questions to which they give rise are demonstrated more clearly in each succeeding age as we advance in true knowledge. For example: all the facts deduced by successive investigations into the abnormal workings of our fallen nature and its hereditary transmission take their Christian position as exponents of the "law of the flesh," which warreth against the law of the Spirit; because, if the record of Redemption be true, the fact of a fall must be true also; if "in Christ all are made alive," it is equally true that "in Adam all die." So, too, the area of the field assigned to human freedom by Divine Providence, and its limitation by the laws of the human constitution and of the constitution of the universe, by the necessary operation of the various faculties of man, by the diverse circumstances in which he is placed, and the influence of those circumstances upon him, are legitimate objects of philosophical observation and analysis; but they must be apprehended in their true connection with the coming of Christ and the truths of the Gospel. Thus all inquiries in the field of human science will enlarge our knowledge and make it more accurate by showing us the positive effects of the Fall upon the various parts of our being, the limitations of our freedom and their nature, because of which we are finite and not infinite beings, the laws of the Creation which supplement the facts of Revelation, and the means by which our position and our laws of action and receptivity may be made auxiliary to the designs of the Gospel for our restoration. If human nature be finite, its limitations may be inquired into; if it be fallen, the nature and extent of its deterioration in the individual or the mass is a subject of possible study; and if it be capable of Providential government and ultimate restoration, the laws under which the restoration is applied and in harmony with which it works, are at least probable additions to our Christian knowledge, as industry and faith together explore the regions of human science. But in such investigations the totality of truth can never have been arrived at until the result comprehended is the Divine system of which Christ is the Head, "Who is over all from the beginning," and "in Whom all fulness dwells."

The Incarnation of the Son of God, again, is the one fact which must be considered, in order to decide the questions that have been raised concerning the successive communications of the Divine Creator to His human creatures. We cannot obtain a true knowledge what Holy Scripture is, or how to interpret it, unless we study it "according to the analogy of the faith." In this relation, as in deciding upon the present condition of human nature, the Incarnation has the power of a *fact* in relation with other facts, of an act which has its historic place among the affairs of the world. Every fact has an absolute power of evidence which cannot be contradicted when it is apprehended in its true relation with its fellows. All our philosophy begins with the observation of them, proceeds with their classification, and seeks its end by induction or deduction from them. They control us by the laws of our intellectual being, according to which we must allow every fact its place in the system of truth, and accept it as defining the relations of others with itself and with each other. Hence facts are evidence. And if this be true of subordinate facts, how much more of the Incarnation, the principal, the all-controlling fact of human history! Hence, before we can enter upon the examination of the Revelation purporting to come from God, we must accept this fact, we must have the faith in Christ, and it must guide our studies, or no research and no ingenuity will lead us to a true conclusion.

All persons of any theological reading are familiar, to some extent, with the (so-called) Rationalistic hypotheses put forth of late years, concerning the origin and nature of the books of Holy Scripture, and with the methods of reasoning by which it is endeavored to support them. Whether any minor truths are brought to light or not, by these methods, they all start with a *petitio principii;* they assume at the outset, as the base of the argument, the conclusion to be arrived at, and therefore reason in a circle. However careful the reasoning, false premises must issue in false conclusions; but few sophisms are as transparent as those of the Rationalistic commentator on Holy Scripture. Assuming that the books of Holy Scripture are naturally produced, he argues thence to the conclusion that they are not supernaturally produced. He sets them on the same level with other ancient documents, and from that premise urges a denial of their superior authority; then, because those documents are condemned of advancing myths or fables when they treat of the supernatural, he refuses to receive the supernatural intimations of Holy Scripture on the ground of this assumed analogy. But the analogy itself is the very thing to be denied on the ground of the Incarnation, since those books which are inseparably connected with the Incarnation, either in the way of prophecy or inspired history, are, by that relation, removed from the level of all other writings. If the Rationalist begin by denying that the Incarnation as a *dogma* should have any influence upon his judgment of the Bible, he will naturally throw out every reference of prophecy, every record of miracle, which refers to the Incarnation as a *fact;* whereas, if he accept it as a fact, it must have its influence as a dogma.

The way in which Rationalism approaches Holy Scripture is this: It first investigates the traditions, remains, and records of the various heathen nations of antiquity, and, observing that in them there are many things incredible as they stand, many legends, allegories, and myths,—it accounts for their existence by the operation of certain real or supposed tendencies of human nature, as the love of the marvellous, or national feeling, or the attempt to supply lost links of tradition by imagination, or the tendency to cast moral and religious teaching into a dramatic form. It then draws by induction the inference that *all* human records and traditions are necessarily wrought over in the same way, and therefore that *all* supernatural relations are to be accounted for by the same principles. Hence it argues, because matters of a supernatural aspect, which are clearly false, are contained in the myths of antiquity, therefore matters supernatural in Holy Scripture are to be judged only by the light derived from the study of heathenism. And it is evident that if Holy Scripture is the product of humanity only, it must be judged by the analogy of other human writings; hence the supernatural relations it contains will be discredited, unless it can be shown that the books it contains are *not of the same class* with those other writings from which the critical rules have been derived.

But the evidence that Holy Scripture does thus differ the Rationalist altogether refuses to receive; he will not permit it to be offered. He protests that the dogma of the Incarnation of the Son, and the Inspiration of the Spirit of God, ought not to influence the investigation. Whereas, if they are facts (as they are), they *must* influence the investigation; for if the Scripture is only human, it may be mythical, but not if it be Divine. If it is only human, there is no more evidence of the supernatural in Scripture than in the traditions of heathenism, beyond the verisimilitude of the story,—

whereas, if it be Divine, it must of necessity contain supernatural relations. It is a preliminary question, therefore, whether Holy Scripture is Divine or human, —or rather, whether it is exclusively human, or both human and Divine. If it be a special Divine Revelation, it is separate from other records, above their analogies, not to be judged by them; it is the criterion by which they are to be judged. Now the fact which does separate the Bible from all other books, is its relation to the Incarnation of our Lord Jesus Christ, to which all the record points, and with which it closes. The Incarnation is a fact. It cannot be a *myth*. It belongs to times confessedly historic; and therefore the Gospels cannot be clouded as the Book of Genesis is, with doubt and disputation. It is a fact never reproduced in the history of the world; and therefore it places the records of the Jewish people, among whom He came, in a class by themselves, with respect to the supernatural, subjecting them to higher than merely human laws. This fact *must* guide our judgment of Holy Scripture. If the Son of God were made man for the salvation of the world (as He was) His life demanded an inspired record; and the inspired record must be altogether a true record.

Nor is it reasoning in a circle to say that we believe in the Son of God on the testimony of Holy Scripture, and that we believe the Inspiration of Holy Scripture, because we believe in the Son of God. For the great facts which prove Christ to be the only-begotten Son of God, His miracles, His Resurrection, corroborating His claims made throughout the whole of His teaching, were such as would be remembered by the original witnesses, by the natural powers of memory, even without inspiration. But these main facts being true, and the Divinity of our Lord acknowledged on their evidence, there was evident need of Inspiration to recall, and guard from misconception, the less memorable details of the teaching He intended to transmit to posterity. We argue from the truth of the greater facts, naturally observed and naturally remembered, to the Deity of our Lord; from His Deity to the Divinity and uniqueness of His Gospel; from that to the truth of the minor details; and so to the Inspiration of the whole. And this argument is irrefragable. For, if God sent His Son to be the object of faith, it is certainly most reasonable that He should send His Spirit to inspire a true record of Him who is to be believed in,—even did we not possess the actual promise of the Saviour that the Spirit should be sent to "recall all things to the remembrance" of the Apostles. Thus our faith in Christ proves the Inspiration of the New Testament (for the same reasoning must be extended to the Acts, and to the Epistles, and Apocalypse); and from the New Testament we reason back to the Old; since its inspiration is everywhere inferred by the New. Hence, before the inquirer after truth can approach the record of Holy Scripture, he must assign it its place *alone*, as a Divine Revelation; and thus the truth of our Lord Jesus Christ enables us to get at the truth of all Holy Scripture. Then, with this guiding light, it becomes a subject of legitimate inquiry, how far the Divine will permitted the laws of the human mind to find expression in the word; how far knowledge was conveyed to the Inspired writer by ordinary avenues of information, how far by extraordinary, and in what state the text has been transmitted to our own times.

The inquiries entered upon in this spirit will add further meaning to the declaration "I am the Truth," by showing that our Lord, the ever-blessed Word, is the object ever before the eye of faith in all the varied contents of both Old and New Testaments; that He is the Person who reveals Himself and the Godhead therein, both immediately and mediately; that He is (so to speak) the *substance*, of which Holy Scripture is the *phenomenon*.

This is self-evident in the New Testament and needs no demonstration. It is equally true of the Old. The Old Testament History, for example,—what is it but a Divine Epic, having, for its twofold argument, man's sin in the past, and his redemption then future? The Fall is its beginning, the Redemption its end, its middle the result of the one and the preparation for the other. The Creation of the world and of man, the temptation and the fall, the promise of a Redeemer, the increase of the human race and the development of sin, the division of mankind into two parts,—worshippers of God and apostates,—children, respectively, of Seth and Cain, the mingling of the two, the consequent corruption of the better by the worse, the destruction of the world by the flood, the salvation of Noah, that the promise might not fail, the second corruption of man by the workings of his fallen nature, the choice of the family of Abraham to be the repository of true religion, the increase of that family into a nation, the promise of Christ again in that family and nation, their law, the Divine intercourse with them, their various transgressions, punishment and repentance, the renewal of the promise from time to time, the guardian care of God over them, until, in "the fulness of time," He sent forth His Son,—this is the course of that history. Is it not all summed up in the one sentence of St. Paul, "As in Adam all die, so in Christ all are made alive?"

In like manner the prophecies and the religious writings of all kinds which make up the collection preserved with so great care by the Jewish Church, with their types, their ceremonies, their hopes, their aspirations, all refer to the coming of Christ, and the kingdom to be set up by Him. The bond of union of all the varied contents of the Old Testament is the anticipation of the advent of our Lord Jesus Christ. In the eloquent language of one[a] not long dead: "Expectation is the inward spirit of the Old Testament, as fulfilment of the New. Wonderful itself, its function clearly is to testify wonders more august to come. From Moses to Malachi, these Hebrew Scriptures are, as it were, one long-drawn sigh of *sorrowful hope;* while, to make the purposed lesson of imperfection more complete, the same testimony is uttered from *every* rank and state of humanity; for of what variety of human fortune will you not find an example there? Not from Jeremiah in his dungeon alone, but from the gorgeous palace of their mightiest king, at the most consummate hour they record of earthly prosperity, comes forth the mournful strain (it is the voice, not of

---

[a] The Rev. Wm. Archer Butler, Sermon XIV, vol. i.

Jewish, but of human nature): 'Vanity of vanities, all is vanity. . . . I have seen all the works that are done under the sun; and behold *all* is vanity and vexation of spirit.' . . . Not from insulated predictions alone, not from separate types alone, not from occasional allusions, but from the whole spirit and tendency and bearing of the Hebrew Scriptures was the Lord Jesus Christ justified when He declared that 'They are they which testify of Him,' that, disjointed from Him, they were a fair and elaborate structure, doubtless, but shadowy, nevertheless, and unsubstantial; while, seen in the light that His coming flashed back upon that strange story of four thousand years, every page sparkled with illumination, every sentence quickened with meaning."

There is still another view to be taken of the relation of our Lord to the Holy Scripture. He is not only the one prophesied of and pointed to, but He is also the Revealer of all the Truth made known by them; so that He is the beginning and the end, "the first and the last" of Holy Scripture in every sense.

Various passages in the earlier records intimate that God was manifested to human vision before the Son was *born* into the world. He appeared to Abraham on various occasions, as at the time of the destruction of Sodom and Gomorrah; to Jacob, as when He wrestled with him; to Moses in the burning bush and on Mount Sinai; to all the congregation of Israel at the time of the giving of the ten commandments. There are several accounts of the appearance of an uncreated "Angel of the Lord," who speaks in the person of God Himself. These all have been abundantly proved by the theologians to have been revelations of the Godhead in the person of the Son, under such form as He was pleased to manifest Himself; and they lead us to expect that He would be the direct Revealer of the great body of supernatural truth which the Bible contains.

Accordingly, we are to understand that the generality of those places where it is said, "The Word of the Lord came" unto one or other of the prophets, assert that the matter following was directly revealed by that Person whom St. John, in his gospel, calls "the Word," that is, by the Son, our Lord Jesus Christ. That "The Word" is a personal being was discerned by older Jews, the Chaldee paraphrasts, Philo, and others, and is placed beyond a doubt by the declaration of St. John. For we must interpret the older books of Holy Scripture by the newer. That which in the older is more obscure, in the newer is more clear; and though the expression "the word of the Lord," might at first seem to be but a figure of speech, its true interpretation is disclosed with certainty when St. John tells that the Everlasting Word is the only-begotten Son of God.

In treating of the Divine element in Holy Scripture, we must distinguish between *Revelation* and *Inspiration*.[a] Holy Scripture is said to be revealed, and also to be inspired; but the latter term is perhaps less properly applied to the written words than to the writers of the Word. They were inspired, and to them the Word was revealed. Now *Revelation* is the

---

[a] Lee on Inspiration.

The Grace of the Son. 133

agency of the Son in giving Holy Scripture, and Inspiration the agency of the Spirit. Inspiration is subjective; Revelation is objective. Correct apprehension rests upon two things, an external presentation of truth, and an internal fitness to receive that truth. Revelation secured the first condition; Inspiration the second. The prophet's mind was made capable of receiving the ray of light without refracting or discoloring it, by the Inspiration of the Spirit; that ray was sent into the mind from without by the Revelation of the Son.[a]

It follows, therefore, that wherever there is Revelation in Holy Scripture there is the manifestation of the Son; that is, of Christ our Lord; He is "the Truth," which is beheld.

It is not asserted, however, that everything contained in Holy Scripture is *immediately* revealed by the Son. Revelation may be either *immediate* or *mediate*. The supernatural truth of Holy Scripture was revealed immediately to the prophets and Apostles, mediately through them to us. So truth might be given mediately to the prophets themselves; it might be set before their minds by other agencies which stood between them and God, as well as be given directly by God. Truth which could not be known, except by supernatural means, was necessarily revealed, either immediately by the Son of God Himself, or mediately by the

---

[a] The distinction of Revelation and Inspiration is clearly shown in the Apocalypse, where the objective and subjective operations are referred to the Second and Third persons of the Blessed Trinity. Cf. Ch. i. 10, 11.

agency of angels performing His commands. We have accounts of the first mode in the passages introduced by the formula already alluded to. Of the mediation of angels we have several accounts, as in the visions of Daniel and Zechariah. But in this case also the Revelations were mediately from the Son; the angels received them from Him, and were His agents to communicate with the children of men; He is the Principal, visible to the eye of faith, as if He were personally present.

In like manner, the matters related in Holy Scripture, which seem not to be supernatural,—the references to events of the natural world, or of tradition or history,—are to be counted a part of Revelation proper, and therefore from the Son of God, though the ordinary avenues of knowledge were the mediate channels by which the writer obtained information of them. They have their place as essential parts of the one whole; they were recorded as such under the Divine guidance. As Inspiration wrought according to the matter to be recorded, in the measure appointed by the Spirit,—as Providence works by constant law or special interposition, according to the will of God, so Revelation wrought, supernaturally, or naturally, according to the measure necessary to give us the mind of God.

Thus, the objects for which *Inspiration* was given did not necessitate that it should be exerted to the full extent of correcting the language of the apparent into the language of the real, in cases where the sensible perceptions of mankind, or their philosophical beliefs respecting natural phenomena were at variance with the final conclusions of merely physical science. "God works," says Hooker, somewhere, "according to the end to be attained," and here the end to be attained was spiritual, not scientific Revelation. Had Inspiration, in fact, wrought to the full extent of rectifying every ordinary belief respecting natural phenomena, to which Scripture refers, it would practically have defeated its own end; for, while it is as easy for us to translate the apparent in Holy Scripture into the real (as we now understand it) as it is to apprehend by the terms sunrise or sunset, the real motion of the earth, it would have been very difficult for the minds of the first ages of the world to have divested themselves of their philosophy of the apparent, in order to accept a revelation of the philosophy of the real; and therefore the result would have been to them both unintelligible and incredible. Inspiration, therefore, increased the power to perceive truth, only so far and on such subjects as was necessary in the Divine plan of the record.

So *Revelation* wrought, in measure suited to the matter to be recorded,—*supernaturally*, so far as truth unattainable by ordinary avenues of information was to be revealed; *naturally*, by those avenues, when they sufficed for the purpose God designed. It was direct and immediate, so far as the truth could not otherwise be known; but when it could, God permitted the writer to obtain it by natural means,—observation, tradition, or documentary research; the whole Scripture being thus an union of the natural and the supernatural, both blended together, both from the same author; in the same manner as God's Providence in the world at large is the perfect blending of His natural laws, and His immediate oversight of, and care for His creatures. But whether the truth were matter of history, of observation, of experience, or of supernatural communication, it was none the less Divine Revelation,—none the less the work of the Word, the Son of God,—either immediately, or mediately from Him; for "the whole Creation is the Lord's;" "all things were made by the Son, and for Him;" and the records of the Inspired Word were selected by God's overruling care; they are revelations of Him who reveals the Godhead by the Creation, and in every other way.

3. And this introduces another fact contained in this inexhaustible name of our Lord; that the Creation itself is a revelation of Him its Creator. The book of God's Word, and the book of God's Works (as the natural world has been called), though separate are not disconnected volumes, any more than the Old and New Testaments. They are parts of one mighty whole, by which God is completely manifested; and the Revealer of the whole is the same Divine Word, who became man. The natural under Inspiration, in Holy Scripture, is the transition from Nature in the Creation to the Supernatural in Revelation; just as Providence in the midst of human affairs is the transition from the constant course of nature under law to the miracles by which Revelation was authenticated,—all being nicely blended parts of the one Divine plan.

Our Nicene Creed instructs us to confess faith in "one God, the Father Almighty, Maker of Heaven and earth, and of all things visible and invisible." This has been already explained to mean, that as God the Father is the source and origin of all being, He is the source and origin of the created universe. But the same Creed also instructs us to confess, "Our Lord Jesus Christ, the only-begotten Son of God, . . by whom all things were made." The Son is the active agent in the Creation. So St. John declares in his Gospel, "All things were made by Him, and without Him was not anything made, that was made;"[a] and again, "The world was made by Him."[b] The true doctrine therefore is, that God the Father created the world by the Son as the active agent, of whom (it must be added to make the statement complete) the Holy Spirit is the energizing power.

Now the world is not God, nor is it the body of which He is the soul. It is a system of things and powers distinct from God, created by Him, differing, therefore, from Him as the created from the uncreated. It is under His government. We know God through the world, therefore, not by perception of things themselves, but by knowledge of the wisdom with which they are formed, and made to harmonize together, and ordered to a common end. We know God through nature, by means of the law under which nature consists. The world can tell us nothing of its creation; it can only give us to infer that it was made according to a preconceived pattern or *idea*, and that it continues in being, in motion, and in development, according to universal and necessary *laws*. These ideas and laws[c]

---

[a] John, i. 3.   [b] John, i. 10.

[c] An *idea* is the *constitutive law* of a thing; a *law* is the *regulative idea* of the activity of a thing. In reason, therefore, there

are not the world, they are above it, they govern it; they are, therefore, so far as they are truly apprehended by us, the manifestation to us of God as the Governor of the Universe. If, then, we could, by the Creation, attain a knowledge of laws and ideas as they exist in the mind of God, we should know God perfectly, as manifested in the creation; and so far as we can appoximate to it, so far we approximate to a knowledge of God. The knowledge of ideas and laws, so far as we can reach it, is Reason. The world, therefore, as a work of God, reveals itself as a work of Wisdom or Divine Reason; it reveals the *Wisdom* of God more clearly than any other attribute. For, being a finite world, it tells us only inadequately of infinite Power; without Revelation, only inadequately of infinite Love; but in every adaptation of means to ends, in every realization of an idea or a law, in every provision for growth, increase, reproduction, in every effect produced by any cause, it tells us of perfect Wisdom. But the special attribute of the Second Person of the Holy Trinity is the being the Word, or Wisdom, or Reason of the Father, beholding and knowing His eternal, universal, constitutive, all-penetrating, perfect law, and working all things subordinate to that law. The Creation, therefore, is in Holy Scripture and the Creed, attributed to the Son; and the manifestation of God which is made through the Creation is a manifestation of the Son, and of God through Him; since the only true knowledge of God's law of crea-

---

is no essential difference between ideas and laws; both have the character of universality and necessity.

tion which we can attain is thrown upon the world by the Son, as the mirror of the Father's perfection.

And this is true, whether the Divine law, which it is the object of philosophy to reach, is given objectively or subjectively,—whether there is really any distinction between intuition and induction or not; whether it is elicited from our own being in contact with external phenomena, or is inferred from the phenomena of the rational mind. For, in considering the Creation, we must remember that we, too, are created beings, and therefore, wherever laws and ideas are placed for our beholding, whether in the mind or out of the mind, they are placed there by the one Creative Wisdom, they are in us (if we apprehend them truly) the image of the Divine Wisdom, the vision of God the Father in and by the Son. The object of philosophy, whether natural or metaphysical, is to attain the knowledge of these laws, to comprehend them in their totality, to destroy isolation, and to know everything in its relations to the system of the whole,—that is, under all its laws,—and so to attain the mind of its Governor. It is a well-known dogma of philosophers, that "Truth consists in abstractions," which is but a less religious way of saying that truth is above the world of things,—that "it resides in the bosom of God."

Hence every fresh advance in philosophy, every certain truth attained, is a further approximation to the knowledge of God through His Son, capable of bearing its part in the enlargement of our Christian faith, if we can trace its connection with the central truth of our Redemption. And that is the true system of the Creation which beholds in all its parts the continuity of all God's laws and doings, and their complete agreement with the Revealed Word and the Gospel of His Son. But if it be separated from that centre, if it be set up in opposition to it, then, however accurate may be the knowledge of the isolated truth, it is, as regards its relations to the complete system, a falsehood the more pernicious according to its magnitude.

Of all this body of truth, however, the work of Christ, the Word Incarnate, is the centre and the most necessary part. The initial need of man is a Redeemer. Without His atonement and mediation, whatever other knowledge we might have, whether of God above, or of earth below, would not avail for our happiness, if, indeed, without Him, we could have any knowledge. To be held under condemnation and given the knowledge that we are so, would be simply to know our own misery, and the impossibility of escape; while to know other things, and yet be ignorant of this, would be not to know the truth of anything. To penetrate the mysteries of science and of art, and to take our pleasure in them, lying under such a doom without knowing it during life, would but make the unveiling of the future world by death the more awful and crushing in the intensity of terror and despair; while, on the other hand, the illusory pleasures of this transitory world would be turned all to gall, by the accuracy of a knowledge which, without a mediator, possessed a revelation of the coming eternity, and every accession of insight into our true condition, would be but a foretaste of the final punishment. The unbeliever, to enjoy even the fleeting moment, must seek a "refuge of lies,"[a]—ignorance, not knowledge, delusion, not truth.

Christian faith, then, is formally the apprehension and reception of our Lord Jesus Christ as the Truth, in this wide latitude of meaning, so far as we have the capacity to take it in—as the object of religious contemplation, the foundation of religious trust, wherever we turn, whether to God above or to earth below, whether we search for truth in the word of Revelation or in the knowledge of our own nature, and the experience of our own condition and duty,—as the circumference of the sphere of religious thought, which alone is thought that reaches truth. He reveals to us the Father, He sends us the Holy Spirit, He makes us to know ourselves, He is the origin and end of the Creation, of human history, of all things; and therefore that only can be a truly religious life which beholds Him everywhere, and in all, and the world in Him.

But if all that is were known, except the mediation revealed in the Gospel, it could never avail to give us hope of salvation; whereas, clinging to Christ the Mediator, it is possible for the Christian to have all the comfort, and assurance, and joy of true religion, however otherwise illiterate and ignorant. This knowledge, then, is not only the most necessary, but the only necessary part. To know God the Father reconciled in Christ, to know ourselves according to our calling as redeemed Christians, to know what to do as such, and to have the happy consciousness of duty done by the rule of Christ,—this is sufficient for the Christian

---

[a] Isaiah.

as a Christian, and the rest is added on as he expands in knowledge and in power.

Finally, as we have seen that Repentance, to be complete, must include faith and regeneration, so Faith must *include* repentance and regeneration and the walk of the regenerate, to be perfect and saving faith. To preach Christ the Truth, then, is but to proclaim Him as the Way and the Life,—for He is Truth realized *in* the person *for* whom He is saving Truth. Such a person has repented of the sin and the falsehood of his natural life; he has sought the grace of Regeneration; he "lives by the faith of the Son of God." Hence faith, like Repentance, has its two stages, the one preceding the other following Regeneration.[a] In the first stage, the penitent sinner beholds Christ (as it were) afar off, as *the* Mediator, indeed, and *the* Redeemer, but cannot yet say, "Christ is *my* Redeemer;" for the personal appropriation of the Redemption rests upon the communication of the Divine life of Christ to the individual at his regeneration. The second stage is when the believer is regenerate and lives as becometh the regenerate; then he is made one with Christ, his redemption is assured, he is "alive from the dead," he has within himself the assurance of forgiveness, and all the other benefits of Christ's passion. Then his faith is perfect, and so long as he retains, by a holy walk, the life implanted at his regeneration, so long he has the confidence of salvation, he knows in his own soul that he is "justified by faith," and through the merits

---

[a] These are the *fides informis* and *fides formata* of the old theologians.

of his Redeemer can stand in the presence of God the Father.

III. We are sent, therefore, to the consideration of the mystery of "Christ our Life,"[a] to complete the circle of Scripture teaching respecting the grace of the Son. By the life-giving operation of His grace, He is the centre of our being, as in His presentation of Himself to faith He is its circumference and spiritual horizon. He thus enters into a still closer relation with the regenerate, into a vitalizing union, by which He becomes the active principle of their life, the inward revivifying influence of their spiritual natures. He enters (if we may so say) into the substance of the soul, He communicates to it life from Himself, He resides in the soul of the regenerate, which, by this union with Him, is "dead to sin," and "alive to God."[b] Our regeneration, then, is our entrance into this so close union, by which "He dwelleth in us, and we in Him," by which "we are members of His body, of His flesh, and of His bones."[c]

I do not know that it is formally stated, but it seems to be tacitly, perhaps unconsciously, assumed, by our modern theological writers, that our Lord Jesus Christ is in us by the presence of His Spirit in our hearts, and in no other sense. It is true, and (as will be hereafter seen) a truth of most momentous importance, that the Holy Spirit is indwelling in the regenerate, and that He is (in the language of the Nicene Creed) the "Giver of Life;" but it is no less true that our blessed

---

[a] Col. iii. 3.   [b] Rom. vi. 11.   [c] Eph. v. 30.

Saviour Himself is also present, that He is the Life which the Spirit gives, that the Son Incarnate, in His own person, in some mysterious way, dwells in and is the life of the Christian. Our "life" is the indwelling grace of the Son; the indwelling grace of the Holy Spirit is the means by which this life springs up, and is brought to maturity in our sanctification,—it is (as it were) the light, the heat, the air, the rain, by which the seed of life fructifies in righteousness of Christian thought and deed. "Know ye not your own selves," says St. Paul, "how that Jesus Christ is in you, except ye be reprobates?"[a] On this fact, indeed, more than on any other depends the whole doctrine of threefold grace, which makes faith in the Holy Trinity of so great practical necessity.

Further, God the Son is the life of the Christian, not simply as Divine, but as Divine and human. For, as Hooker remarks, "That which quickeneth us is the Spirit of Christ, and His flesh that wherewith He quickeneth." And again he asks: "Doth any man doubt but that, *even from the flesh of Christ,* our very bodies do receive that life which shall make them glorious at the latter day, and for which they are already accounted parts of His blessed body?" For Christ, being God and man in one person, His grace being His personal efficacy in us to eternal life, and His assumption of humanity being the means to our

---

[a] II. Cor. xiii. v. ἀδόκιμοι, "spurious," said of coin which has the color and appearance, but not the substance of gold and silver; hence of Christians who have the semblance, but not the substance of the Christian,—who have lost "the life," and therefore are *reprobate.*

Redemption, there is the same conjoint operation of the Divine and human natures in this respect, which we have seen in the parts of His grace already treated of. There is a mystical conjunction, therefore, of all true Christians with the humanity, as well as with the Divinity of their head. Not only is there that substantial conjunction with him, through the presence of His Spirit, which rests upon the unity of essence in the Deity, but there is also a personal conjunction with Himself, in His own person, in which He partakes of the Divine and the human nature,—a conjunction wrought by the operation of the Holy Spirit when we are made regenerate; and it is in respect of this that He is said to be the Life of His people.

Upon so important a subject as this, it is impossible that a theologian whose authority is as deservedly great as that of Hooker should misunderstand or misstate the doctrine of the Church of God. As an example, therefore, of the testimony of her doctors and fathers, I shall set down his statements at some length, requesting attention to the forcible, unmistakable, and unhesitating precision of his language.

"We are by nature the sons of Adam. When God created Adam He created us, and as many as are descended from Adam, have in themselves the root out of which they spring. . . The sons of God have God's own natural Son, as a second Adam from Heaven, whose race and progeny they are by spiritual and heavenly birth. . . Life, as all other gifts and benefits, groweth originally from the Father, and cometh not to us, but by the Son, nor by the Son to any of us in particular, but through the Spirit. For this cause, the Apostle wisheth to the Church of Corinth 'the grace of our Lord Jesus Christ, and the love of God, and the fellowship of the Holy Ghost.' Which three St. Peter comprehendeth in one, 'the participation of Divine Nature.' . . But in God, we actually are, no longer than only from the time of our actual adoption into the body of His true Church, into the fellowship of His children. . . Our being in Christ by eternal foreknowledge saveth us not, without our actual and real adoption into the fellowship of His saints in this present world. For in Him we actually are, by our actual incorporation into that Society which hath Him for their Head, and doth make together with Him one body (He and they in that respect having one name), for which cause, by virtue of this mystical conjunction, we are of Him, and in Him, even as though our very flesh and bones should be made continuate with His. . . We are, therefore, adopted sons of God to eternal life by participation of the only-begotten Son of God, whose life is the wellspring and cause of ours.

. . . "The Church is in Christ as Eve was in Adam. Yea, by grace we are every of us in Christ and in His Church, as by nature we are in those our first parents. God made Eve of the rib of Adam. And His Church He frameth out of the very flesh, the very wounded and bleeding side of the Son of Man. His body crucified, and His blood shed for the life of the world, are the true elements of that heavenly being which maketh us such as Himself is of whom we come. For which cause the words of Adam may be fitly the words of Christ concerning his Church, 'flesh of my flesh, and bone of my bones,' *a true native extract of mine own body*. So that in him, even according to His manhood, we, according to our heavenly being, are as branches in that root out of which they grow. . . . . Adam is in us as an original cause of our nature, and of that corruption of nature which causeth death, Christ as the cause original of restoration to life; the person of Adam is not in us, but his nature, and the corruption of his nature derived into all men by propagation; Christ, having Adam's nature as we have, but incorrupt, deriveth, not nature but incorruption, and that immediately from His own person into all that belong unto Him. As therefore we are really partakers of the body of sin and death received from Adam, so, except we be truly partakers of Christ, and as really possessed of His Spirit, all we speak of eternal life is but a dream. . . . .

"Thus much no Christian man will deny, that when Christ sanctified His own flesh, giving as God, and taking as man, the Holy Ghost, He did not this for Himself only, but for our sakes, that the grace of sanctification and life, which was first received in Him, might pass from Him to His whole race, as malediction came from Adam unto all mankind."[a]

Confirmed by these statements of our great divine, we proceed to inquire into the teachings of Holy Scripture respecting the communication of spiritual life from our Lord to His faithful followers.

The word *life*, besides having its twofold physical use to denote the bodily vitality and the outward state

---

[a] Hooker, Ec. Pol., b. v. ch. lvi.

or condition of man, is used in four different but related senses in Holy Scripture, to express, 1, the eternal life of our Lord as a Divine Person, residing in His separate Personality, received by Him from the Father, dwelling in Him as God before His Incarnation, after His Incarnation as God and Man; 2, the grace of which that Personal life is the fount, communicated as an inward, active, vivifying power to the soul of man, as the spiritual life both of soul and body; 3, the outward working of that inner life, its growth and development into the outer walk of the Christian; and 4, the continuance of that life in consummate blessedness in the eternal happiness of Heaven. Examples of these senses (except the third, which is singular) are most distinctly apparent in the writings of St. John; in those of St. Paul two or three senses are frequently combined.

1. The first meaning appears in the opening of the first chapter of St. John's Gospel, "In Him was life, and that life was the light of men."[a] The Son, as a person distinct from the Father, has life in Himself; this life He has from the Father, and it is the light of men, their joy and hope of salvation; because on the possession of a Personal life in Himself depends His power to mediate between the Father and man; by it He is a third party, able to merit from the Father what He gives to man, able to give to rebellious man of His own, that He may make him acceptable to His Father. So the Saviour Himself declares: "As the Father hath life in Himself, so hath He given to the Son to have life in Himself,"[b] where the sense unquestionably is that the

---

[a] John, i. 4. [b] John, v. 26.

Father hath given to the Son the subsistence of a distinct personality, by giving Him His own divine life. And this truth our Saviour further uses as an analogy by which to show the spiritual subsistence of the Christian through participation of Him: "As the living Father hath sent Me, and I live by the Father, so he that eateth Me, even he shall live by Me."[a] The Divine life of the Son, indeed, is the foundation of St. John's teaching; he begins his Epistle with it, as well as his Gospel: "That which was from the beginning, which we have heard, which we have seen with our eyes, which we have looked upon, and our hands have handled of the word of Life: for the Life was manifested, and we have seen it, and bear witness, and show unto you that eternal life which was with the Father, and was manifested unto us."[b] Here "the Life," and the "Word of Life," are names of our Lord derived from His possession of life in Himself, and His giving us to partake of it. And as this is the beginning, so it is the end of St. John's doctrine; for he closes his Epistle with the words, "We are in Him that is true, even in His Son Jesus Christ. This is the true God, and eternal life."[c]

2. The second sense, in which it denotes the communication of the grace of Christ as a power of spiritual life in us, is as clearly and distinctly to be perceived in St. John. The testimony of John the Baptist, set down by the Evangelist in his third chapter, is: "He that believeth on the Son hath everlasting life: and he that believeth not the Son shall not see life; but the wrath

---

[a] John, vi. 57.   [b] I. John, i. 1, 2.   [c] I. John, v. 20.

of God abideth on him."[a] The words "everlasting life" may combine the fourth sense with the second, but the present tense of the verb shows conclusively that the life itself is a present possession,—now begun, and everlastingly continuing,—an inner, spiritual resurrection of the soul from its death in sin. So our Saviour Himself says: "Verily, verily, I say unto you, He that heareth my words, and believeth on Him that sent me, hath everlasting life and shall not come into condemnation, but is passed from death unto life."[b] And again, "I am come that they might have life."[c] These passages prove that the word "life" has the sense of an inner spiritual power in man; but they do not prove, with the clearness necessary to demonstration, that this power is derived personally from the Son Incarnate. This, however, is evident, beyond gainsaying, by the following: "The bread of God is He which cometh down from Heaven, and giveth life unto the world."[d] "I am the bread of life."[e] "The bread which I will give is my flesh, which I will give for the life of the world."[f] He would not represent Himself under the figure of bread—"bread of life"—unless He intended us to understand that He would be given and received in order to be life to the world. Hence, further on in the chapter whence the foregoing quotations are made, He declares, "Except ye eat the flesh of the Son of Man, and drink His blood, ye have no life in you."[g] And when the manner of this reception

---

[a] John, iii. 36.
[b] John, v. 24.
[c] John, x. 10.
[d] John, vi. 33.
[g] John, vi. 53.
[e] John, vi. 36.
[f] John, vi. 51.

was in doubt by His disciples He explained that it would be a spiritual reception, a reception of the life,— the "incorruption" (to use Hooker's word) of His body and blood: "The flesh profiteth nothing; the words that I speak unto you, they are spirit and they are life."[a] Hence, also, St. John says in his first Epistle, "He that hath the Son hath life, and He that hath not the Son of God hath not life."[b] The union of the Christian and his Lord, by which he derives his spiritual life, is represented also by the growth of the branches in the vine: "I am the vine, ye are the branches. As the branch cannot bear fruit of itself, except it abide in the vine; no more can ye except ye abide in me."[c]

3. It is somewhat remarkable that the word seems not to be used by St. John in its third sense, in which it seems to be most commonly (I might almost say, exclusively) used in our modern theological literature. For the verb "to live," in this sense, the Evangelist substitutes "to walk," as in the following from his first Epistle: "He that saith he abideth in him, ought himself also so to walk, even as He walked;" from his second, "This is love, that we walk after His commandments;" from his third, "I have no greater joy than to hear that my children walk in the truth." A clear example of this sense, however, is St. Paul's declaration, "The life which I now live in the flesh, I live by the faith of the Son of God, who loved me and gave Himself for me."[d]

---

[a] John, vi. 63.
[b] I. John, v. 12.
[c] John, xv. 54.
[d] Gal. ii. 20.

4. Of the fourth sense, containing the notion of eternal blessedness, examples are so numerous that it is not necessary to set any down; all those passages where *eternal* or *everlasting life* is spoken of have this sense, and how many they are, may be seen by turning to the concordance.[a]

From this analysis of the meanings of the word, we perceive the history of the grace of Christ the Life to be as follows: 1. He is, in Himself, the Divine Life, having received it from the Father. This life He first communicated to His human nature by His Incarnation, and completed its effect upon it by His Resurrection from the dead. 2. To mankind in His Church He communicates the grace of life from Himself (by the agency of His Spirit) as an inward principle of Regeneration,—a seed (as it were) of eternal life. 3. That seed of eternal life, the indwelling grace of Christ, springs up in the Christian and develops, by the assimilation to itself of the whole man, his thoughts, feelings, affections, actions; it becomes active by the co-operation of the will and affections under the Divine influence of the Holy Spirit, which are to it as soil, and air, and light, and heat, and moisture to a plant, and so grows outwardly into the life and walk of holiness, justice, charity, and purity; and finally, 4, having brought forth fruit unto holiness in perfection, it is transplanted into the Heavenly Kingdom of the

---

[a] Between the second and fourth senses comes in the whole world of Christian faith and practice. We first receive it, we live according to it by faith and grace influencing our wills; and so we make our calling and election sure. This explains such texts as John, iii. 15, vi. 40, 47, etc.

redeemed, there to flourish and abide in eternal blessedness.

This account agrees with all the passages in the New Testament which speak of our spiritual life. And since that entire accordance with Scripture is the proof of the doctrine, the rest of this chapter will be occupied with its verification—1, in those places (more abundant, especially, in the writings of St. Paul) in which the word "life," or the verb "to live," embraces a combination of two or more of the senses above assigned to it, and 2, in those places where the doctrine is assumed as the ground of other forms of speech.

1. Passages in which the word combines two or more senses are these which follow:

Rom. v. 17. "If by one man's offence death reigned by one; much more they which receive abundance of grace and of the gift of righteousness shall reign in life by one Jesus Christ." Without entering into questions regarding the rendering of the very difficult context of this verse, it is evident that the Apostle argues *a fortiori* from Adam to Christ, in favor of universal Redemption, and the salvation of the Redeemed through partaking of the grace and life of Christ. This is well brought out in the rendering of the verse in Conybeare & Howson's Life and Epistles of St. Paul (vol. ii. p. 168): "If the reign of death was established by the one man [Adam], through the sin of him alone; far more shall the reign of life be established in those who receive the overflowing fulness of the free gift of righteousness, by the one man Jesus Christ." But this translation omits the point of the antithesis of the two parts of the sentence,—the change of giving a personal nominative to the verb "reign," in the second clause. The exact sense is that by the original sin of the first man, death reigned over us and enslaved us; but by the gift of Christ we are restored, not only to liberty, but to dominion in life. It is not merely that *righteousness* reigns in us to life, but that *we* reign, being alive, now and forever, spiritual life being eternal life—the verb in the future ("shall reign") having a present force (as is evident by the nature of St. Paul's argument), and carrying on this present dispensation of grace to the future dispensation of glory. The idea of "reigning in life," therefore, combines the second and fourth senses of the latter word; to which the third sense is added in the next verse: "Therefore, as by the offence of one, judgment came upon all men to condemnation; even so, by the righteousness[a] of one, the free gift came upon all men to justification[b] of life"—the meaning being, I conceive, that the grace obtained for us by the righteousness of Christ, avails for all who receive it, to a threefold justification[c] of life: 1. Justification, by infusion of the life of Christ (our *being alive* being the justifying fact); 2. Justification by the righteousness of a *life* or *walk* according to grace; 3. Justification availing to eternal life. The same idea is expressed in v. 21: "Where sin abounded, grace did much more abound: that as sin hath reigned unto death, even so might grace reign through righteousness unto eternal life, by Jesus Christ our Lord."

---

[a] δικαίωμα.   [b] δικαίωσις.

[c] δικαίωσις, the act in progress, as distinguished from δικαίωμα, the act completed.

Rom. vi. 2, 3, 4. "How shall we, that are dead to sin, live any longer therein? Know ye not, that so many of us as were baptized into Jesus Christ were baptized into His death? Therefore we are buried with Him by baptism into death: that like as Christ was raised from the dead by the glory of the Father, even so we also should walk in newness of life." The word is used here in the third sense, the Apostle exhorting Christians, as baptized into the death and resurrection of Christ, to act and walk according to the commandments of God, in a new outward life. If we are dead to sin, we cannot live or walk any longer therein; hence our *outward* life is a new one, the fruit of a new *inner* life. In v. 8, "If we be dead with Christ, we believe that we shall also live with Him," this passes over into the fourth sense—life completed at the Resurrection. And that the union with Christ in baptism is the ground, both of the exhortation in v. 4, and of the hope in v. 8, is manifest from the use of the word in the second sense, in v. 11: "Christ being raised from the dead dieth no more; death hath no more dominion over Him. For in that He died, He died unto sin once; but in that he liveth, He liveth unto God. Thus,[a] also, reckon ye yourselves to be dead indeed unto sin, but alive unto God, through Jesus Christ our Lord."

Rom. viii. 2. "The law of the Spirit of life[b] in Christ Jesus hath made me free from the law of sin and

---

[a] οὕτω καὶ "thus also," not "*likewise*" as in the authorized version.

[b] τῆς ζωῆς " of *the* life" in Christ Jesus.

death." The sense evidently is, "the law of the Spirit who giveth the life in Christ Jesus;" for the "Spirit of life," or "of *the* life," is the "Spirit who maketh alive,"[a] and the life is "the life in Christ Jesus." The word is therefore to be taken in its widest application, as including the second, third, and fourth significations; according to which view, "the law of the Spirit of life" will be, 1. the law of the Spirit, written upon the heart, when the Christian receives the inner life; 2. the law of the Spirit governing the outward life according to God's will; and 3. the law of the Spirit, by obedience to which, having received the initial life on earth, we shall attain its consummation in heaven. In the same way, the "Spirit who maketh alive," is the Spirit, 1. by whose agency we receive "the life in Christ Jesus," 2. by whose help we live the life in Christ Jesus, and 3. by whose power we are raised to the life everlasting.

Rom. viii. 10. "If Christ be in you, the body is dead because of sin; but the Spirit is life because of righteousness." The inner life is presupposed, and the fountain of it declared to be the Second Person of the Holy Trinity, in the postulate: "If Christ be in you." The expression, "the Spirit is life," therefore can only mean that the Holy Spirit is the agent developing and perfecting the outward life of righteousness by His action on the heart, thus opposing and overcoming the deathful influences of the carnal nature, and assuring us power to continue in the grace we have received to eternal life. This text, therefore, is a clear

---

[a] το πνευμα το ζωοποιον—Nicene Creed.

testimony to the fact that the grace of life is personally derived from the Son, our Lord Jesus Christ. Nothing could be stronger than the expression "If Christ be in you."

In the twelfth and thirteenth verses of the same chapter the word is used three times, twice to denote the outward walk in this world, and the third time the final consummation in the future world: "We are debtors, not to the flesh, to live after the flesh. For if ye live after the flesh ye shall die; but if ye through the Spirit do mortify the deeds of the body, ye shall live."

II. Cor. iii. 6. "Our sufficiency is of God; who also hath made us able ministers of the New Testament; not of the letter, but of the spirit; for the letter killeth, but the Spirit giveth life." The life here declared to be given by the Spirit is the life of Christ, which is communicated by His operation, whose agents and ministers (the Apostle asserts) are the commissioned ministers of the Gospel. St. Paul contrasts this ministry with that of the law, which, having no such regenerating grace and spiritual power to give as would enable men to perform its commands, was but a "letter" not a "spirit," and so, as it is called in the next verse, a "ministration of death."

The next place in which the word occurs is in the tenth and eleventh verses of the fourth chapter of this Epistle, where the Apostle refers to the hardships endured in the exercise of his ministry, and draws attention to the source of the strength which sustains him under them: "Always bearing about in the body the dying of the Lord Jesus, that the life also of Jesus might be manifest in our body. For we which live [this natural life of hardship, want, and suffering] are always delivered unto death for Jesus' sake, that the life also of Jesus might be made manifest in our mortal flesh." That is, that the life communicated by the grace of Christ might be made manifest in the fruits of fortitude, patience, and endurance which the Apostles were enabled to exhibit—that the inner life might be manifest in the outer life.

II. Cor. v. 4. "That mortality might be swallowed up of life"—the eternal life succeeding the Resurrection.

Gal. ii. 20. "I am crucified with Christ: nevertheless I live; yet not I, but Christ liveth in me; and the life which I now live in the flesh, I live by the faith of the Son of God, who loved me, and gave Himself for me." In this passage, note the accuracy of the Apostle's language, as interpreted by the doctrine here expounded. "Not I, but Christ liveth in me,"—this in the second sense above assigned to the word. The grace of Christ is the inner life-power. The Apostle has an inner spiritual life because "Christ liveth in him." The word then passes over to the next sense, the outer life of act and deed: "the life which I now live in the flesh, I live by the faith of the Son of God." Note the words "by *faith* of the Son of God." A new element is here introduced. The grace of Christ is the inner life; but in order for that life to develop outwardly, it must be assimilated by the sanctified will and other spiritual powers. But the will needs to be stimulated to action by the "faith of the Son of God," and therefore the Apostle so expresses himself in relation to the outer life.

Gal. iii. 11. "The just shall live by faith." This quotation from the prophet Habakkuk cannot be understood, except by remembering that "faith" here is inclusive—equivalent to the acceptance of the whole Gospel dispensation, with its spiritual grace, as well as its preaching of the Atonement. "The just shall live,"—be made alive, and so continue to all eternity,—by the grace of the Divine life, the condition of receiving which is "faith."

Gal. v. 25. "If we live in the Spirit, let us also walk in the Spirit." The gift of the Holy Spirit is simultaneous with the gift of life from the Son; we cannot have the latter without the former; therefore "to live in the Spirit" is "to live in Christ" and *vice versa*.

Eph. iv. 17, 18. "This I say therefore, and testify in the Lord, that ye henceforth walk not as other Gentiles walk, in the vanity of their mind, . . . being alienated from the life of God, through the ignorance that is in them, because of the blindness of their heart." The "being alienated from the life of God" is equivalent to the being "without God in the world," in ch. ii. v. 12,—being without the life of Christ in their souls, having no power in themselves to do what is right, and therefore living an outward life contrary to the law of God.

Phil. ii. 15, 16. "That ye may be blameless and harmless, the sons of God, without rebuke, in the midst of a crooked and perverse nation, among whom ye shine as lights[a] in the world; holding forth the word of life,"—preaching the truth of the inner life by your

---

[a] φωστηρες.

outward conduct, and setting forth by the beauty of your holiness, the blessedness of your hope of eternal life.

Col. iii. 3, 4. "Ye are dead, and your life is hid with Christ in God. When Christ, who is our life, shall appear, then shall ye also appear with Him in glory." Note here, again, how it is said that "Christ is our life,"—how all that is said of our spiritual life in other passages is to be understood of His presence in us.

I. Thess. v. 9, 10. "God hath not appointed us to wrath, but to obtain salvation by our Lord Jesus Christ, who died for us, that, whether we wake or sleep, we should live together with Him." The word is here used in the last sense assigned to it above. The Apostle has previously instructed the Thessalonians, that at the last day, those Christians who remain in the body will be partakers of the Lord's glory together with those who rise from the dead. He exhorts them, therefore, to be steadfast in their profession, since it will make no difference whether they "wake or sleep"—the same eternal life will be theirs in heaven.

II. Tim. i. 1. "Paul, an Apostle of Jesus Christ by the will of God, according to the promise of life which is in Christ Jesus." A more correct translation is: "Paul, an Apostle of Jesus Christ by the will of God, according to the promise of the life[a] in Christ Jesus." Our translators, by inserting the words "which is," have confused the sense, making it possible to read it as if the clause "which is in Christ Jesus," referred to

---

[a] ζωης της εν Χρ. Ιη.

"the promise." The Greek shows that it refers to "the life." St. Paul is an Apostle carrying out the fulfilment of the promise made long ago by the prophets of "the life in Christ Jesus." This promise is now fulfilled by the grace of, not now promised by, the Gospel.

II. Tim. i. 10. "Our Saviour Jesus Christ, who hath abolished death, and hath brought life and immortality to light by the Gospel." He has abolished spiritual death, in the Redeemed, has brought forth life and immortality from their hidden place in the secret counsels of God, made them manifest by the preaching of the word, and given them in possession to His people by the grace of the Gospel. The word "life" is here used to denote the inner grace of the regeneration, the beginning on earth of the immortality of blessedness assured to believers in heaven.

Titus, ii. 11, 12. "The grace of God that bringeth salvation hath appeared unto all men, teaching us that, denying ungodliness and worldly lusts, we should live soberly, righteously, and godly in this present world." The word in this passage needs no comment. The third sense is apparent.

These are the most (if not all) of the passages in the Epistles of St. Paul in which the word "life" is used in a spiritual sense. Taken together, they agree completely with and prove fully the doctrine advanced in these pages. Indeed, the interchange and mingling of senses in the pregnant language of the Apostle, is one of the strongest proofs of the doctrine which could be advanced; for it is impossible to understand him, without attending to this fulness of meaning.

2. But if we confine the evidence of the doctrine to the passages in which the word "life" itself occurs, we lose much of its support from Scripture. Strong as its authority would be, even with this limitation, it is doubly confirmed, when we note the equivalent expressions, the modes of speech, the course of argument, of which the root-idea is the vital union of the regenerate with Christ, through His personal indwelling grace. The following are examples of this kind of evidence:

John, i. 12, 13. "As many as received Him, to them gave He power to become the Sons of God, even to them that believe on His name: which were born, not of blood, nor of the will of the flesh, nor of the will of man, but of God." In this passage a new birth is spoken of, and that by the power of the Son, given to as many as received Him. The idea is evidently the same as that contained in the class of texts before discussed, since a new birth implies a new life. It is reproduced no less clearly in v. 16 of this chapter: "Of His fulness have we all [*i.e.* all Christians] received, and grace for grace."

John, xiv. 19, 20. "Yet a little while, and the world seeth me no more; but ye see me: because I live, ye shall live also. At that day ye shall know that I am in my Father, and *ye in me, and I in you.*" V. 23. "If a man love me, he will keep my words; and my Father will love him, and we will come unto him, and make our abode with him."

John, xv. 1, 2. "I am the true vine, and my Father is the husbandman. Every branch in me that beareth not fruit He taketh away; and every branch that beareth fruit, He purgeth it, that it may bring forth more fruit." V. 5. "*I am the vine, ye are the branches:* he that abideth in me, and I in him, the same bringeth forth much fruit." V. 7. "If ye abide in me, and my words abide in you, ye shall ask what ye will, and it shall be done unto you." The expression "*my words* abide in you" is not the exact equivalent of the "I in him," above. "Christ in us" is the source and beginning of life, "His word in us," governing our conduct, is the means whereby that life comes to maturity. The retaining His word is within the compass of *our* wills, aided by the grace of the Holy Spirit; hence He says, "If ye abide in me, and my words abide in you," as intimating the responsibilities and contingencies of our action. There is no "if"—no subjection to the receiver in His own presence. That, *He* gives or withdraws.

John, xvii. 19-23. This is from the sacrificial prayer with which our Saviour consecrated Himself to be the Atonement for our sins. He is praying for His Church: "For their sakes I sanctify myself, that they also might be sanctified through the truth. Neither pray I for these alone, but for them also which shall believe on me through their word; that they all may be one; as thou, Father, art in me, and I in thee, that they also may be one in us; that the world may believe that thou hast sent me. And the glory which thou gavest me I have given them; that they may be one, even as we are one. I in them, and thou in me, that they may be made perfect in one." V. 26. "I have declared unto them thy name, and will declare it: that the love wherewith thou hast loved me may be in them, and I in them." The life-giving union of Christ and His redeemed is surely the ground of these solemn utterances.

Acts, xxii. is an account of St. Paul's defence before his countrymen at Jerusalem. In relating the story of his conversion, after telling them of the miraculous light which he beheld, he says: "I fell unto the ground, and heard a voice saying unto me, Saul, Saul, why persecutest thou me? And I answered, Who art thou, Lord? And He said unto me, I am Jesus of Nazareth, whom thou persecutest." Can any words express more forcibly the union of the saint and his Saviour, than this identification of the two? Christ is persecuted in His saints—and why, but because He *is* in them?

Rom. vii. 4. "Ye are become dead to the law by the body of Christ; that ye should be married to another, even to Him who is raised from the dead, that we should bring forth fruit unto God." The Church is represented in Holy Scripture as the bride, the spouse of Christ; the spiritual union is as close as the union of husband and wife, who "are no more twain, but one flesh."

Rom. viii. 16, 17. "The Spirit itself beareth witness with our spirit, that we are the children of God; and if children, then heirs; heirs of God, and joint heirs with Christ; if so be that we suffer with Him, that we may be also glorified together." The "partnership" with Christ, being fellow-heirs, fellow-sufferers, and partakers of His glory, and the consequent suggestion of the union with Him in His Church, by the partaking of His life, is more plain in the original than in the translation.

Rom. viii. 28–30. "We know that all things work together for good to them that love God, to them who are the called according to His purpose. For whom He did foreknow, He also did predestinate to be *conformed to the image*[a] *of His Son*, that He might be the first-born among many brethren. Moreover, whom He did predestinate, them He also called: and whom He called, them He also justified: and whom He justified, them He also glorified." Without entering into the predestinarian controversy, which does not affect the particular subject now under consideration, we may perceive that the text evidently states the process of God's grace in leading us to ultimate salvation. It is His will that we should be "completely made over in the image of His Son,"[b] first by being made partakers of His life; then by being trained to righteousness after His example; and lastly, by being raised to the glory of the life eternal—"called" at baptism, "justified," by grace enabling us to walk in righteousness and holiness; "glorified" at the Resurrection.

I. Cor. i. 30. "Of Him are ye in Christ Jesus, who of God is made unto us, wisdom, and righteousness, and sanctification, and redemption." "Of Him," that is,

---

[a] συμμορφους της εικονος.

[b] This, perhaps, expresses the force of συμμορφους, though the text is an exact and literal translation. In the ancient philosophy, things being considered to consist of *matter* and *form*, the *matter* was held to be an inert, and the *form* an active, vivifying principle. To be συμμορφος, therefore, is to be subject to the active form or formative influence, and by it to be brought into conformity with the archetype. How well this expresses the operation of the grace of the Son.

"born of God," as St. John expresses it—"in Christ Jesus," being made "members of His body, of His flesh, and of His bones." Being thus closely united to Him, He is made unto us "wisdom," enabling us by His grace to receive the truth, "and righteousness," giving us the ability to walk justly in this present world, "and sanctification," imparting inward holiness of heart, "and redemption," as gaining the final victory over death, by raising our bodies to immortality.

II. Cor. v. 17. "If any man be in Christ, he is a new creature: old things are passed away; behold, all things are become new." To be a "new creature" is equivalent to being "new born," "regenerate," "made alive unto God,"—a man is this by being "in Christ." And as far as in *his* life the life of Christ within him is realized, so far the old is passed away," and "all things are become new." To the same effect also, in Gal. vi. 15, the Apostle says: "In Christ Jesus neither circumcision availeth anything, nor uncircumcision, but a new creature." And in Ephesians, ii. 10: "We are His workmanship, created in Christ Jesus unto good works."

Gal. iii. 24-27. "The law was our schoolmaster to bring us unto Christ, that we might be justified by faith. But after that faith is come [that is, the dispensation in which faith is made perfect by grace given from Christ;—for it is evident that "faith" is here used as a comprehensive name for the whole Gospel covenant] we are no longer under a schoolmaster.[a] For ye are

---

[a] παιδαγωγος, that is, the servant who attended children of rank to their teacher. The English word "*page*" is the same word

all the children of God by faith in Jesus Christ. For as many of you as have been baptized into Christ have put on Christ." "Being baptized into Christ," and "having put on Christ," are clearly equivalent to being made partakers of the life of Christ, as well by participation of His grace as by profession of His calling.

Ephesians, ii. 4, 5. "God, who is rich in mercy, for His great love wherewith He loved us, even when we were dead in sins, hath *quickened us together with* Christ." The union,—nay more than this, the *oneness* of Christ and His saints, the Head and the Body, is so vividly impressed upon the Apostle's mind that he speaks as if the Church were raised from the dead at the very resurrection of her Lord,—as if it were partaker of His lot, not only in the manner of His life, but at the time. The Apostle's vehemence carries him into this use of the figure *hyperbole*, and gives intensity to his meaning. The same is the case in all other places where we are said to have or to do anything "together with Christ."

Col. ii. 20. "If ye be dead with Christ from the rudiments of the world, why, as though living in the world, are ye subject to ordinances?" The Christian grace and profession is a partnership with Christ in His death, by which He is severed from "the world that now is." It may be well to remark, that, generally, when the Apostle speaks of death, he does not consider it in the heathen way, as a state of the body, a state of dissolution or non-existence; but as a state of

---

shortened. The translation "schoolmaster" gives a wrong sense to the entire passage.

the man, and therefore as a state of existence; so that to pass from life to death or from death to life, is not to pass out of existence, and *vice versa;* but to pass from one state of existence to another.[a] To be dead with Christ to the world, therefore, is to be alive with Christ to spiritual and eternal verities,—to have received the grace of spiritual life from Him. The Apostle tells Christians that if they be thus regenerate, they must live accordingly; their actions must correspond to their state.

Col. iii. 9, 10. "Ye have put off the old man with his deeds; and have put on the new man, which is renewed in knowledge after the image of Him that created him." This is parallel with, "As many of you as have been baptized into Christ, have put on Christ."

Heb. iii. 14. "We are made partakers of Christ, if we hold the beginning of our confidence steadfast unto the end." That is, we are made partakers of Christ, now, by receiving His grace of life, and shall continue so to be, if we hold this beginning of our confidence, by leading a holy life, steadfast unto the end.

In Heb. x. 1, the Apostle begins a discussion of the efficacy of the life-giving sacrifice of Christ with these words: "The law having a *shadow* of good things to come, and not the very *image* of the things, could never, with those sacrifices which they offered year by year continually, make the comers thereunto perfect." This passage is produced to note the antithesis of the legal "shadow" and the "image" which, it is implied, the Gospel is. The law, according to the teaching of the Epistle to the Hebrews, was an inefficacious *type*, or

---

[a] Cf. Rom. vi. 2; vii. 4; xiv. 9; I. Cor. xv. 12; Eph. v. 14; Col. i. 18; and many other passages.

bare representation of the mysteries of the heavenly world, prophesying of a future dispensation (the Christian), which should be the "image," or embodied form, the heavenly mysteries themselves being the true substance. Three things, then, are here implied, the "shadow," the "image," and the substance. The "shadow"[a] differs from the "image" as a picture from a statue. Figures painted have no substance; they are represented only by their surface colors, with no body underneath; the statue or "image" bodies it forth, filling out the form with substance, yet not substance of the same nature with that which is represented. So, the Christian dispensation is the "image" of the heavenly world, differing from it, as grace differs from glory. The Christian "image," therefore, differs from the Mosaic "shadow," in having the grace of Christ,—the life of Christ realized in us on earth, as the image of the life of Christ realized in heaven. It is in such expressions as this that the all-pervading evidence of this doctrine is noticed.

I. Peter, i. 22, 23. "Seeing ye have purified your souls in obeying the truth through the Spirit, unto unfeigned love of the brethren, see that ye love one another with a pure heart fervently: being born again, not of corruptible seed, but of incorruptible, by the Word of God, which liveth and abideth forever." Four statements are implied in this passage: 1. that Christians are born again; 2. that this new birth is "by the Word of God,"—that is, by the grace of Christ, the Son of God, the "Word, which liveth and abideth

---

[a] σκια.

forever;" 3. that obedience to the truth advances the purification of the soul, being the means by which the "incorruptible seed assimilates the soul to itself; and 4. that this progress from the beginning of the new birth to the perfection of the Christian character, is "through the Spirit," that is, by His abiding grace, acting in co-operation with the grace of the Son.

These passages corroborate the evidence contained in the former group. They contain the same doctrine in different words. We read as clearly in them, that Christ our Lord is the source of our spiritual life; that we possess that life by His indwelling; that our outward life and conduct as Christians is the outgrowth or development of the inward life received from the Redeemer, and that the eternal life of Heaven is its further development, its consummation, and its reward.

We see also in the Scripture which has been brought forward, the confirmation of the assertion advanced at the beginning of this section: that we derive our life from the Son of God, not only as Divine, but as Incarnate. Take, for instance, the sixth chapter of St. John: "The bread which I will give is my flesh, which I will give for the life of the world," and the whole discourse of which this is an example. It asserts clearly the connection between our spiritual life and the partaking of Christ Incarnate. Nay, every text of the whole *catena* proves it, speaking, as they do, of our Lord as Jesus Christ. The Word did not take His name Jesus, nor his official designation, Christ, until He took flesh; and this constant use of His human name informs us by implication that He first filled His own humanity with the Divine Life, and thence derives His grace to His followers by mystical union with Himself; so that Christ, the Son of God, made man, is the fountain of our life, as He is the truth of our faith and the way of our repentance.

It will now, also, be seen more clearly why Repentance and Faith, in their first stage, are so necessary for those who seek the life of Christ, having come to the knowledge of their need of it, after having committed actual sin ; and why, at the same time, this life itself is the bringing of repentance and faith to perfection. In the case of those who are regenerate before they have committed actual sin—infants who attain the election— a preparatory repentance and faith are not necessary, as they are not possible; the repentance and faith of their after-years are that forsaking of sin, and knowledge of a present Redeemer, which follow after their regeneration, and which must be acted while life lasts, that they may not lose the gift. But from adult persons, a preparatory repentance and renunciation of their past sins, and a faith in Christ the Redeemer, are required, that they may have in themselves no "root of bitterness,"—no bar to the operation of grace; because the life is a restoration from the death of sin, which must be left behind when they rise new-born in spirit ; and because it is a making over to them the merits of the Redeemer, which they must plead by faith in Him. In such persons, therefore, repentance and faith in the first stages begin the work, which is carried forward by the communication of life in their regeneration ; and then repentance and faith, containing within themselves all added Christian graces, complete the work, by the life of holiness which ensures its continuance and increase, till it grows "to the measure of the stature of the fulness of Christ."

It remains to be said that, since the true beginning of the Christian life is the communication of the grace of Christ as an inward gift at our regeneration, its *growth* consists in its development *from within outwardly*, in heavenly affections and works of righteousness. This has, indeed, been spoken of; but it needs to be insisted upon, in order to call attention to Scripture testimony bearing upon this point, the strength of which might be lost were it mingled with that which has been brought forward in another connection. It will be seen also, that by the mercy of God this grace may continue for a time at least in those who do not show in themselves the full fruits of its presence; though it will finally be taken away, to their eternal loss, unless they eventually "give diligence to make their calling and election sure."

In the third chapter of the first Epistle to the Corinthians, St. Paul writes: "I, brethren, could not speak unto you as unto spiritual, but as unto carnal, even as unto babes in Christ. I have fed you with milk, and not with meat: for hitherto ye were not able to bear it, neither yet now are ye able. For ye are yet carnal: for whereas there is among you envying, and strife, and divisions, are ye not carnal, and walk as men?" From this we collect that the Corinthian Christians had the gift within them, though it had not yet brought forth fruit according to its full measure, it had not yet cast out "envyings, strifes, divisions;" hence they were but "babes in Christ;" their infancy consisted in the discrepancy of the outward life, with the profession of

Christ; and therefore the full stature of manhood would consist in the subjection of the outer life to the obedience of "faith working by love." So to the Galatians, who were in danger of being led away by legalizing Jews to the bondage of the law of Moses, he writes in the same spirit, but with expression of more intense emotion: "My little children, of whom I travail in birth again until Christ be formed in you, I desire to be present now, and to change my voice; for I stand in doubt of you."[a] He counts them "little children," because they are, indeed, new-born; but he fears that "Christ is not formed within them," or their life would correspond more closely to the Gospel, and not be led away to follow the dead ceremonies of the law, which are now abrogated.

To the same effect, in the chapter of I. Corinthians above quoted, by a change of the figure, the Apostle says: "Other foundation can no man lay than that is laid, which is Jesus Christ. Now if any man build upon this foundation gold, silver, precious stones, wood, hay, stubble; every man's work shall be made manifest: for the day shall declare it, because it shall be revealed by fire; and the fire shall try every man's work of what sort it is. If any man's work abide which he hath built thereupon, he shall receive a reward. If any man's work shall be burned, he shall suffer loss: but he himself shall be saved; yet so as by fire."[b]

Of the various meanings of this passage, it is surely one, that the building upon the foundation, "Christ in

---

[a] Gal. iv. 19, 20.   [b] I. Cor. iii. 11–15.

them," with "gold, silver, precious stones," *i.e.* imperishable good works, is equivalent to the growing to the full measure of holiness in the other figure; while the building with "wood, hay, stubble" is like remaining a babe,—yet, in this case, if the foundation still remain, if Christ be in the man, "he shall be saved, yet so as by fire."

In still another way the same thing is expressed in II. Cor. iii. 18: "We all, with open face beholding as in a glass the glory of the Lord, are changed into the same image from glory to glory [that is, from one height of holiness to another], as by the Spirit of the Lord."

In the Epistle to the Ephesians the Apostle explains the labor of the members of the Church in their several offices to be, "for the perfecting of the saints, for the work of the ministry, for the edifying the body of Christ: till we all come in the unity of the faith, and of the knowledge of the Son of God, unto a perfect man, unto the measure of the stature of the fulness of Christ: that we henceforth be no more children, tossed to and fro, and carried about with every wind of doctrine, by the sleight of men, and cunning craftiness, whereby they lie in wait to deceive: but speaking the truth in love, may grow up into Him in all things, which is the head, even Christ: from whom the whole body fitly joined together and compacted by that which every joint supplieth, according to the effectual working in the measure of every part, maketh increase of the body, to the edifying itself in love." And so he goes on to the exhortation: "That ye put off concerning the former conversation the old man, which is corrupt according to the deceitful lusts; and be renewed in the spirit of your mind; and that ye put on the new man, which after God is created in righteousness and true holiness." And then he ends with certain practical exhortations; from which we gather that in his mind the progress of the Christian life is from within outwardly, and that the means of progress is the earnest endeavor to make the outward life correspond with the law of God; by which means the whole heart and character is assimilated to the Divine seed implanted at the beginning.

The same idea is expressed in the exhortation to the Colossians: "As ye have received Christ Jesus the Lord, so walk ye in Him: rooted and built up in Him, and established in the faith."[a] "Rooted" of the inner life, "built up" of the outer.

So again, and lastly, in the fifth chapter of the Epistle to the Hebrews: "Every one that useth milk is unskilful in the word of righteousness: for he is a babe. But strong meat belongeth to them that are of full age, even those who by reason of use have their senses exercised to discern both good and evil,"[b]—that is, who by practice have made the outer life correspond with the inward gift. These are grown to manhood in Christ.

Now the grace of Christ, by which He is the life of His people, corresponds to His kingly office. As He is "the Way," by His priesthood, and "the Truth," in his prophetical character, so He is "the Life," in His kingly relation to His people. For the type of

---

[a] Col. ii. 6, 7.   [b] Heb. v. 13, 14.

the kingly office which represents His reign is not that with which we are acquainted in modern times; but it is the patriarchal type, and therefore includes, besides rule and judgment, the idea of family relationship, of a common nature, and of nourishment and preservation as well as of subjection. The patriarchal king was the "first-born among many brethren." He was "the head of the body;" it was he who fed and sustained and preserved his people, as the defender of the common weal, and the administrator of the common store. So our Lord Christ is the King of those whom He has made His brethren, by giving them to partake of His nature in their regeneration; He is the head of the corporate body, His Church; He feeds His people with the Divine food of His body and His blood; and these acts are as essential to His kingly office, as the watchfulness of His providence, and the scrutiny of His judgment.

But the offices of Christ are inseparable; and therefore His kingly grace confirms and makes operative His grace as Prophet and as Priest. His priestly actions are, for the most part, those of one not immediately present in the soul; a part of them were performed while He was on earth in the flesh; another part are performed by Him now present in heaven. His prophetical grace is, for the most part, external; by it He is to us as the world of sight around us, presenting Himself, and all things in Himself, as the object to the spiritual eye of faith. But by this grace He enters into our nature, makes us His own, and applies to us personally the merits of His priestly acts, and the hopes, comforts, consolations, and joys of His prophetical teachings. For it is this imparted grace which separates those who are the saved from those who are not. While Christ made a "full, perfect, and sufficient sacrifice, oblation, and satisfaction for the sins of the whole world," yet, without the communication of a gift of grace, which draws with it the application of the atonement to them individually, men are not redeemed from their sins, nor released from the consequences of them. Nor, though men "believe and tremble," as do the fallen angels with a dead faith, are they thereby justified; but they require a grace imparted, which shall make it a living faith, quickened with hope, joy, love, and good works. That gift of grace is the Divine life of Christ our Head. Its possession alone gives the sacrificial and mediatorial acts their efficacy for the recipient, causes them to terminate in individuals for their salvation, gives faith its power for justification, its energy for good works. And thus, by fitting this part into its place, the doctrine of the grace of Christ becomes an ensphered and perfect whole.

The effects of the grace of the Son, so far as they belong to Christian experience—so far as they enter into the consciousness of the Regenerate—are connected so intimately with the grace of the Holy Spirit, that they will best be considered in that connection in the next chapter. We have still to consider here, however, the relation of the grace of the Son to the grace of the Father, and the effect of the former upon our position before God.

The priesthood of Christ has been hitherto considered as sacrificial and intercessory. It has been shown that He offered up Himself as a Sacrifice and Atonement, and that now, by virtue of that atonement, He intercedes within the veil of the heavens on our behalf. The virtue of His intercession extends to all mankind so far as this, that God grants to them, in respect of it, the opportunity of pardon and reconciliation, dependent upon their action in accepting the grace of Christ. Where, without the Atonement, all must have been lost, now, because of it, all may be saved, if they will avail themselves of the offer of mercy, and come unto God in the way which He has appointed. The intercession of Christ in this aspect is represented in Holy Scripture by that parable of our Lord's in which He represents Himself as the gardener pleading for the barren fig-tree, "spare it this year also," thus averting the immediate sentence. Though the first and most obvious application of this parable may be to the case of the unprofitable members of the Church, it is certainly susceptible of the widest interpretation, as applying to the whole world in its natural estate, and thus it represents the universality of Christ's mediatorial action in delaying the execution of the sentence, and giving opportunity for its reversal.

But the priesthood of our Redeemer assumes a new and higher aspect for those who accept the Gospel, and are regenerate and renewed by His grace and the grace of the Holy Spirit. It is not only sacrificial and intercessory, but Eucharistical and perfective of the new relation between man and the reconciled Father. He not only obtains us from the Father and makes us His own, but He offers us again to the Father, as an acceptable gift, having taken away our sins; and thus as our great High Priest, in our regeneration and renewal, He acts towards the Father—not terminating our relation to the Godhead in Himself. Hence in that holy, sacrificial prayer recorded in the seventeenth chapter of St. John, He dwells more upon this exercise of His office than upon any other; since it is this which completes the other acts, and makes them operative and effectual. "For their sakes I sanctify myself, that they also might be sanctified through the truth. Neither pray I for these alone, but for them also which shall believe on me through their word; that they all may be one; as thou, Father, art in me and I in thee, that they also may be one in us: that the world may believe that thou hast sent me. And the glory which thou gavest me, I have given them; that they may be one, even as we are one: I in them, and thou in me, that they may be made perfect in one; and that the world may know that thou hast sent me, and hast loved them, as thou hast loved me. Father, I will," He proceeds, "that they also, whom thou hast given me, be with me, where I am; that they may behold my glory, which thou hast given me: for thou lovedst me before the foundation of the world. O righteous Father, the world hath not known thee: but I have known thee, and these have known that thou hast sent me. And I have declared unto them thy name, and will declare it; that the love wherewith thou hast loved me may be in them, and I in them."

Now the first effect of the fully imparted grace of Christ, in this function of His priestly office, as operating upon our relation to the Father, is to secure "*the remission or forgiveness of our sins*,"—those which we commit before our regeneration, at our regeneration, and those which we commit after,—provided they be not such, nor so many as to provoke the entire withdrawal of the grace of the Son, on our sincere repentance and amendment. "The God of our Fathers raised up Jesus. . . . Him hath God exalted with His right hand, to be a Prince and a Saviour, for to give repentance to Israel and forgiveness of sins;"[a] so preached St. Peter. And so St. Paul: "Be it known unto you, men and brethren, that through this man is preached unto you the forgiveness of sins."[b] And so St. John: "The blood of Jesus Christ, His Son, cleanseth us from all sin."[c]

The second effect is our *justification*, or our being accounted just before God, for the sake of His merits. "Being justified freely by His[d] grace, through the Redemption that is in Christ Jesus."[e] We are "justified by faith."[f] There is, perhaps, no declaration of Holy Scripture which has been the subject of so much controversy as this. But at this stage, we are able to obtain the true meaning with a few words. To be "justified" is a forensic term, and is, undeniably, "to be declared just." In its forensic use, it has two applications: first, to the sentence of the judge, acquitting the defendant—either accounting him innocent of the charge, or admitting the atonement or restitution as sufficient; and secondly, to the declaration of the defendant, setting forth his innocence, or pleading satis-

---

[a] Acts, v. 30, 31.
[b] Acts, xiii. 38.
[c] I. John, i. 7.
[d] *i.e.* the Father's.
[e] Rom. iii. 24. See Titus, iii. 4-7.
[f] Rom. iii. 28.

faction. With respect to the former meaning, faith is the title to justification. In the judgment which passes upon every human soul, God accepts the true faith of those who are truly united to Christ, as members of His mystical body (since no one can be thus in vital union with that body who has not true faith), as equivalent to complete righteousness, and so declares them just, appropriating to them the merits of the Redeemer to cancel their guilt, and counting His obedience as theirs. In the second sense, man, trusting not in his own works, which, though he be regenerate, are still imperfect, is empowered to declare himself justified, as before the bar of God, with a certainty equal to his faith in the Redeemer, his knowledge that he has fulfilled the conditions attached to the gift of the grace of Christ, and his assurance that that grace is his possession.

The ground of justification, then, is union with Christ.[a] The gift of His Divine life carries with it all the benefits of His sacrificial acts, and causes them to terminate in the recipient for his salvation. This union is so intimate—it is so completely a oneness of the

---

[a] It is a proof of the essential unity underlying all apparent theological differences, that Bishop McIlvaine quotes with entire approval, in his "Righteousness by Faith," S. Bernard's expression of this doctrine of justification as follows: "Since the Apostle [says?] if one died for all, then were all dead; meaning that the satisfaction made by one should be imputed to all, even as one bare the sins of all; *so that there should not be found one distinct person who incurred the forfeit, and another who made satisfaction; because truly the head and the body are one Christ.* The head satisfied for its members: Christ for His own bowels."— *Righteousness by Faith*, p. 108, note.

members of the mystical body with their head, that it pleases God to count as ours the merits of the sacrifice of Christ, as He placed upon Him our sins. It is (to speak as forcibly as we can, if we may do so reverently) as if, being made one with Him, the atonement belongs to us and the sin belongs to Christ, so unreserved is the communion, so entire is the transfer of properties between Him and the members of His mystical body, the Church. The Apostle Paul speaks of our union with our Lord, as being "dead with Him," being "buried with Him," being "risen with Him," being "set with Him in heavenly places"—as being "members of His body, of His flesh and of His bones," so that what is His is ours and what is ours is His—His righteousness takes away our sins and God accepts us as fully justified in Him.[a]

The third effect of the grace of the Son is to secure our *adoption* as the Sons of God. Though we had forfeited by sin our title to be counted the children of God, by creation, God adopts us again through Christ, receives us into His family, "the general assembly and Church of the first-born," makes us "fellow-heirs" with His only-begotten Son, and so pours upon us the fulness of His love, that we may stand before Him with joy to all eternity.

Thus the mediatorial work is accomplished;—the

---

[a] This simple Church statement cuts away all disputations respecting the application of the Atonement, the imputation of Christ's righteousness, the nature of vicarious sacrifice, etc., and substitutes in place of the scholastic refinements which have darkened the subjects, the firm faith *in the reality of the union* of the members with the Head.

grace of the Son being for remission of sins, for regeneration of nature, for justification of life, for adoption into the heavenly household of God the Father.

In conclusion. It must be remembered, by way of warning, that, being of so transcendent benefit, so fully efficacious to eternal life,—the grace of the Son, if it be once lost, can never be restored. Those who fall away totally from the grace of Christ fall away forever. Degrees of it may, by the mercy of God, be regained; but if all be gone, there is no new imparting. As it required Christ to restore what we lost of the perfection in which Adam was created; so it would require a second Christ to restore the loss of the new creation. Such a second Redeemer there cannot be; and therefore there cannot be a second regeneration. This is the sense of such passages of Scripture as the following: "It is impossible for those who were once enlightened, and have tasted of the heavenly gift, and were made partakers of the Holy Ghost, and have tasted the good word of God, and the powers of the world to come, if they shall fall away, to renew them again unto repentance; seeing they crucify to themselves the Son of God afresh, and put him to an open shame."[a] "For if after they have escaped the pollutions of the world through the knowledge of the Lord and Saviour Jesus Christ, they are again entangled therein and overcome, the latter end is worse with them than the beginning. For it had been better for them not to have known the way of righteousness, than, after they have known it, to turn from the holy commandment delivered unto them."[b]

---

[a] Heb. vi. 4–6.   [b] II. Peter, ii. 20, 21.

CHAPTER IV.

THE GRACE OF THE HOLY SPIRIT.

AS the grace of the Son is subordinate to the grace of the Father, and is directed to restore man to a state of acceptance with the Father, so the grace of the Holy Spirit is auxiliary to the grace of the Son, and operates to the end of making man able to receive and retain that grace, and the benefits it confers. The communication of the grace of the Son (to all except those whom God regenerates in infancy, and takes out of the world before they reach the age of consciousness) depends, as we have made clear, upon the willingness and co-operation of the recipient, both for its initial reception and subsequent growth and increase. Since the natural state of man, however, "is such that he cannot turn and prepare himself by his own natural strength and good works to faith and calling upon God,"—such that he cannot at first dispose himself to desire and seek the gift, nor afterwards do without further help, those good works will ensure its continuance, nor shun those evil deeds which would cause its withdrawal, he has need of other grace, given independent of, and before the operation of his will and his affections, to restore these faculties to their freedom of choice, and enable him to seek the saving grace of Christ, and to co-operate with it when acquired. That other grace is the help of the Holy Spirit. It has pleased God, in arranging the economy of salvation, to assign the Holy Spirit the part of the work of man's restoration proper to His attributes. It is our duty now to inquire what that part of the work is.

In entering upon this inquiry, it will help us towards understanding how there is need of the grace of the Spirit, to remember that our Lord Himself, in His human nature, was actuated by the influence of the Third Person of the Blessed Trinity, though He is Himself, as to His Divine nature, the Second. There is an analogy in this respect between the Christian's participation of Christ, and Christ's participation of Divinity; and if the inherent Divinity of our Saviour did not exclude His human inspiration by the Holy Ghost, neither does the Christian's possession of Christ exclude the necessity of the grace of the Spirit. The two Persons of the Blessed Trinity have their different spheres of operation, one of which is supplementary to the other.

When the time came at which our blessed Lord was to be born into the world, the Angel Gabriel, we are told, was sent to the Virgin Mary, with the announcement, "Behold, thou shalt conceive in thy womb, and bring forth a Son, and shalt call His name Jesus;" and when Mary, in her astonishment, inquired: "How shall this be, seeing I know not a man?" the angel answered: "The Holy Ghost shall come upon thee, and the power of the Highest shall overshadow thee; therefore also that Holy Thing which shall be born of thee shall be called the Son of God."[a] It appears

---

[a] Luke, i. 31–35.

from this, that though our Lord was in His Divine nature pre-existent to His birth in the flesh, and possessed in His own person all Divine power, yet the operation and agency by which He took flesh of the Virgin, was that of the Holy Spirit. And we learn, also, that though the Father was the Father of our Lord Jesus Christ according to His human nature, as well as according to His Divine, yet He performed the miraculous operation which enabled the Virgin to conceive, by the agency of the Holy Spirit. We may infer from this, that God the Holy Ghost is the immediate agent in the operations of Deity in the Creation. For surely if in any case the Father and the Son would operate directly in their own persons, that case would be the Incarnation; yet it was the Holy Ghost who effected the conjunction between the human and the Divine, by which the Son, who is "Perfect God," became "perfect man, of a reasonable soul and human flesh subsisting."

Further, the Holy Ghost, in separating from the Virgin that substance which was to become the man Christ Jesus, cleansed it from all impurity and defilement of original sin, so that our Saviour, who "did no sin, neither was guile found in His mouth," was born without sin, "a lamb without blemish and without spot." The Holy Ghost thus appears as the agent of all sanctification in man; since He sanctified the humanity in which the Son was pleased to dwell, that it might be His acceptable tabernacle.

The Spirit who was thus present and operative at the Incarnation of our Lord was, moreover, present with Him during all His earthly life. We learn this from our Lord's own exposition of the prophecy of Isaiah:

"The Spirit of the Lord is upon me, because He hath anointed me to preach the Gospel to the poor; He hath sent me to heal the broken-hearted, to preach deliverance to the captives, and recovering of sight to the blind, to set at liberty them that are bound, to preach the acceptable year of the Lord." "This day," said He, as He read this passage in the synagogue at Nazareth, "is this Scripture fulfilled in your ears."[a] Hence, when He went into the wilderness to be tempted, He was "led by the Spirit;"[b] and when He returned, He "returned in the power of the Spirit."[c] So St. Peter, preaching to the Centurion, told him "how God anointed Jesus of Nazareth with the Holy Ghost and with power: who went about doing good, and healing all who were oppressed with the devil; for God was with Him."[d]

The anointing of our Saviour is specially referred to two occasions: the first (which has been already spoken of) at His Incarnation, by which he was made a man without sin, and so remained, which was (if we may so distinguish it) a personal unction; the other at His baptism by John in the Jordan, which was His ministerial unction to be prophet, priest, and king of God's people. "Jesus, when He was baptized, went up straightway out of the water; and lo, the heavens were opened unto him, and He saw the Spirit of God descending like a dove, and lighting upon Him."[e] After this He commenced the active exercise of His ministry, to which the baptism and unction was His

---

[a] Luke, iv. 18–21.   [b] Luke, iv. 1.   [c] Luke, iv. 14.
[d] Acts, x. 38.   [e] Matt. iii. 16.

solemn consecration; and in the exercise of that ministry Scripture testimony is clear that He was aided by the Holy Ghost. From the words of John the Baptist we learn this in respect to his *prophetical* office: "He whom God hath sent speaketh the words of God; for God giveth not the Spirit by measure unto Him."[a] And of His exercise of His *kingly* power by the same Spirit our Lord Himself testified in His answer to the Pharisees, who blasphemously said: "He doth not cast out devils but by Beelzebub, the prince of the devils." "If I," He replied, "by Beelzebub cast out devils, by whom do your children cast them out? therefore they shall be your judges. But if I cast out devils by the Spirit of God, then the kingdom of God is come unto you."[b] And the Epistle to the Hebrews says the same of His *Priestly* office: "If the blood of bulls and of goats, and the ashes of an heifer sprinkling the unclean, sanctifieth to the purifying of the flesh: how much more shall the blood of Christ, who through the eternal Spirit offered Himself without spot to God, purge your conscience from dead works to serve the living God?"[c] It is evident from these passages of Holy Scripture that Christ, though He is God the Son, was, while on earth as man, under the influence of the Holy Spirit, and without Him did nothing. We may not be able to solve the mystery why it was so; but such is the fact.

The truth seems to be this: The Holy Spirit, being the third Person of the Blessed Trinity, proceeding from the Father and the Son, is, as it were, the nearest to the Creation; and therefore the carrying forth of all

---

[a] John, iii. 34.   [b] Matt. xii. 24, 27, 28.   [c] Heb. ix. 13, 14.

Divine operations into the created universe is ascribed to His immediate agency; the power of the Father and the Son is shed forth upon the world by Him. The Father communicates His power to the Son; the Father and the Son communicate it to the Holy Ghost; and the Holy Ghost communicates it to the world to produce the effect designed by the Divine will. The world itself was created at the beginning by His active operation, so receiving and communicating the creative energy of the Father and the Son. "By His Spirit," says the book of Job, "He hath garnished the heavens:"[a] and the Psalmist sings: "By the Word of the Lord were the heavens made, and all the host of them by the breath of His mouth," or by His Spirit;[b] and again, "Thou sendest forth thy Spirit, they are created; and Thou renewest the face of the earth."[c] And so we read, "The Spirit of God moved upon the face of the waters," when the primordial matter was about to be ordered into the fair beauty of the world which now is. And so in all Divine operations upon the world and among created beings, the Holy Spirit is the Divine Person who places Himself in immediate contact with the world. Hence when the Son was to come into the world, and, by taking a human nature, become a part of the Creation, He took the substance whereof He was made man by the operation of the Holy Ghost; and the Third Person of the Trinity cleansed and sanctified that substance that it might be His habitation; so that, while it was the Son who became man, and in whose person (and not in the person

---

[a] Job, xxvi. 13.   [b] Ps. xxxiii. 6.   [c] Ps. civ. 30.

of the Holy Ghost) humanity was united to Divinity; yet the Holy Ghost accomplished the union, that act being His proper operation.

After the Incarnation, our Lord Himself was, as respects His human nature, a created being, and in that nature was therefore subject to the same limitations as others, sin only excepted. In the intimate union of the Divine and human natures in one person, the Divine nature did not yield any of its properties to the human, nor did the human subject the Divine to any of its limitations. The Person was all which was Divine and human; but both natures of that Person retained their respective properties as distinctly as if they were separate. As body does not cease to be body on being united with spirit in the composition of man, so the human soul and body of our Saviour did not cease to be such in every attribute by being the soul and body of a Divine person. His Divine Wisdom was the attribute of His Divine Nature; but His human soul possessed human wisdom, which was capable of increase as He advanced from childhood to maturity. His Divine Power belonged to His Divine Nature; His human nature had but the natural powers and capacities of a perfect and sinless man. The Divine Love inherent in His infinity had its counterpart in the affections of a human nature. His Divine Will was one; His human will was another. There was no transfer or confusion of properties in consequence of the personal union. Hence, when His human nature was the recipient of a Divine impulse, that impulse was communicated according to the conditions of other humanity by the Holy Spirit; and, in like manner, whatsoever

He operated in the way of miracle, upon beings other than Himself, was performed by the same agency. In the exercise of His Divine power in healing the sick, in liberating the possessed, in feeding the hungry, in controlling the elements of the natural world, He wrought by the Holy Ghost, as he would have done had He not been Incarnate; and in like manner, when He acted upon Himself as a created Being, transferring from His Divinity to His humanity any supernatural gift, He illuminated it with supernatural wisdom, or increased its power, or made efficacious in miracle his human acts, as He would have given such gifts to any other prophet, by the Holy Ghost,—the difference between Him and any other prophet in this respect consisting in this, that being the Son, " God gave not the Spirit by measure unto Him." And so, also, since a perfect man, not needing the grace of regeneration and renewal, would nevertheless find his perfection in the communion of the Holy Spirit, He lived in that communion in moral and spiritual perfection while He was on earth, and in that communion "by the Eternal Spirit offered Himself without spot to God."

Such being the facts with respect to our Blessed Lord Himself, it will at once be seen that His communication of Himself and the efficacy of His grace to His followers for their salvation, does not exclude, but infers the grace of the Holy Spirit, in preparing man to receive it, in applying the gift, and in leading the recipient to full sanctification. As it was necessary that the substance taken of the Virgin should be sanctified to become the manhood of Christ, so the man who is joined to His mystical body must first be so far sanctified as to be made penitent and believing by the grace of the Holy Spirit. As that Spirit operated to conjoin the Divinity of our Lord with His humanity, so He operates in regeneration to convey the life of Christ into the soul of man. As our Lord's perfection in manhood consisted in the communion of the Holy Ghost, so the Christian reaches full sanctification in the same communion. And as our Lord was anointed to His ministerial office by the Holy Spirit, so those who are Divinely employed to minister in the Church, receive from the same source the special gifts by which their labors are made efficacious.

Now as the unction of our Saviour was both official and personal, so the influence of the Holy Spirit upon the members of His mystical body is both official and personal,—official, so far as particular persons are called to minister to the rest; personal, as it is given to each for his own personal, spiritual good. Hence is suggested an obvious division of the operations of that influence into two classes named, in accordance with Scripture authority, "gifts" and "graces,"—gifts being those influences which conduce to efficiency in ministering to the edification of the Church; graces, those which operate to the sanctification of the recipient.

The "gifts" of the Holy Spirit are not generally counted a part of His grace; since, by the latter, we understand that which operates to personal sanctification. For though, ordinarily, the gifts of God were given to holy men, they were not causative of holiness, nor were they universally joined with holiness. There are instances in Holy Scripture where unrighteous persons have been made instruments of ministration to others, they themselves, by their unrighteousness, being cut off from any benefit of their gifts. An example is Balaam, who, though he was entrusted with the gift of prophecy, nevertheless loved "the wages of unrighteousness" and taught Balak to tempt Israel to sin. Strictly, therefore, the consideration of the "gifts" belongs not to the present inquiry; but it will enlighten us as to the "graces" to touch upon them briefly, and to note the points in which all the influences of the Spirit bear an analogy to each other.

The most extended catalogue of the "gifts" in Holy Scripture is that contained in the twelfth chapter of the First Epistle to the Corinthians: "To one is given by the Spirit the word of wisdom; to another the word of knowledge by the same Spirit; to another faith by the same Spirit; to another the gifts of healing by the same Spirit; to another the working of miracles; to another prophecy; to another discerning of spirits; to another divers kinds of tongues; to another the interpretation of tongues: but all these worketh that one and the self-same Spirit, dividing to every man severally as He will." In this list we may distinguish two classes of gifts,—those analogous to Inspiration, which transcend the ordinary intellectual power of man; and those which can all be counted together as the "working of miracles," which transcend ordinary physical power, or ordinary command over the phenomena of nature.

Inspiration is the means by which Holy Scripture was written, and is to be studied in its product.

The distinction has been drawn between Inspiration

and Revelation; by which it appears that Revelation is the operation of the Son and Inspiration of the Holy Ghost. The supernatural facts set before the mental vision, relating to the future of this world or to the invisible things of the heavenly world, were so placed as objects of spiritual intuition, mediately or immediately, by the Son; they were beholdings or reflections of His light, and so Revelations; but the influence on the mind itself, which raised its powers to behold, comprehend, remember, and judge correctly of the matter set before it, was that operation of the Holy Ghost which we name Inspiration. The Divine illumination of the inspired men of old consisted (as we have said) in the two facts that to them was *revealed*, by symbol, by dream, by angelic ministration, or by the Word of God, what was not given to other men; and that their intellectual and moral faculties were *inspired* to a supernatural clearness of vision, correctness of judgment, and accuracy of memory, and stimulated to action by an irresistible impulse from above. In the variety of matter contained in Holy Scripture the following cases are to be distinguished:

1. When the inspired writer was required to record such history as enters into the sacred volume. In this case it is permitted to understand, that personal observation, reliable tradition, documentary evidence, furnished the objective fact which, in matters supernatural, was supplied by Revelation; Inspiration, therefore, would operate to give accuracy to the memory in retaining a knowledge of events; to aid the judgment in selecting proper matter and rejecting extraneous; to perfect the moral perceptions, so as to present the

truth in the right moral and spiritual aspect and connections.

2. When the subject-matter was prophecy, by symbol or vision, in the extatic state. The personal appearance of the Son, as the "Angel Jehovah," was withdrawn after the idolatry of Israel in worshipping the calf at Mount Sinai. After that He veiled His communications, giving them by the agency of His Spirit, or by angelic ministry, or in dreams, visions, and symbols. The objective fact is, nevertheless, a revelation of the Son, so veiled and farther removed from His people. But in visions and symbolic representations, the Holy Spirit may have been—doubtless was—the agent operating on the mental or bodily organism, so as to produce the impression in the mind. This, however, as a function of Revelation, must be separated from the Inspiring act, which consisted in inducing the elevation of soul, suspension of bodily sense, and strengthening of spiritual insight that gave the prophet power to behold the vision and to receive the Revelation,—that condition of the spirit which is called in Holy Scripture "having the eyes opened." This seems to have been the inspiration also when angelic ministers were made the means of communicating Divine knowledge, as in the prophecies of Daniel and Zechariah, and in the Revelations. In other cases Inspiration and Revelation seem to coincide more closely, and prophecy to be the object rather of inward intuition than of vision, as in the Messianic prophecies of Isaiah.

3. When the present is made the type of the future. It has been remarked of prophecy, that "each prediction, with scarcely an exception, proceeds from, and

attaches itself to, some definite fact in the historical present. In other words, when the future is to be foreshadowed, certain events of the time, historical or incidental, are selected as occasions on which may be founded the several disclosures of the Divine will." Hence prophecy has a double sense, a nearer and more remote; oftentimes both a literal and a figurative fulfilment. In this case, the form of the prediction is given by the present circumstance, and that furnishes the object before the prophet's mind; the Inspiration consists in the Divine afflatus, which raises the prophet's conception of the event, and gives his language an apparent exaggeration, but real meaning far in the future, of which the prophet himself may not have been immediately conscious; but which the Holy Ghost intended from the first.

4. The inspired writer is himself oftentimes the type of Christ, and speaks in his person. In this case, the prophecy is rather, Christ, speaking by His Spirit, through the mouth of the prophet; the Divine influence moulding him, for the time being, into the likeness of Christ,—he being to himself, as he is to us, the immediate objective element of the Revelation, and being supernaturally endowed with the subjective element by the Inspiration of the Holy Spirit. An example of this is the second Psalm, in which David speaks of himself in words which can find their truest fulfilment only in our Lord.

5. When the inspired writer touches the facts of human nature in its fallen and redeemed estate,—giving utterance to prayers, praises, penitential bewailings, spiritual aspirations. The Psalms of this character

were doubtless written under that measure of Inspiration which consisted in bringing the soul into the right moral and spiritual state, in which it would obtain true views of human needs and of God's goodness, and a full expression of its devotional feelings.

Under these various manifestations of the Spirit's influence, there is discernible a unity of the Divine impulse. Leaving aside that part of the operation which belongs to Revelation, Inspiration remains as a quickening of the soul into supernatural activity, involving an elevation of all its faculties, their emancipation, while under the influence, from the imperfections of nature, and their introduction into a higher world. Upon this state of Inspiration Revelation supervened.

As an operation on and through human nature, Inspiration wrought in harmony with its constitution and laws. The inspired men of old remained in possession of their natural faculties; but those faculties were strengthened and raised to a supernatural degree of power and activity; and thus were guarded by the Divine influence against the mistakes to which, if left to themselves, they would have been liable. Hence their natural characteristics are preserved by the writers of Holy Scripture; at the same time the truth is infallibly communicated by them, and shown in all its bearings. The operation of the Holy Spirit was not merely mechanical; the prophets were not mere instruments to write down, word for word, without any personal interest in the matter; the Spirit spoke through them, as through persons, and therefore exercised His influence upon their personal qualities, energizing *them*, and so giving "the word of God in the language of men."

Inspiration supernaturally stimulated the spiritual nature, opened senses ordinarily closed, co-ordinated the spiritual faculties with each other, withdrew them from thraldom to the bodily organization, urged them to fulfil their mission, gave accuracy to the memory in recording history and vision and prophecy, and so ensured us a Scripture "profitable for doctrine, for reproof, for exhortation, for instruction in righteousness."

The chief part of the effect seems to have been the arousing the moral powers—the affections, the conscience, the judgment—to perfection of action in respect of those matters which were to be treated of. Hence the strict impartiality and straightforwardness of the history. Hence the stern denunciations of the sins of Israel and Judah, of which so large a proportion of the prophetical writings consists; from which it is evident that the prophet's moral nature was laboring under an irresistible impulse, and that he spoke with a personal interest which identified him with the message, as a co-worker with the Spirit. Hence, also, the penitential and meditative psalms, in which human nature is mirrored, are both the Divine declaration of the right thoughts and feelings of the heart, and the human appreciation and expression of those thoughts and feelings. And so, too, where, as in so many portions of the Epistles, the writer enters into argument, it is clear that the spiritual reason has been illuminated, and the Apostle is so filled with the Divine Spirit that he has for his own, the truth he proves and imparts. On the other hand, being under the guidance of an intelligence higher than his own, the words of the inspired man may oftentimes have had a reach beyond his comprehension of them. The prophecy revealed to him by type met its fulfilment in the antitype, of which he had but dim, uncertain vision; himself (like David) oftentimes the type, he spoke in language designed by the Inspiring Spirit to be prophetic of other times and circumstances, and another Person,—unconscious, it may be, of the fulness of the message he was delivering to future generations. Hence "prophecy came not of old time, by the will of man, but holy men of God spake as they were moved by the Holy Ghost."

Nor is this account invalidated, but rather confirmed by the instances in which the moral perceptions of the prophet did not continually influence his own conduct. He was, in this respect, under the same laws of moral conduct with other men. Inspiration was a temporary gift for a special purpose; it was a "gift," not a "grace;" the exalted perceptions necessary for official accuracy in prophesying or recording were results of the Divine afflatus, given in a measure beyond that vouchsafed for the ordinary guidance of mankind, and withdrawn when the occasion ceased. The example of Balaam is in point. His prophecies are an epitome of all Revelation, and Inspiration is evidently the source of their moral coloring; the noble sentiments, the aspiration for the death of the righteous indicating that for the time the man was possessed of a judgment respecting the good, which enabled him to give his prophecies in their organic connection with the spiritual intent of the Word of God. But when the Inspiration was withdrawn, he relapsed into his meaner self; when actuated by the will of God, he appears holy; but when left to his own will and put upon his responsibility, he shows what manner of man he is, and perishes for his unworthiness.

The gifts of "wisdom," "knowledge," "prophecy," "discerning of spirits," imparted to the early Church, are doubtless to be regarded as different degrees of Inspiration, directed towards supplying the need of special Divine guidance which the Christian communities felt in their incipient state. "Knowledge" and "wisdom" were evidently something more than sanctified natural endowments; like the other gifts, they were Divine operations on the minds and souls of special instruments for special purposes, at a time when the Church had not gained the mastery over its situation in the midst of hostile Jewish and Gentile tradition, learning, and philosophy, and while the canon of the New Testament was incomplete. A different manifestation of the same power was the "divers kinds of tongues," and the "interpretation of tongues," concerning which it is not necessary nor convenient to theorize.

The analogue of this gift in the permanent constitution of the Church is the Divine aid granted to the ministry in the execution of their office as teachers of God's word. Holy Scripture stands to the Church in place of the direct immediate Revelation granted to the prophets of old; but the right apprehension of it, the influence by which the ambassadors of Christ are enabled to preach "with power," is the aid of the Holy Spirit,—given, not indeed in supernatural measure, but in degree suited to the ordinary and continuous work of preaching the Gospel to the world at large.

Of a different nature was the Divine influence in that class of gifts which are grouped under the general title of "the working of miracles." In this class the power of the Holy Ghost, it is more reasonable to believe, was exercised not *through*, but *in connection* with the act of the person who is said to be endowed with it. It is difficult to understand that any special efficacy was given to the act or word itself which was the immediate visible or audible antecedent of the miraculous effect— that the outward sign, whether of words spoken, or hands imposed, or whatever else it were, had in itself the power it signified. We rather conclude that by the Divine will there was a conjunction of the act of the Holy Spirit with that of the human agent, and that, for His own wise purposes of confirming the Church in the faith, the Omnipotent Spirit chose thus to honor His special instrument, by operating in time and place according to that conjunction.

Analogous to this gift, in the permanent constitution of the Church, is that operation of the Holy Spirit by which the Sacraments and ordinances, administered by lawful authority, are made means of conveying spiritual blessings to the faithful recipient. Not that the effects of the operation are visible, or wonderful, as in the miracles of the natural world; but that the operation itself is in the same manner performed by the Holy Ghost in conjunction with the ministerial act. The effect is in the spiritual world, and therefore invisible.

These two gifts, that of teaching (with the possession of Holy Scripture) and that of administering the Sacraments and ordinances of Christianity, given to some persons in the Church for the edification of the whole, are the *external* means of influence of the Holy Spirit upon the individual Christian, ordained for the purpose of bringing him into union with other Christians, and so building up the Church as the visible body of Christ. But the grace of the Holy Spirit proper is *internal* and direct upon the heart, and in large part given without Sacraments and ordinances. To the consideration of this we now address ourselves.

First. The Holy Spirit is the agent in working the Regeneration of those who embrace the Christian faith,—that is, of conveying to them the life-giving grace of Christ treated of in the last chapter. The ordinary means of conveying this gift (as will be fully proved in the next chapter) is by sacramental participation. The Holy Sacraments of Baptism and the Lord's Supper were ordained, the one for the initial, and the other for the continuous communication of the grace of the Son. A collateral benefit of their faithful reception is an enlarged measure of the Spirit's aid ; but their principal intention has relation to the person of Christ. Their efficacy, to that end, rests upon the will of Christ, pledged in their institution and in the various declarations of Holy Scripture concerning them ; and that will is carried into effect by the operation of the Holy Spirit in time and place with the ministerial act in which the outward form of the Sacrament consists. It is this operation, which we said was the analogue in the permanent constitution of the Church, of the "gift of miracles." As the Holy Spirit was the agent in uniting the humanity and the Divinity of our Lord, so in Baptism He works in the faithful recipient that union with the Redeemer, by which the life of Christ is made his, with the benefits and blessings it confers. In the Lord's Supper, also, the Holy Spirit operates to confer the spiritual sustenance and increase of the Divine life which our Saviour Himself calls "His body and blood." Hence, in the Nicene Creed, we profess Him to be "the Giver of Life." The Scripture proof rests upon our Saviour's own words: "Except a man be born of water and of the Spirit, he cannot enter into the kingdom of God. That which is born of the flesh is flesh, and that which is born of the Spirit is spirit."[a] This connects clearly our Regeneration with the operation of the Spirit in Baptism. The same inference follows, with respect to the communication of the body and blood of Christ in the Holy Communion, from the close of our Saviour's discourse in the sixth chapter of St. John, where, His disciples having missed the spiritual sense of His words, He says: "It is the Spirit that quickeneth, the flesh profiteth nothing: the words that I speak unto you, they are Spirit and they are life,"—intimating (whatever may be the precise exegesis of the words) that that Divine food of the soul is communicated by the Holy Spirit, and spiritually received.

Now in the case of infants who are brought to the Sacrament of Regeneration before they have committed actual sin, there is no bar to the communication of the grace of Christ; that unconsciousness which prevents sinful deeds renders repentance and the active exercise of faith unnecessary, as it renders them impossible. Their regeneration, therefore, is the first operation of

---

[a] John, iii. 5, 6.

the Holy Spirit, and His subsequent action upon their souls is directed to preserve them in life, and build them up upon the foundation already laid.

But in those who have grown up to years of maturity unregenerate, and are therefore stained with the guilt of actual sin, there must be wrought that sorrow for sin, that repugnance to it, that disposition and determination to put it away, that appreciation of and endeavor after holiness, that desire and will to return unto God by Christ, "the way, the truth, and the life," which will inspire them to seek and enable them to approach the Sacrament in a receptive state of the soul; otherwise their sin interposes a bar to its efficacy. Man cannot produce in himself this repentance and faith without aid from on high; and therefore the prevenient grace of the Holy Spirit is given to convict and convert him. By submission and obedience to His influence man is brought into the right spiritual state to receive the gift of regeneration.

While the grace of the Son, then, is, as we said in the last chapter, of voluntary reception (except in the case noted above of infant regeneration), and therefore sacramental, since Sacraments are the acts by which God gives and man takes,—the prevenient grace of the Holy Spirit is extra-sacramental and involuntary; because it is the initial step in man's restoration, which must originate with God. Its object is to enable us "to will and to do according to God's good pleasure" —to will, as well as to do; and therefore it is given antecedent to any religious exercise of the will of man. Man may voluntarily follow or resist the grace of the Holy Spirit after it is received; but it is not voluntary with him whether he shall receive it; otherwise the will so to do would be of his own strength, and he could originate in himself the good will which would dispose him to its reception. He can receive, voluntarily, the grace of Christ, because the Holy Spirit predisposes his will; but there is no predisposing grace before that of the Spirit, and therefore its reception is involuntary. That it is so, Scripture testimony is clear. It is true, St. Paul says in one place, "I know that in me, that is, in my flesh, dwelleth no good thing; for to will is present with me, but how to perform that which is good I know not;"[a] but here he is speaking of the man as under the influence of the Spirit, and his assertion of the presence of a will to do what the natural man lacks power to accomplish, is predicated upon that influence. Under it, the state of the natural man is thus described in the Epistle to the Galatians: "The flesh lusteth against the Spirit and the Spirit against the flesh; and these are contrary the one to the other, so that ye cannot do the things that ye would."[b] Such texts are not contrary to the reasoning by which the Apostle enforces the advice: "Work out your own salvation with fear and trembling"—"for," he proceeds, "it is God which worketh in you both to will and to do of His good pleasure." And although this is said to regenerate Christians, it is true *a fortiori* of all others; for if God's help is necessary that Christians should will the good, much more is that help necessary for the unregenerate; if nature in the one is not renewed so as to do or to will that which is right of its own power, cer-

---

[a] Rom. vii. 18.   [b] Gal. v. 17.

tainly neither the act nor the will is in the power of nature unrenewed. When God was about to destroy the world by the flood, we read that He said, "My Spirit shall not always strive with man," from which it is to be inferred that the Spirit had striven with him hitherto. So our Lord, making promise to His disciples of the Comforter, tells them, "When He is come, He will reprove [or convict] the world of sin, of righteousness, and of judgment," referring to that exercise of Divine grace which operates upon the world (as distinguished from the Church, and therefore as unregenerate), to open its heart to the Gospel, or to leave it without excuse. And the Apostle to the same effect: "By grace are ye saved, through faith; and that not of yourselves: it is the gift of God;"[a] and again: "Through Christ we both (that is, Jew and Gentile) have access by one Spirit to the Father;"[b] and more particularly in the first Epistle to the Corinthians: "Ye know that ye were Gentiles, carried away unto these dumb idols, even as ye were led. Wherefore I give you to understand, that no man speaking by the Spirit of God calleth Jesus accursed: and that no man can say that Jesus is the Lord, but by the Holy Ghost."[c] The confession of Christ is a necessary condition precedent to admission into the Church; and therefore the grace of the Holy Spirit is given beforehand to enable men to exercise faith. Indeed, though the mass of New Testament teaching respecting the grace of the Holy Ghost is directed to inform Christians of their blessedness in Him, being regenerate, so

---

[a] Eph. ii. 8.   [b] Eph. ii. 18.   [c] I. Cor. xii. 2, 3.

that it is difficult to produce passages bearing immediately upon the present subject, yet the argument is all the stronger; for if Christians who have received the grace of the Son need also the grace of the Spirit, those who are unregenerate need that grace to produce in them the motions towards virtue and religion.

The Holy Spirit, therefore, is the author of conversion, producing repentance and faith in those who come to their regeneration after having committed actual sin. The reader will remember that faith and repentance were said to be *acts*, or rather different parts of one and the same complex act,—not mere emotions or impressions; and that, as acts, they implied a motive in the heart, a perception in the mind, and an effort of the will, terminating in the performance of the deed or deeds required. The motives to repentance and faith are: fear of the consequences of sin, hatred of sin itself as repugnant to the law of God, desire after good, love of God, gratitude to the Saviour, hope of attaining heaven. The mental element is knowledge of the Gospel. The effort of the will is to forsake sin, to receive the sacrament of regeneration, to perform all good and right actions. The Holy Spirit is a Helper in each part of the act; His influence, therefore, is exerted on the mind, the heart, and the will, giving each the power and the conditions necessary to enable it to perform its religious functions.

The will (it was also said) is defective,—partly by a loss of its own power, and partly by its connection with the other fallen faculties of our nature. Without right perceptions in the mind, without right desires, affections, and motives in the heart, it cannot act rightly, even if it possessed the necessary power to carry its resolves into effect, because it could not form the right resolves. But in addition to this fault of association, it is itself weakened by the fall, so that the lower parts and passions of our nature, which it ought to hold under control, are naturally unruly and insubordinate. The influence of the Holy Spirit in adding power to the will as weakened in itself, so as to enable it more and more fully to act up to the law of God, I conceive to be *sacramental*—the communication of the life of Christ,[a] which, being received efficaciously, enables the soul to grow up into the condition and power it lost at the fall, by a gradual increase through life perfected at the resurrection. His influence on the faculties auxiliary to the will I conceive to be, on the mind, *external;* on the heart (in which, in accordance with the Scripture use of the word, I include the conscience), *internal* and immediate.

The sacramental operation has been spoken of. So far as the will depends upon it the repentance and faith preceding regeneration is defective, and but preparatory to a better state. The two operations of Divine grace now claiming attention are, therefore, the *external* and the *internal*.

One part of the *external* work of the Spirit in inducing faith and repentance in the unregenerate is performed by the revelation of the Law and the Gospel,

---

[a] Hence the religion of those denominations which deny the virtue of the Sacraments is observed to be emotional, resting in the excitable parts of the nature, not in the will, and therefore not steady and constant.

through the teaching of the ministry, and the giving of the Holy Scripture which He inspired. By this means He sets before the mind the facts and laws of truth and righteousness, reveals the Saviour, and the way to come to God by Him. "Faith cometh by hearing," says the Apostle; and so does Repentance, —for it will be admitted that to be real and valid repentance it must be actuated according to the Gospel, and therefore infers a knowledge of the Gospel. It is not to be denied, indeed, that heathen have had perceptions of the law of nature, and feelings of self-condemnation because they could not keep it; but true repentance, in the Gospel sense, implies more than this,—it implies a knowledge of sin which Scripture alone, or teaching founded on Scripture, can give. "The Word," says St. John, "was in the world, and the world was made by Him, and the world knew Him not." The reason and conscience of man, apart from revelation, even though we admit him to be inwardly gifted with that measure of the Holy Spirit's grace given to the unregenerate, are so imperfect that whole communities are habitually addicted, without compunction, to their particular sins; and there is probably no sin condemned in Scripture which has not been approved and openly practiced by some community or other among the heathen. We depend upon God's word for the mental element in repentance and faith; and therefore Holy Scripture and the gift of teaching granted to the ministry are operations of the Holy Spirit for the conversion of the world.

The other external means of influence is the Holy Spirit's use of the circumstances of our life, the providential disposition of our temporal and social condition, and of the occurrences which happen around us, to awaken us to the truth. It is in vain to attempt a classification of the means and modes in and by which these circumstances are made instrumental in working conviction and conversion. "The wind bloweth where it listeth, and thou hearest the sound thereof, but canst not tell whence it cometh nor whither it goeth; so is every one that is born of the Spirit."[a] All God's influence in nature and society is an act of Divine grace upon the soul, the end of which is our salvation. Besides the modifications of circumstances themselves by Divine Providence, the aspects which they are made to present are adapted by Divine grace to our moral and spiritual state. They influence us not only as they are in themselves, but as we are permitted to behold them. The same event is differently viewed by different men; and as circumstances strike upon us at different angles, or range themselves around us in different combinations, it is not to be doubted that our perceptions of them are arranged by the Divine Spirit, so as to forward our discipline in our state of probation. One man sees a way open in a certain situation which another does not observe; they are conscious of different possibilities, they discover dif-

---

[a] The precise force of the Greek can scarcely be expressed in English, because we have no word combining the two senses of the Greek πνευμα. Our Saviour not only expressed a truth, but illustrated it by an analogy, combining the force of these two sentences: "The wind bloweth, etc.; so is that which is produced of the wind," and "The Spirit breatheth (πνει), etc.; so is every one that is born of the Spirit."

ferent connections, some missing of one and some of another. Hence the varieties of spiritual experience are as numerous as the individuals in the world. Some men are led to God by observation of the works of nature, some by the orderly influences of the society in which they are placed, some are awakened by special circumstances,—an accident (as it is called), an escape from death, the loss of friends, the influence of times of special religious interest, intercourse with religious people, solitary hours,—all things are made means, by the Holy Spirit, of impressing our souls, weaning us from the world, and setting our thoughts on our religious calling and duty, thus becoming external auxiliaries to the Gospel.

The *internal* influence of the Holy Spirit He exerts directly upon the heart itself, developing the affections, the conscience, the sense of sin, the holy desires by which man is enabled to accept the Gospel and seek the Regeneration. The motives on which we adopt any line of conduct, the possibility or feasibility of which is perceived, are drawn from the fears, or desires, or affections, or principles of the heart. Of the infinite multitude of facts set before us by our perceptions, we select as important and of practical interest those only with which we have an affinity, by reason of some desire or affection tending that way; others are passed by as irrelevant and without interest, and are not recalled. The Gospel is presented under this law of human nature. If man were to hear it without any affection or desire towards it, without any motive in the heart urging him to adopt it, it would have no more effect upon him than a fiction,—he would never follow it. The truths that enter the soul through the mind are photographed (so to speak) upon the background of the heart, and those lines and colors only are fixed with which the heart has an affinity. Conscience and feeling, and good and bad affections, are in every picture, and, as they are, so is the picture. The will stands as spectator, not of the reality without, but of the transcript within, and from it makes the choice which way the man shall go. A holy and pure heart will color the world with the hues of heaven, and enable us to see the means and opportunities of right action in all things and in all situations; the unholy and impure heart will shadow the picture with its own gloom, and lust, and selfishness.

Now, left to itself, the natural heart has nothing holy or heavenly within it, and therefore no affinity with the holy and the heavenly in what is set before the mind. The spiritual affections are torpid, dormant, dead. Hence, were there no internal grace, the heart would have no affinity for the Gospel, it would make no impression upon it,—it would appeal to the will upon no motive; neither its promises nor its threatenings would have any weight, and the will would turn away from it to follow the things the heart lusted after in the world. To overcome this natural deadness to spiritual things, and to implant again, or develop the latent germs of the holy and heavenly affections which are the acceptable motives to repentance and faith, to arouse the conscience, and so give man an aptitude for the Gospel, the Holy Spirit exerts His influence directly and internally upon the heart. With the effectual preaching of the word, and with the providential use of circumstances to enforce reflection and conviction, an inward grace and operation upon the soul is wrought, calling forth into activity the conscience and the spiritual affections, and thus enabling the man, who otherwise would be unable, to repent and believe, and seek the gift of the new life. Yielding himself to these influences, he receives a new view of his present condition and past conduct, his conscience is roused to activity and bears witness against him, his higher affections seek after good and God and Christ, he forsakes and renounces the evil he has heretofore followed, and by this means is made a capable recipient of the Sacrament of regeneration.

The Spirit's influence upon the heart, then, is directed to arouse in it the love of God, and of good, and by this means to create an affinity for the Gospel, and induce that "godly sorrow which worketh repentance to salvation not to be repented of," and that "faith which worketh by love."[a] For only a repentance and faith, actuated by the love of God, is valid and real, and acceptable with Him. Fear of the punishment of sin, I suppose, might be wrought in the soul by the preaching of the word without internal grace; but under this motive alone, there would be no real repentance, no *contrition*, no forsaking and hating of sin, as sin, no faith but that of the devils, who, without any grace at all, "believe and tremble." Fear is and must be an ingredient in repentance, and doubtless is, in many cases, the most powerful and the prime mover in the conviction of the sinner; and the attempts at reformation which it causes may, by the mercy of God,

---

[a] II. Cor. vii. 10.

have the effect of opening the heart to the influence of the Spirit, which infuses the higher principle of love, both to define sin, and to show its vileness. But that fear, in all actual cases which result in conversion, is always a collateral effect of the grace of the Spirit; it cannot be an element of progress unless it be allied with hope, and hope follows from a persuasion of the goodness and mercy of God in Christ that cannot exist without calling out love, and which has love for the foundation of the belief in its possibility. The conscience, witnessing of guilt, if untouched by love (as we may see by the dealings of man with man), works rather hatred of the being against whom we have sinned; whereas, let there be love in the heart, there is genuine and sincere repentance and self-accusation. It is this love which is the foundation of true "godly sorrow" for sin, of endeavors after a holy life, of living faith and trust, of the right fear of God, and of all Christian progress; and this love it is the object of the internal grace of the Holy Spirit to produce.

In speaking thus of the *internal* influence of the Spirit as exerted on the heart; of the *external* as directed to inform the mind; and of the *sacramental* operation as giving back, in measure and degree, the lost power to the will, I do not wish to be understood as denying that each faculty receives benefit from each operation. The soul, in truth, is one and indivisible, whole in every part; and therefore whatever influence is exerted upon it by Divine grace is exerted upon all the faculties, or rather upon the soul itself in all its functions; for those which we call faculties are but functions of the soul. To speak of the heart, or the mind, or the will as a faculty, is not to assert that each is a separate division of the soul, but that each is the soul itself in different relations. They are no more separable from each other than are length, breadth, and thickness in space. The heart is the soul itself in relation with things to be desired or shunned; the mind is the soul itself in relation with things to be perceived; the will is the soul itself in that relation in which deeds are to be done. As the three dimensions of space everywhere interpenetrate, and there is no position in length which has not position in breadth and thickness, so these three functions everywhere interpenetrate,—each is in all and all in each. The simplest exercise of the mind, attention, whether observant or recollective, has in it, however unconsciously, a desire of the heart, and an effort of the will. And as it is with the soul actively, so it is with it passively. Hence, when the Divine Spirit exerts His influence upon it, in whatever way, He touches all alike,—He touches the soul itself, the one indivisible essence, and therefore excites and exalts every faculty. But as the grace is diversely exhibited, it has relation to one and another function or faculty, in developing which it chiefly acts, acting on the other subordinately. Thus, while the *external* grace influences the heart by giving it the object without which the internal grace would excite only a blind and aimless instinct of affection, its principal relation is to the soul as perceptive and knowing; and so, also, while the *internal* grace operates upon the mind, quickening it to attend to and receive the external presentations of the Word, its principal effect is to arouse the soul to the love of things divine; and, in like manner, while the *sacramental* communication of the life of Christ is to restore, as far as may be, what Adam lost of all spiritual power, both of heart and mind, as well as of will, yet as this power works outwardly principally in Christian acts, it is rightly assigned chiefly to the will. The results, the phenomena are apparent in these relations; by them, therefore, we have made the division necessary in treating the parts of the subject in consecutive order.

In further prosecuting the inquiry respecting the grace of the Holy Spirit as given to the regenerate, we meet the question : What are the respective spheres and what is the mutual connection of the grace of the Son and that of the Spirit, both being possessed by the child of God?

And first it may seem to require explanation how—if the communication of the grace of the Son is, as we have said, the regeneration of the Christian, that is, the true beginning of his spiritual life—how the soul can be the recipient of spiritual influence before it is thus spiritually alive—how it possesses the capacity, under the grace of the Spirit, of repenting and believing, while yet unregenerate, and therefore dead. The explanation is the more necessary because the want of it is the foundation of that popular misconception which confounds conversion with regeneration, and both with the renewal and sanctification of the Christian believer. The three things are, in truth, distinct: Conversion is the term appropriated in Holy Scripture[a] to denote a turning to obey the prevenient grace

---

[a] In the form of the verb; the noun, I believe, does not occur except in Acts, xv. 3.

The Grace of the Holy Spirit. 217

of the Holy Spirit from a former life of sin; Regeneration is the communication of the life of Christ in the Sacrament, to which conversion (in the adult) is preparatory; and Renewal or Sanctification is the subsequent growth into complete holiness. That the last is the act denoted by renewal is plain from the admonition of St. Paul, several times repeated in other forms, and addressed, it is important to observe, to regenerate Christians: "Be renewed in the spirit of your mind; and . . . put on the new man, which, after God, is created in righteousness and true holiness."[a]

The difficulty arises from pressing the metaphor of life and death, which the Scripture applies to the spiritual state of man, as if it were taken from the physical condition, with the heathen opposition of existence and non-existence. The description of the state of the Christian as a spiritual life has for its correlative idea that the natural man is in a state of death; and this is directly asserted by St. Paul in several places, as in the fifth chapter of Romans, "If through the offence of one, the many be dead,"[b] etc.; in the fifth chapter of II. Corinthians, "We thus judge that if one died for all, then were all dead;"[c] and in the second chapter of Ephesians, "You hath He quickened, who were dead in trespasses and sins."[d] But the use of the word "dead" does not amount to a declaration of annihilation, or total paralysis of the spiritual powers of man; but it rather implies that total separation from the kingdom and family of God, which is wrought by innate unrighteousness. It is easy of

---

[a] Eph. iv. 23, 24.   [b] Rom. v. 15.   [c] II. Cor. v. 14.   [d] Eph. ii. 1.

verification by any one who will look, with the help of his concordance, over the passages in which the Apostle speaks of natural death, that he does not give the word the heathen meaning of dissolution, even as referred to the body; but, viewing it in the light of the Christian faith in immortality and the resurrection, he contemplates it as another state of existence—a state of separation from that world in which the man existed while a tenant of the body—another sphere in which the dead are as truly existent as are the living in this. From this point of view he transfers the word to the mysteries of religion. Death and life, therefore, are terms of opposition, describing states which exclude each other, in the former of which, existence is as real as in the latter, the application of either term to either member of the opposition being determined by the relation to the other of the party spoken of. Hence the Apostle's apparent indifference in calling either a state of death or life. The unregenerate are "dead in sin," as being in a state of separation from the kingdom of God, and under the dominion of the devil, heirs by nature of that punishment which is called eternal death. Christians are "dead with Christ," being by their membership in the Church, separate from the world. Indeed, Christians are more often said to be dead, in relation to the world, than sinners in relation to God—thus marking more plainly the Apostle's sense to be "existence in separation"—life in another sphere—a relative, not a real dissolution—as the meaning of the word.

But if the man exists, while thus spiritually dead—especially if he exists with a capacity to be restored—it is evident he must possess the essential qualities and necessary faculties and powers, however weakened and debased, without which his soul would no longer be a spiritual nature. These faculties may be weakened and shrivelled up, and what remains of them may lie torpid and dormant, but they are there; and therefore, according to the measure of existence which remains in them, they are capable of responding to the Divine grace. At the same time it cannot be doubted that in the application of the figure of death to express the state of the sinner, there is reference to the loss which his spiritual nature has sustained by original sin. There is an evident discrimination of the means which define the separation from the worlds respectively of righteousness and of sin. The Christian is dead to the world, because he is possessed of a higher hidden life, in which the world has no share; the sinner, on the other hand, is dead in sin because of the depravation and degradation of his spiritual powers, consequent upon the fall; he is thrown out of relation to the kingdom of God, by inherent inability to work righteousness according to God's law. Hence his state of spiritual death is defined by these two facts, that he still exists as a spiritual nature, possessing all the essential powers and faculties of a soul; but that all those faculties are weakened and depraved by sin. As possessed of these powers and faculties, however, he has a capacity, while unregenerate, of being acted upon by the Spirit of God,—a capacity, not only of receiving the regeneration, but of receiving and answering to those impulses of grace which are preparatory to the regeneration; just as the souls of the dead, though unable by their own power to reassume their bodies, have a capacity of receiving the Divine impulse which will call them forth clothed with bodies at the Resurrection.

Here, however, is the distinction between the response to the Divine grace in the state of death and the state of life. Just as we must suppose the dead, while without the body, to be capable of some of the acts of life, as consciousness, thought, the communication of ideas with each other, and yet to lead a maimed, imperfect existence, bereft of the natural power of the united soul and body: so the soul of the man dead in sin, though to some extent responsive to the Spirit's influence, answers to it in a maimed, imperfect, powerless way, incapable of that steady, continuous righteousness which God requires. Nor is it capable of sustaining the weight of the Divine impulse, and the blaze of the Divine light, in such measure as is granted to the holy after regeneration. It must receive an inward strength, a reorganization of its substance (so to speak), to be enabled to respond perfectly to the motions of grace. The owl's eye must be made the eagle's, the strength of the shadow of Hades must be made that of the new man of the resurrection, by a new birth. It needs, therefore, for continuous holiness, besides the Divine impulse *upon* it, the replanting of the lost strength in the soul, the communication of the power to bear that influence. Hence the possession of the grace of the Spirit by the regenerate is called His "indwelling"—a closer personal presence than is granted to the unregenerate, to whom this term is never applied; and consequently, conversion is an event of far less magnitude than the subsequent renewal or sanctification; while regeneration stands between the two, as the restoration from the glorified Divine humanity of Christ our Lord, of that life and power which enables the converted sinner to "go on to perfection." Not, indeed, that all the "infection of nature" is removed by this gift; but that the grace of Christ enables the soul, under the influence of the Spirit, to overcome it, and live no longer to the flesh, but to God.

We may see from this discussion what are the respective spheres of operation of the grace of the Son, and the grace of the Spirit. The grace of the Son in the soul operates *in* its inmost nature, is directed to restore it in its essence which underlies all the phenomena of its activity; while the operations of the grace of the Spirit is *upon* the soul, directed to elicit the spiritual phenomena, and to call forth into action the qualities it possesses as a spiritual being, whether in its unregenerate or its regenerate estate. The grace of the Spirit acts upon it as a breath from above, stimulating and exciting its powers, as the pure air stimulates and invigorates the bodily organs; the grace of the Son enters into the soul and reconstitutes it, as bread and wine enter into and reconstitute the wasting body. The one acts *within* the soul, the other acts *upon* it.

And this, so far as relates to the grace of the Son, I conceive to be the sense of Hooker in this passage (before quoted): "The person of Adam is not in us, but his nature, and the corruption of that nature derived into all men by propagation; Christ, having Adam's nature, as we have, but incorrupt, deriveth not nature, but incorruption, and that *immediately from His own person* into all that belong to Him." This view is confirmed, and at the same time guarded, by another passage on a succeeding page: "His Church, and every member thereof, is in Him by original derivation, and He personally in them by way of mystical association wrought through the gift of the Holy Ghost, which they that are His receive from Him, and together with the same [gift] *what benefit soever the vital force of His body and blood may yield;* yea, by steps and degrees they receive the complete measure of all such Divine grace as doth sanctify and save throughout till the day of their final exaltation to a state of fellowship in glory with Him whose partakers they now are in those things that tend to glory. *As for any mixture of the substance of His flesh with ours, the participation which we have of Christ includeth no such kind of gross surmise.*"

At this point the reason will be observed for the statement made in the last chapter that the grace of the Son, as "the Life" is, like all other of His grace, a derivative from Him as now existing in the two natures, Divine and human. It is needless to remark that the last sentence in the preceding paragraph is directed against the Romish figment of transubstantiation—a notion as gross and low in divinity as it is absurd and baseless in philosophy. If the substance of the flesh of Christ entered into ours, it would not, as such, be in us that "life" which His grace is said to be. But it has pleased God that the reparation of the loss which our nature sustained at the fall should be derived from Him, the Redeemer; and therefore that His grace should be given to humanity after the analogy of the derivation of life from man to man. "For as in Adam all die [that is, are born in the natural state subject to death], even so in Christ shall all be made alive." Hence this economy implies a derivation of grace from Him as man to us as men; from His humanity, purified and glorified, to our corrupt and fallen humanity. And this is the reason that we are said to be "members of His body, of His flesh, and of His bones," vivified by His life, as His own body is. What is the mode in which the regeneration is wrought we do not know. The gift and the manner of its communication are transcendent mysteries. The means by which it is communicated and the reality of the operation are made known to us in Holy Scripture; but the manner how is as mysterious and impenetrable to human thought as the mystery of His birth, of His Resurrection and Ascension. That a vital power is given by Him to the regenerate, through the operation of the Spirit in regeneration, the result of which is a "new birth," a "new creation,"—this is certain; more than this is no subject of speculation to the devout and humble Christian.

While the grace of the Son, as "Life," however, works that change in the substance and essence of the regenerate, which underlies the phenomena of consciousness, the grace of the Holy Spirit, it is next to be observed, is connected more consciously with the phenomena themselves of the religious life. We are conscious of the effects of the one, while we are not immediately conscious of the effects of the other.

The substance and the phenomena being distinguished, that which works in the substance can reveal itself to the consciousness only in the intuition of substance, while that which elicits the phenomena will manifest itself by the phenomena. But the soul is only conscious of itself as substance in the affirmation of its indivisible unity, as the *ego* which, as an idea, is incapable of intensive or extensive increase or diminution; and this being the full expression of the soul's substantial existence, it cannot go back to what enters into and underlies this consciousness,—to what brought it into being and makes it what it is from time to time. It cannot get behind the affirmation, "I am;" and there is no combination of facts in that affirmation, the analysis of which will tell it what lies behind it. Whatever faculty or power of the soul is in activity, it presents to the consciousness but the one intuition of an existing substance, which is the subject of that activity, and of which that activity is the phenomenon. The intuition of self-consciousness is the same precisely in its affirmation of myself whether I say, "I love," "I hope," "I believe," "I think," or "I act." How the various powers whose acts are expressed by these words coexist in the indivisible unity of myself as revealed to my consciousness, I am ignorant. I can gain no intuition of them. In other words, what powers or faculties underlie the affirmation of being are concealed from direct consciousness. And therefore, *a fortiori*, that Divine grace of the Son which lies still deeper than these powers, operating, as it were, from underneath to revivify and regenerate, must operate unconsciously. Its results may be apparent at last in the magnified phenomena of the soul's active life; but itself is contained in the affirmation of substance, "I am," which suffers neither increase nor diminution, whether I am equal to an atom or to a world; whether the spiritual life is that of the babe or of the strong man in Christ.

Underneath this simple consciousness of an indivisible entity lie, it is not to be doubted, powers and faculties, or attributes of the soul, which are the subjective elements of the phenomena that reveal themselves to that entity. But the phenomena themselves, whether affections, or thoughts, or intuitions, or sensations, whether moral or mental, cannot be produced by their own self-activity; they are dependent upon influences from without, and the consciousness of the diverse powers is all contained in the consciousness of the phenomena, as phenomena, and therefore as distinguished from self. The phenomena of the soul's regenerate active life, therefore, as objects of spiritual experience, testify rather of the influence brought to bear from without itself than of that which takes place within its substance; they testify of the grace of the Holy Spirit upon the soul. That I exist is the testimony of consciousness to my substantial being; that I love, that I hope, that I believe, that I think and act is the testimony of consciousness to the phenomena supervening upon my substantial existence—inferring within me, indeed, the powers, or faculties, or capabilities of love, hope, faith, thought, action; but implying also another influence besides myself, acting upon me, and always referred by consciousness to that influence. Outside of the phenomena, I am not conscious of the powers or faculties they suppose, as I am, or conceive myself to be, of my existence; those powers never reveal themselves immediately to my consciousness as my existence does; I can in thought separate from myself not only the phenomena but the powers, but I cannot separate from myself in thought, my existence; I do not separate the "I" which loves from the "I" which believes; but I do separate the "I" which loves from the love which I feel. Hence the internal phenomena of the soul are always, in immediate consciousness, contemplated on their objective side and in their objective relations. Under this law, therefore, the *phenomena* of the spiritual life are naturally referred to the grace which operates *upon* us, rather than to that which operates *within* us; for it is in more immediate connection with the grace of the Spirit than with the grace of the Son. There is a love-faculty and a faith-faculty, as well as a love-phenomenon and a faith-phenomenon; but the grace which is more immediately concerned with the production of the phenomenon will in ordinary thought be counted its cause, rather than that whose operation is in the faculty,—whose immediate effect is unconscious, and of which the result is not apparent till the third or fourth remove. In this sense, then, it is to be understood that the grace of the Son is substantial and the grace of the Spirit phenomenal.

These remarks are valuable, chiefly as showing us the grounds on which in Holy Scripture the graces which are in one view an outgrowth of the life derived from our Saviour, are more immediately referred to the grace of the blessed Spirit as produced by His immediate influence on the regenerate nature. Thus, St. Paul tells the Galatians: "The fruit of the Spirit is love, joy, peace, long-suffering, gentleness, goodness, faith, meekness, temperance." And so our Saviour promised Him to be a "Comforter" to His disciples, bringing forth in them the joy, and hope, and peace in believing, which is the source of the Christian's satisfaction in the Gospel. These passages, and such as these, are not contrary to the doctrine of the grace of the Son; but they add to it that of the grace of the Spirit.

In this manner, also, is explained that view of the grace of the Spirit, according to which it is opposed to "the flesh," as a ruling principle of the active life. For this opposition supposes this grace to operate *upon* the soul, as a force from without, in the same manner as "the flesh" does. For the flesh, although it is a part of the complex being of the man as a whole, is external to the soul, in which the essence of his being consists, and therefore operates *upon* it, in conveying to it its own disorderly and unruly desires. It would be manifestly less symmetrical in the analogy, therefore, to oppose to "the flesh" that grace whose operation is *within* the soul, a part of its very being,—where the object is to draw attention to the Christian calling, as implying obedience to the rule of a power consciously distinct from itself. The soul is considered in this relation as placed between two powers, of which the one is the "flesh" or carnal nature, and the other the "spirit" or the grace of the Holy Spirit; and from the one or the other of these, and the emotions, affections, or passions which are its fruits, the will assumes the motive on which it acts. Thus St. Paul exhorts the Galatian Christians: "Walk in the Spirit, and ye shall not fulfil the lust of the flesh. For the flesh lusteth against the Spirit, and the Spirit against the flesh: and these are contrary, the one to the other; so that ye cannot do the things that ye would."[a] Here it is to be noted that "the Spirit" is not the natural desires of the spiritual nature of man (as if the Apostle were advancing some Manichean doctrine), but the motions of the grace of the Holy Spirit in the soul; and that to "walk in the Spirit" is equivalent to the phrase "to walk after the Spirit" in the eighth chapter of the Epistle to the Romans, where the Apostle draws out this opposition at great length: "There is therefore now no condemnation to them which are in Christ Jesus, who walk not after the flesh, but after the Spirit. For the law of the Spirit of life in Christ Jesus hath made me free from the law of sin and death. For what the law could not do, in that it was weak through the flesh, God sending His own Son in the likeness of sinful flesh, and for sin, condemned sin in the flesh: that the righteousness of the law might be fulfilled in us, who walk not after the flesh, but after the Spirit. For they that are after the flesh do mind the things of the flesh; but they that are after the Spirit the things of the Spirit. For to be carnally minded is death; but to be spiritually minded is life and peace. . . But ye are not in the flesh, but in the Spirit, if so be that the Spirit of God dwell in you. Now if any man have not the Spirit of Christ he is none of His. And if Christ be in you, the body is dead because of sin; but the Spirit is life because of righteousness. . . Brethren, we are debtors, not to the flesh, to live after the flesh. For if ye live after the flesh, ye shall die: but if ye through the Spirit do mortify the deeds of the body, ye

---

[a] Gal. v. 16, 17.

shall live." So to the Ephesians: "Be not drunk with wine, wherein is excess; but be filled with the Spirit; speaking to yourselves in psalms and hymns and spiritual songs."

The mutual relation, then, of the grace of the Son and the grace of the Spirit is that of the seed and the conditions of its growth. The heart is prepared to receive it by prevenient grace, working repentance and faith; the good seed is then implanted in regeneration, and after that the grace of the Spirit is as the air, and heat, and light, and moisture, causing it to spring and grow up, and bring forth fruit,—assimilating to itself in the process all the powers and faculties of the nature of man.

The carrying forward this process is called in Holy Scripture renewing or sanctification,—renewing, as it is the gradual assimilation of the disorganized elements of our nature to the Divine seed implanted in us, and their reorganization in the likeness of Christ; sanctification, as it is that restoration to holiness, that advancement of the consecration to God, that acceptableness before Him which is the result of the inherency and operation of Divine grace.

The words sanctification and renewal, however, are not precisely equivalent; because the former is used in Holy Scripture in two senses, to denote (1) a consecration or separation of the person to God; and (2) the being made holy in heart and life,—in which last sense it is the equivalent of "renewing." In the first sense, sanctification is attributed to Christ, in the second to the Holy Spirit. It may be well to verify this by an examination of passages.

1. "Paul, . . . unto the Church of God which is at Corinth, to them that are sanctified in Christ Jesus, called to be saints." This is the opening of the first Epistle to the Corinthians, and the ground on which they are said to be "sanctified" is evidently their baptismal consecration. So, in the thirtieth verse of the first chapter: "Of Him are ye in Christ Jesus, who of God is made unto us wisdom, and righteousness, and sanctification, and redemption,"—which text, so far as the present subject is concerned, may receive illustration from such passages as these: "Both He that sanctifieth and they who are sanctified are all of one: for which cause He is not ashamed to call them brethren."[a] "Then said He, Lo, I come to do thy will, O God. . . . By the which will we are sanctified through the offering of the body of Jesus Christ once for all. . . . For by one offering He hath perfected forever them that are sanctified."[b] The connection of this sanctification with baptism is seen again in Ephesians, v. 25, 26: "Christ loved the Church, and gave Himself for it; that He might sanctify and cleanse it with the washing of water by the word, that He might present it to Himself a glorious Church, not having spot or wrinkle or any such thing; but that it should be holy and without blemish." In this passage, however, the first sense passes over into the second, the Apostle looking forward to the completion of the work of redemption in the glory of the Church triumphant. The same combination of the two senses is evident also in the following: "Know ye not that the unrighteous

---

[a] Heb. ii. 11.   [b] Heb. x. 10, 14.

shall not inherit the kingdom of God? Be not deceived: neither fornicators, nor idolaters, nor adulterers, nor effeminate, nor abusers of themselves with mankind, nor thieves, nor covetous, nor drunkards, nor revilers, nor extortioners, shall inherit the kingdom of God. And such were some of you: but ye are washed [a reference to baptism], but ye are sanctified, but ye are justified in the name of the Lord Jesus, and by the Spirit of our God."[a]

2. In the second sense in which the word is generally used in theology, it occurs in the following places: I. Thes. iv. 3: "This is the will of God, even your sanctification." Ib. v. 23: "The very God of peace sanctify you wholly; and I pray God your whole spirit and soul and body be preserved blameless unto the coming of our Lord Jesus Christ." II. Thes. ii. 13: "God hath from the beginning chosen you to salvation, through sanctification of the Spirit and belief of the truth." St. John, xvii. 17, 19: "Sanctify them through thy truth: Thy Word is Truth." "For their sakes I sanctify myself, that they also might be sanctified through the truth." These, with the exception of Heb. x. 29 (in the same sense as Heb. x. 10, 14), are all the passages in which the word "sanctify" or "sanctification" is used in the New Testament with any bearing on this subject. But the same root appears in all the words translated "holy," "holiness," "saints," etc., and the connection of our sanctification with the Spirit is expressed in His very name, "the Holy Spirit."

3. That our "renewal" is the same with our sanctification, in the second sense, is plain, from the fact

---

[a] I. Cor. vi. 9–11.

that St. Paul exhorts those who are already Christians to labor for it as not yet attained in its perfection. This he does in such passages as the following: "I beseech you therefore, brethren, by the mercies of God, that ye present your bodies a living sacrifice, holy, acceptable unto God, which is your reasonable service. And be not conformed to this world: *but be ye transformed by the renewing of your minds*, that ye may prove what is that good, and acceptable, and perfect will of God."[a] "This I say therefore, and testify in the Lord, . . . that ye put off concerning the former conversation the old man, which is corrupt according to the deceitful lusts; and be renewed in the spirit of your mind; and that ye put on the new man, which after God is created in righteousness and true holiness."[b] "Lie not one to another, seeing that ye have put off the old man, with his deeds; and have put on the new man, which is renewed in knowledge after the image of Him that created him."[c] This admonition recalls to the Colossian Christians their Christian profession, and exhorts them to live up to it, truly "putting on the new man" as they have professed. These texts (the two first more particularly) fix the meaning of that much-controverted one, Titus, iii. 5: "Not by works of righteousness which we have done, but according to His mercy He saved us, by the washing of regeneration and renewing of the Holy Ghost;" where the "washing of regeneration" is the baptismal grace, and the "renewing of the Holy Ghost" another and subsequent operation, carrying on

---

[a] Rom. xii. 1, 2.   [b] Eph. iv. 17, 22–24.   [c] Col. iii. 9, 10.

the baptismal state to the perfection of the Christian life.

The grace of the Holy Spirit in this relation is named by theologians aiding, or assisting grace.

It is further to be observed that this grace is given in larger measure, and with a more intimate and constant presence of the Holy Spirit, as an endowment of the estate of regeneration,—a presence which is called the "indwelling" or constant abiding of the Spirit with the accepted members of Christ. "I will pray the Father, and He shall give you another Comforter, that He may abide with you forever; even the Spirit of truth, whom the world cannot receive, because it seeth Him not, neither knoweth Him: but ye know Him, for He dwelleth with you, and shall be in you."[a] So St. Peter, preaching to the multitude on the day of Pentecost: "Repent, and be baptized every one of you, for the remission of sins, and ye shall receive the gift of the Holy Ghost;"[b] where the increased measure of the Spirit's presence is connected with the sacrament of initiation into the Church. "The love of God is shed abroad in our hearts by the Holy Ghost, which is given unto us."[c] "Ye are not in the flesh, but in the Spirit, if so be the Spirit of God dwell in you. Now if any man have not the Spirit of Christ, He is none of His."[d] "Know ye not that ye are the temple of God, and that the Spirit of God dwelleth in you?"[e] And many others to the same effect, all predicated upon the membership of the Church which is the body of Christ.

---

[a] John, xiv. 16, 17. [b] Acts, ii. 38. [c] Rom. v. 5.
[d] Rom. viii. 9. [e] I. Cor. iii. 16.

The operation of the Spirit upon the regenerate, therefore, is more powerful than upon the unregenerate, and reaches farther in its effects, producing in the soul which is obedient to it, all the graces, comforts, hopes, joys, and works of the spiritual life. But it is not necessary to understand that it differs in kind from that before treated of. The altered relation of the Christian to his Saviour changes the conditions of reception; the grace differs in degree, not in kind,— just as the same air passing through the pipes of an organ produces in one one sound and in another another, according to its volume and velocity. Hence the same division applies here which we before made use of. The sacramental influence is realized in the Holy Communion, conveying to the worthy recipient the spiritual food of the body and blood of Christ which that Sacrament was ordained to exhibit. The external influence is as necessary to instruct the disciple more fully in faith and duty as it was to awaken him to the first knowledge of the Gospel; it enforces the instruction and carries it home, by the constant operations and special dispensations of Divine Providence, and bears upon him and moulds him to the Christian pattern by the social organization of the Church of which he is a member. By the internal grace, the heart and conscience are cultivated and renewed, developing those holy affections, that devout fear, that tender conscience, those manifold phenomena of the heart which are all generalized under and contained in the expression, "the love of God." Under these influences in the regenerate state, the faith which before the gift of the grace of Christ was but a preparatory, imperfect, provisional faith, now becomes "faith working by love;" repentance loses its need of sorrow, and becomes the continual renunciation of sin, the habitual purity of self-watchfulness, and the constant holiness of a heavenly walk; the act which previous to regeneration could reach no farther than the Sacrament, becomes the communion with God in the beauty of an acceptable life. And in this way the grace of the Holy Spirit is the indispensable auxiliary by which the inner life of Christ develops into the outward life of the Christian.

The mediation between the grace of the Son and the grace of the Spirit, however, is the will of the Christian; and therefore the actual results in the Christian life at any given time are complicated with the imperfections of his obedience and also with the remains of original sin. The theoretical beauty of the Divine economy falls short of practical realization by so much as the man has yielded to adverse influences or suffered himself to be tempted to sin. "The infection of nature doth remain in the regenerate also," is the language of the Church, and the experience of every individual proves its truth. The tendency to sin is only gradually overcome by earnest endeavors after perfect obedience; and therefore Christian improvement and sanctification is progressive, following upon growing habits of well-doing, and corresponding conquest over the motions and temptations of the flesh, and its abettors, the world and the devil. Besides, the Divine grace operates not to a compulsory, but to a free obedience, and therefore leaves the will of the regenerate in a freedom which it is possible to abuse. Hence it is not to be wondered at if the results are only partially manifest in this world; they were never intended to be more perfect than is consistent with the designed economy. Nor is it to be argued from the evil lives of some who have received the Sacrament of regeneration, that the doctrine fails by the test of experience, since all the lapses and falls are fully accounted for by the perversion of their freedom and neglect of their privileges on the part of those who fall back into condemnation. The Christian standing of every one at any given time is the result of the combined action of grace and self; and since all actions have a reflex influence upon the agent, the acts of sin will operate to freeze the heart against the germination of the seed of life, and to render it unresponsive to the grace of the Spirit; while the acts of righteousness and obedience will open the heart to those influences and accelerate the growth of the "tree of righteousness."[a]

There is one effect of the grace of the Spirit which has not yet been noticed,—the co-ordinating the members of the Church into one body, so that each is edified by the other and all work in common. "By one Spirit are we all baptized into one body."[b] This is the work of the Spirit, because the Spirit is essentially the love of God, which, being shed abroad in the hearts of men, produces in us the love to our neighbors. Thus, in the harmony of divine love, the peculiarities of each individual character, subordinated to one common principle, assign the different labors and positions to each member of God's Church—to one being

---

[a] Isaiah, lxi. 3.   [b] I. Cor. xii. 13.

given "the word of wisdom," to another "the word of knowledge,"—some being "Apostles," and some "Evangelists," and some "pastors and teachers,"—the very imperfection of one member being balanced by the imperfections of another; the tendencies of one in one direction being balanced by the opposite tendencies of another, and so, all co-operating to carry on the work of the Church on every side, in complete harmony and mutual subordination of part to part. He who will study the influence of individual and national intellectual tendencies in preserving the faith whole and entire, as evidenced in the history of the Ecumenical councils, will there see one illustration of the scriptural representation of the one body having many members.

The other effects of the grace of the Spirit, the "comfort" of the Paraclete, the "helping our infirmities," the "witness with our spirits," the strength, and peace, and joy, and whatsoever other fruits are brought forth in the Christian heart, may easily be assigned their places in the system of which the principles are here developed. It is not needed to carry the inquiry any farther. The effects are as various in manifestation as individual men, and as manifold as the circumstances of life; and an attempt at a full classification would be as presumptuous as impossible. Only, let it be remembered, that though the grace of the Holy Spirit is "extra-sacramental," yet it is given in increasing measure, in prayer, in reading Holy Scripture, in public worship, in all religious duties, and especially in the Apostolic rite of confirmation, and that its withdrawal is consequent upon the neglect of these means of grace and upon continuance in sin.

CHAPTER V.

THE PLACE OF THE SACRAMENTS IN THE SYSTEM OF GRACE.

THAT the grace of Christ, the Son, is of voluntary reception, is the ground of the institution of the Holy Sacraments as parts of the Divine economy. It remains, therefore, to assign them their place in that economy.

It has been sufficiently shown in the preceding chapters how the grace of the Son differs in respect of voluntary reception from the grace of the Spirit. The latter being the prime mover in drawing man to the way of life, operates upon the will before any exercise of its activity. It is the condition by which he is able to exercise his will in the reception of Christ. It has for its object, whether as prevenient or as assisting grace, to free the enslaved will, to lead man to seek for and lay hold upon the grace of Christ, and to prepare him for its reception; and therefore it must be given antecedently to, as well as together with every human act. But the grace of the Son of God, being the gift offered to the sinner to accomplish his redemption, is made of voluntary acceptance, that his restoration may be wrought under the conditions of his freedom as was his fall. The one is a gift forced,[a] as it were, upon man,

---

[a] Gen. vi. 3. "And the Lord said, My Spirit shall not always *strive* with man."

though not so but that he can resist it; the other is a gift so offered that it may be freely appropriated. Hence, while the internal grace of the Spirit is given without as well as in means, the grace of Christ is imparted in connection with certain acts appointed by our Lord, which have the twofold design of being, on the one hand, tests of the faith and obedience of the recipient, and so of his desire and endeavor after saving grace; and, on the other hand, of being seals and vessels of that grace, conferring it upon him in time and place determined by the acts. These acts are the two Sacraments of Baptism and the Holy Communion.

The Sacraments, then, have relation to the grace of Christ, and are the appointed means of its communication. This is their distinctive use in the economy of the Church. They are, in their primary intent, means of applying the grace, not of the Spirit, but of the Son; though the possession of a larger measure of the grace of the Spirit follows necessarily from being made partaker of the grace of Christ. In scholastic language, the grace of the Spirit is an *accidental*, the grace of the Son, the *essential* gift of the Sacrament. And the ground of the institution of Sacraments is, as was said, that they may be acts of voluntary performance, by which the faithful recipient may take to himself this saving grace.

The proof that the Sacraments are thus related to Christ is the language of Holy Scripture, which assigns them this place. With respect to Baptism, we have the words of St. Paul in the sixth chapter of the Epistle to the Romans: "Know ye not, that so many of us as were baptized into Jesus Christ were baptized into His death? Therefore we are buried with Him by baptism into death: that like as Christ was raised from the dead by the glory of the Father, even so we also should walk in newness of life." Here the idea of union with Christ as the result of the Sacrament underlies every expression. So also in I. Cor. xii. 12, 13: "For as the body is one and hath many members, and all the members of that one body, being many, are one body; so also is Christ. For by one Spirit are we all baptized into one body; ... and have been all made to drink into one Spirit." In this passage the three facts are distinctly brought forward, that the Spirit is the invisible agent in the Sacrament; that our baptism brings us into Christ's body—that is, makes us members of Him, conveys to us the grace of His life, and makes us thereby, as it were, "continuate with Him;"[a] and that, as a collateral benefit, we are given a larger measure of the grace of the Spirit. But the whole text turns on the similitude of the body, showing that our union with Christ in the Sacrament is its principal end. The same truth is evident in Galatians, iii. 27: "For as many of you as have been baptized into Christ have put on Christ;" where, if the phrase "have put on Christ" refers to the public profession made in baptism, the other phrase, "baptized into Christ," most certainly asserts the inward oneness of the grace of union. The phraseology of the passage from Romans is reproduced in Colossians, ii. 12: "Buried with Him in baptism, wherein also ye are risen with Him through the faith of the operation of God, who hath raised Him from the dead."

---

[a] Hooker, b. v. ch. lvi. 7.

In view of texts such as these, no difficulty need be felt in regard to our Lord's statement to Nicodemus: "Except a man be born of water and of the Spirit, he cannot enter into the kingdom of God;"[a] nor in regard to that of St. Peter: "Repent and be baptized in the name of Jesus Christ for the remission of sins, and ye shall receive the gift of the Holy Ghost."[b] They harmonize perfectly with the doctrine here delivered. The one text declares the agent by whom the regeneration is wrought; the other, the enlarged measure of the Spirit's presence consequent upon the regeneration. But the regeneration itself consists in the communication of the grace of Christ, and our incorporation thereby into His body.

That the Sacrament of Holy Communion has relation to the grace of the Son is still more clear. It appears in the words of institution: "Take, eat, this is my body." "Drink ye all of this, for this is my blood." "Do this in remembrance of me." The only other passage in which the Holy Communion is openly mentioned in connection with the grace it conveys is, I. Cor. x. xi., where, in the sixteenth verse of the former chapter, St. Paul says: "The cup of blessing which we bless, is it not the communion of the blood of Christ? The bread which we break, is it not the communion of the body of Christ?" But we cannot doubt that this appointment of the way in which the Divine gift is granted was anticipated in the sixth chapter of St. John's Gospel, which records our Lord's discourse in the synagogue of Capernaum, respecting the eating of

---

[a] John, iii. 5.   [b] Acts, ii. 38.

His flesh and the drinking of His blood. All these passages connect the Sacrament specially and distinctively with the grace of Christ.

A more profound reason, therefore, than appears at first sight, underlies the decision of the Reformers, when they rejected the Romish enumeration of seven Sacraments and restricted the word to these two only. If we seek for a definition more inward than they have given us in the Church Catechism, we may say that Sacraments are the outward and visible signs ordained by Christ to convey His personal grace. Those acts, such as confirmation, in which the grace of the Holy Spirit is specially vouchsafed, we call *rites*, as not so closely connected with the special grace of Christ.

The Sacraments having the twofold design of being tests of faith and obedience, and seals and channels of grace, have a corresponding twofold outward character. They are acts of the administrator, and acts of the recipient. The administrator stands on the part of Christ; he is His "steward" and "ambassador," empowered to act on His behalf. Christ acts thus through His minister in that which is visible, because by His ascension into heaven He is Himself invisible. The recipient acts in his own person. The Sacrament, therefore, is of the nature of a covenant ratified openly and visibly by the two parties, each attesting something invisible. The minister, by Divine authority, pledges the invisible grace; the recipient, on his part, confesses his faith and trust in Christ, and shows his purpose of obedience to the law of God.

The force of the act of the administrator rests upon the promise of Christ, pledging that He will honor the commission by which His servant acts, with the aid of His Spirit and the communication of grace. The effect of the act being invisible, it is beheld by faith; it needs, therefore, the Divine promise that faith may have a sure foundation. The formal promise of our Saviour is preserved for us in the Gospels, in the commission of His ministers, and the institution of the acts, in the words by which they are commanded, and in such expositions of their intention as the Apostles afford in their inspired teachings. These last will appear as occasion offers. The commission to baptize, making baptism of universal necessity, is set down in the words: "Go ye and make disciples of all nations, baptizing them in the name of the Father, and of the Son, and of the Holy Ghost."[a] "He that believeth and is baptized shall be saved; but he that believeth not shall be damned." The commission to administer the Eucharist is contained in the words of institution, spoken "in the night in which He was betrayed:" "Take, eat, this is my body." "This is my blood of the New Testament." "Do this in remembrance of me." These are assurances sufficient to the faithful heart that Christ will honor the Sacrament with the grace it is intended to convey.

Such an act, of course, is not necessary on the part of Christ, so far as we can see, to enable Him to confer the gift of grace, or to know the person on whom to confer it. But if it be His purpose thus to confer it, His promise limits to this way our hope of attaining it; just as His promise, attached to any other act, would

---

[a] Matt. xxviii. 19.

require us to perform it. And there does seem to be need of such an act on man's part, if he is to receive grace with consent and by seeking; because the fact of seeking consists in the performance of the prescribed act with the faith that desires to attain the benefit. The grace of the Sacrament is made to depend upon the outward sign; not because the Holy Spirit is under any necessity of working by such means in this, any more than in any other operation, but because man's probation under the Gospel is thus made more accordant with his moral nature as a voluntary agent. Unless there be an *act*, the element of human will necessary to the restoration of man as a moral being is not present. And, unless the act be one determined by Divine appointment, it does not declare the submission to God of heart, and mind, and will, in which the restoration consists. Hence the Sacrament is (as it were) the clasped hands of the Saviour and the sinner, joined in the covenant of grace. The administrator of the Sacrament, and the Sacrament itself, are ordained for the sake of the recipient. They pledge him to God, and in return they pledge and convey the grace of Christ to him.

Hence, on the part of the recipient, the act is in form a receptive act. The intention being to obtain a gift, the form of the transaction is such as to declare its purpose. It is therefore the constant witness against any notion of merit by reason of good works on the part of him who receives it. It testifies that all we can do—all works of penitence, of faith, of charity, of self-denial, are all too little, and nothing worth, until over and above them we have the imparted virtue of the atonement of our Lord. The Christian who relies upon his baptismal adoption into the family of God can do so only because he trusts his Saviour and his Saviour's word. Were it an act of great difficulty, or self-denial, or great visible effect for good, it might be misapprehended. Were it an act of service instead of reception, it might obscure, to a mind not fully enlightened, the truth that our salvation is the free gift of God in Christ. But, consisting as it does in receiving simple elements, administered with a simple rite, it obtains all its value from the faith which rests upon the promise of Christ. It is purely an act of faith. The more implicit the faith, the more unreserved the trust, the more exalted will be the sense of the transaction; the less faith and trust, the less importance will be attached to it,—the infidel will have no motive to seek it.

Hence the objection which is sometimes urged against the doctrine of the Sacraments—that it is unreasonable that such momentous consequences should hang upon transactions outwardly so insignificant—proves only the want of faith of those who make it. If the body of Naaman, the leper, could be healed by the Holy Ghost after washing in the Jordan at the command of a prophet, surely the soul of the sinner will be regenerated by the power of the same Holy Ghost on his being washed in the laver of baptism at the command of Christ Himself.

Every aspect of the act marks its fitness for the end for which it is ordained. Being receptive and not energizing, it shows that saving grace is a received benefit, a *free* gift of God; being a simple act, it declares the unreserved bounty of the Giver; requiring sincere repentance and faith and obedience to the commandments, as conditions precedent to its reception, and being a free gift coming after these, it pledges the Christian to personal holiness, while yet it testifies that all our works fall short in themselves; and finally, it is a continual witness that we are accepted for the sole merit of our blessed Redeemer, by whose commission it is administered.

Baptism is the initial Sacrament. It is the Sacrament of Regeneration, the beginning of the Christian life. What goes before is the preparation of the crude material of human nature, out of which the Christian is to be made. Regeneration is, as has been already much insisted on, the communication of life from Christ our Lord, by the agency of the Holy Spirit, in His sacramental operation, connected through the promise of Christ with the administration of the outward sign by His commissioned minister.

In its outward form, Baptism[a] is the application of

---

[a] To clear the language of theology from misapprehension, it is to be remarked that the word Sacrament, and the names of the two Sacraments, have both a wider and a narrower application. In their wider signification they include the " outward sign" and the "invisible grace." In their narrower signification they are applied to the outward sign alone. In either sense they are said to consist of *matter* and *form*. The " matter" of baptism in the former sense is the invisible grace; the water, with the words of administration, is the " form." In the latter sense the water is the " matter," the words are the " form." So, *mutatis mutandis*, of the Holy Communion. This remark is necessary for students of the works of the Reformers, since, by inattention to the limitation or extension of the word, the reader might be led to draw a wrong conclusion from their language. Thus, if it be said that

water in the name of the Father, and the Son, and the Holy Ghost. That this ceremony is the means in connection with which the life-giving grace of Christ is imparted; and that this imparting is the regeneration of the Christian, which has been all along assumed, is now to be proved.

The proof consists in sustaining the two following propositions:

1. That regeneration in Baptism is taught in Holy Scripture.

2. The baptismal regeneration taught in Holy Scripture is the communication of the life-giving grace of Christ.

1. The word "Regeneration" occurs but in two places in the English version of the New Testament, in both of which it is the translation of the Greek word παλιγγενεσια. The first place is St. Matthew, xix. 28: "Ye which have followed me, in the regeneration when the Son of Man shall sit in the throne of His glory, ye also shall sit upon twelve thrones, judging the twelve tribes of Israel." The other is Titus, iii. 5: "Not by works of righteousness which we have done, but according to His mercy He saved us, by the washing of regeneration, and renewing of the Holy Ghost." In the former passage there is no immediate

---

the Sacraments confer grace, the statement is true on condition that the word is taken to apply to the whole transaction, visible and invisible; taken in the narrower signification, the statement is false. Conversely, when it is said that the Sacraments do not confer grace, then the statement is predicated of the outward form, *in connection with which* the grace is conferred by the Holy Spirit.

reference to the subject under consideration; but the analogy of its use there will explain it in the other passage. "The regeneration when the Son of Man shall sit in the throne of His glory" has the same general signification as "the restitution of all things" in Acts, iii. 21: "Jesus Christ, . . whom the heavens must receive, until the time of the restitution of all things which God hath spoken by the mouth of all His holy prophets, since the world began;" which, again, is explained by II. Peter, iii. 13: "We, according to His promise, look for new heavens and a new earth, wherein dwelleth righteousness." A parallel passage from St. Paul's writings is Rom. viii. 19–23: "The earnest expectation of the creature [*i.e.* the creation[a]] waiteth for the manifestation of the sons of God. . . . Because the creature itself also shall be delivered from the bondage of corruption into the glorious liberty of the children of God. For we know that the whole creation[b] groaneth and travaileth in pain together until now. And not only they, but ourselves also, which have the first fruits of the Spirit, even we ourselves groan within ourselves, waiting for the adoption, to wit, the redemption [*i.e.* by the resurrection] of our body."

From a comparison of these passages, it appears that "the regeneration," in this sense, must be taken of the more glorious estate to which the universe will be advanced at the end of the present dispensation, when this world shall be destroyed by fire, and "new heavens and a new earth" be given as the habitation

---

[a] ἡ κτίσις.   [b] πασα ἡ κτίσις.

of the glorified body of the resurrection. But with this wider meaning, I conceive that there is in our Saviour's words a special reference to the resurrection of the saints. "Ye also (being raised from the dead) shall sit upon twelve thrones," etc. For that the resurrection was counted a "new birth" or "new begetting" is evident from St. Paul's application of Psalm ii. 7, to the resurrection of our Saviour, in Acts, xiii. 33: "The promise which was made unto the fathers, God hath fulfilled the same unto us their children, in that He hath raised up Jesus again; as it is written in the second Psalm, Thou art my Son, this day have I begotten Thee,"—that is, on the day of His resurrection, and therefore by the resurrection.

Now this reference to the Resurrection will help us in our present inquiry so far as this, that as the resurrection of the body is a regeneration, so the "restitution" of the heavens and the earth is also a regeneration; inasmuch as it is, after its kind, a resurrection of heaven and earth, from their death by fire, in which they shall put off "the bondage of corruption" under which they are held by the sin of man, and "put on incorruption." And thus the parallel is perfect with baptism, which is represented in Holy Scripture as a death and resurrection with Christ. "Know ye not, that so many of us as were baptized unto Jesus Christ were baptized unto His death? Therefore we are buried with Him by baptism into death: that like as Christ was raised up from the dead by the glory of the Father, even so we also should walk in newness of life."[a]

---

[a] Rom. vi. 3, 4.

"Buried with Him in baptism, wherein also ye are risen with Him through the faith of the operation of God, who hath raised Him from the dead."[a] In each case the same idea underlies the expression—the idea of the infusion of a higher principle of vitality, in the one case, into the body, in the other case into the soul. The resurrection of the body is a restoration of the same body which died; but not simply a restoration, it is also an advancement to a higher state. "It is sown a natural body, it is raised a spiritual body." We can conceive of the resurrection, therefore, only as the gift of a higher, spiritual life-principle to the body, assimilating it to a spiritual nature,[b] and enabling it to exist in incorruptible immortality. In like manner, the spiritual resurrection of the soul in baptism, asserted in the passages from Romans and Colossians just quoted, is a restoration of the soul from its state of death by the infusion of a higher life,—that is, the grace of Christ our Lord. Hence παλιγγενεσια, regeneration, may be harmoniously applied to the resurrection of the body, the renewal of the world, and the Divine operation on the soul in baptism.

And so we find it applied to the baptismal act, in the only other place in which it occurs, Titus, iii. 5: "Not by works of righteousness which we have done, but according to His mercy He saved us, by the washing of regeneration, and renewing of the Holy Ghost." The "washing of regeneration" is undoubtedly baptism. It

---

[a] Col. ii. 12.
[b] Nicholson on the Catechism. "As near unto the nature of a Spirit as it is possible for a body."

has been shown already, that the two phrases, "the washing of regeneration" and "renewing of the Holy Ghost," denote two different operations; but even admitting them to be the same, the reference to baptism is equally clear. The only place besides this in which "washing" occurs as the translation of λουτρον, is Eph. v. 26: "Christ loved the Church and gave Himself for it; that He might sanctify and cleanse it with the washing of water by the Word." The "washing of water by the Word" is clearly equivalent to the "washing of regeneration," implying the whole transaction of baptism, visible and invisible—viewed differently, indeed, in either case; in the one with a reference to the cleansing efficacy of the grace of baptism, in the other with a reference to its restoring power. No one will deny that baptism is alluded to in the text from Ephesians; and there is as little reason to deny it in the passage from Titus. The plain, unvarnished sense requires that it should be thus understood, and no reasoning is needed to enforce the interpretation. It is a well-known method of St. Paul to bring in the Sacraments allusively (φωνεντος συνετοισιν) in his disquisitions upon grace. Thus the reference to the outward sign is clear in I. Cor. xii. 13: "For by one Spirit are we all *baptized* into one body;" nor is it any less clear in "the washing [or laver] of regeneration."

We are willing to admit that the word παλιγγενεσια does not etymologically signify the raising to a higher state than before, by the infusion of a new and higher life; but in both its applications the things themselves contain this idea of advancement. If, however, a more forcible word be demanded, we have ἀναγεννησις, whose congeners (the noun itself not appearing in the New Testament) are applied to describe the baptismal grace, with a force inclusive of all that is claimed for it; and that though it is not applied to the Resurrection, thus giving a greater prominence to the truth of a new birth in the Sacrament.

It is somewhat unfortunate for the English reader of the New Testament that, our language being a composite formed out of many others, Saxon, Greek, Latin, French, etc., the relation of many words to each other, clear enough in the original, is thereby obscured in the translation. We miss connections of great doctrinal importance, because we are not able to express cognate Greek words by cognate English words. Thus the adjective ἐκλεκτος is rendered nearly always "elect," while the verb ἐκλεγω, from which it is derived, is translated "choose." So, we have ἅγιοι, "saints," ἅγιος, "holy," ἁγιαζω, "to sanctify," ἁγιασμος, "sanctification;" words of the same root in Greek, rendered by Latin, French, and Saxon derivatives. In addition to this defect, very few English words will give the full force of the Greek, and our translators had to choose between encumbering their pages with wordy paraphrases, or the permission of inadequate and vague expressions, by restricting themselves in the number of words. It sometimes happens, moreover, that a Greek word has the sense of two or more English words, and is translated in the one place by the one, and elsewhere by the other, so that the mere English reader is unable to compare passages, with a certainty of arriving at a right conclusion. These three causes operate to make the truth of regeneration in baptism less clear in the translation than it really is in the original.

Sacraments in the System of Grace. 253

The verb γεννάω, from which ἀναγεννάω is compounded, has in earlier Greek the sense to "beget," but in later Greek, the two senses "to beget" and "to bring forth;" its passive, consequently, has the two senses, "to be begotten" and "to be born." It is translated both ways, in relation to the mystery of the new birth, in I. John, v. 1: "Whosoever believeth that Jesus is the Christ is *born* [γεγέννηται] of God; and every one that loveth Him that begat [τον γεννήσαντα], loveth him also that *is begotten* [τον γεγεννημένον] of Him." The last rendering is necessary to preserve the inference of the Apostle, which rests on the active "begat" and the passive "is begotten." But in either place the word contains both senses, and there is no exact equivalent for it in our language; hence our translators use that term which expresses the part of the meaning most necessary to the context. It is, however, very important to remember the whole extent of the word, because it bears with great weight on the question of the initial communication of life in the Sacrament, giving over both these senses to its compound ἀναγεννάομαι.

The latter verb occurs (in participial form) only in I. Peter, i. 23: "Being born again [ἀναγεγεννημένοι][a] not of corruptible seed, but of incorruptible, by the Word[b] of the Lord, which liveth and abideth forever." Ἀναγεγεννημένοι is literally, in its full force, to the learned ear, "being regenerate;" but our translators

---

[a] ἀναγεννήσας in v. 3 of this chapter.

[b] λόγος, not ῥῆμα. See Lee on Inspiration, p. 132-3, American edition.

rightly judged that the plain, homely Saxon would convey more meaning to the mere English reader than the foreign polysyllable. The doctrinal equivalent is, in Saxon, "being begotten and born again;" and even then the full force of the preposition ἀνα is not obtained. In composition it not only implies the *return* signified by "again," but it also retains its own proper signification, "up to," "upon," "from above,"—the compound here being equivalent to γεννηθῇ ἄνωθεν, in John, iii. 3. Hence, to translate adequately, we must read, "being begotten again *from above* [and so begotten *to* the higher life], not of corruptible seed," etc.

The above passage does not connect regeneration with baptism; but if there be one passage in Scripture which does so, that is conclusive for all places where it is spoken of without definition, and must be understood in each. Thus, as we understand ἀνα in St. John's "Which were [new] born, not of blood, nor of the will of the flesh, nor of the will of man, but of God;"[a] and "Whosoever is [new] born of God doth not commit sin,"[b] and "Whosoever believeth that Jesus is the Christ is [new] born of God;"[c] the thing here spoken of being the same new birth which is called by St. Peter ἀναγεγεννημένοι; so, if there be one undoubted passage which adds to this notion, the further particular, ἐξ ὕδατος και πνευματος, "of water and the Spirit," that also enters into the notion of regeneration, and must be understood wherever regeneration or the new birth of the individual is spoken of, upon the self-evident principle that anything, however named, has at

---

[a] John, i. 13. [b] I. John, iii. 9. [c] I. John, v. 1.

all times its essential attributes and parts, and, if it be thought of at all, must be thought of as it is.

The authority of the doctrine of regeneration in baptism finally rests on the discourse of our Saviour to Nicodemus, in which the required phrase, εξ υδατος και πνευματος, is added, to complete the notion, by the Son of God Himself: " Verily, verily, I say unto thee, Except a man be born again [γεννηθη ανωθεν] he cannot see the kingdom of God. . . . Verily, verily, I say unto thee, Except a man be born of water and of the Spirit [γεννηθη εξ υδατος και πνευματος] he cannot enter into the kingdom of God. That which is born of the flesh is flesh; and that which is born of the Spirit is spirit. Marvel not that I said unto thee ye must be born again" [γεν. ανωθεν]. Here to "be born of water and the Spirit" is certainly equivalent to and a clearer explanation of γεννηθη (-ναι) ανωθεν in the preceding and following verses; and as certainly γεν. ανωθεν is the same with αναγεγεννημενοι in the passage quoted from St. Peter. And since the simple verb and its compounds contain the sense of *begetting*,[a] as well as birth, the regeneration of man, in the full force of the Latin term, is here asserted to be wrought in and through baptism.

The only answer to this on the part of those who contravene the doctrine, is that the word "water" is used figuratively, and not materially. But this evasion was

---

[a] The author feels the necessity of insisting upon this truth the more strongly from having heard a clergyman of some ability as a preacher assert, in a convention, that regeneration in baptism was but *birth*, and that "life" must precede birth, apparently in utter ignorance that the Greek verb used is γενναω throughout.

met completely by our great Hooker, nearly three hundred years since, in these memorable words: "I hold it for a most infallible rule in expositions of sacred Scripture, that where a literal construction will stand, the farthest from the letter is commonly the worst. There is nothing more dangerous than this licentious and deluding art which changeth the meaning of words as alchemy doth, or would do, the substance of metals, making of anything what it listeth, and bringing, in the end, all truth to nothing. Or, howsoever such voluntary exercise of wit might be borne with otherwise, yet, in places which usually serve as this doth, concerning regeneration by water and the Holy Ghost, to be alleged for grounds and principles, less is permitted. . . . When the letter of the law hath two things plainly and expressly specified, water and the Spirit,—water as a duty required on our parts, the Spirit as a gift which God bestoweth,—there is danger in presuming so to interpret it as if the clause that concerneth ourselves were more than needeth. We may, by such rare expositions, attain, perhaps, in the end, to be thought witty, but with ill advice."[a]

Two texts above quoted require additional remark to guard against misunderstanding. I. John, iii. 9, and v. 1, were produced incidentally to show that the words "born" and "born again" were identical in sense in this connection, and it was assumed that the "birth" there mentioned is the baptismal regeneration. The former verse (which reads: "Whosoever is born of God doth not commit sin; for his seed remaineth in

---

[a] Hooker, b. V. lix. 2, 4.

Sacraments in the System of Grace. 257

him: and he cannot sin, because he is born of God") must not be taken either as asserting the indefectibility of the baptized, nor as contravening the fact of regeneration in baptized sinners. It is an example of St. John's way of looking at the end from the beginning. At the last, when all imperfection is done away, it will be so; and in view of that final consummation, regeneration is nothing if it do not attain the resurrection of the just. But in respect to this life, it is the mark at which the Christian aims, the rule by which he must guide himself to keep his regeneration, the *definition* of a new-born man, which he must strive to realize in himself,—not the description of him as he actually is; for the same St. John says: "If we say we have no sin we deceive ourselves, and the truth is not in us." The baptized Christian who does not walk by this rule will lose the grace of regeneration, if he have possessed it; he who does walk by it, striving against sin, is not only born of water, but of the Holy Ghost. It does not touch the question when or how the man becomes regenerate, which must be answered from our Saviour's words to Nicodemus, preserved by St. John himself. The other text is: "Whosoever believeth that Jesus is the Christ is born of God;" from which, were it alone, it might be inferred that faith was the only necessary requisite to regeneration. But no one will deny that faith must be joined with repentance; that the faith spoken of is a living, working faith,—since St. James says, "Faith without works is dead." It is faith manifest in the Church, faith confessed in the appointed manner, and therefore faith which has made the baptismal confession, and received the gift of baptismal grace. The Apostle who has preserved to us the most of our Lord's teaching respecting the grace of the Sacraments[a] is not the one to make it of none effect by any "tradition" of his own.

We conclude, then, that our first assertion, that Regeneration in Baptism is taught in Holy Scripture, is fully proved: 1, by the passage in St. Paul's Epistle to Titus; 2, by the words of our Lord to Nicodemus; and 3, by the doctrinal harmony of all other texts which speak of the new birth.

Our next proposition is, that the Regeneration asserted to be wrought in Baptism is the communication of spiritual life by the grace of Christ our Lord.

That the grace of the Son is a Divine life given to the Christian has been proved in the fourth chapter. Conversely, as there is but one imparted life, the Divine life given to the Christian is the grace of Christ. What is now to be proved, therefore, is that the term regeneration, though not explicitly defined in Holy Scripture, is there intended to mean the gift of the grace and life of Christ.

1. Our first argument is that the word itself, whether $παλιγγενεσια$ or $ἀναγεννησις$, implies the communication of life. Regeneration is a second generation; generation is a begetting, and begetting is the communication of life. Dead things, things material, things inanimate, are not begotten. The father has his right of paternity, because his son partakes of his life. Our blessed Lord is the "only-begotten of the Father," because God the Father has given to Him His life. "As the

---

[a] John, iii., vi.

Father hath life in Himself, so hath He given to the Son, to have life in Himself."[a] So, we are sons of God, through Christ, because He "hath begotten us again [ἀναγεννήσας] unto a lively hope, by the resurrection of Jesus Christ from the dead."[b] This idea of "begetting" as well as "birth" is inherent in παλιγγενεσία as well as ἀναγέννησις. The root of the former, γενεσία, is from the obsolete γενω, "to beget," and γέννησις is from γεννάω, which is only a strengthened and later form of the same verb; hence the words are identical in signification, meaning "begetting" or "birth," as including begetting. For the work of grace is instantaneous; the end is not separate from the beginning; there is no need to have one word expressive of the beginning and another of the end; the new birth is the new begetting, and the new begetting is the new birth. The "new birth," therefore, or regeneration of man by grace, is the begetting him to a new life; it is the communication of the grace of life from the Divine humanity of Christ our Lord; the idea of initial communication is inherent in the term; and, since the grace of Christ is the only principle of life in the Christian, we conclude that regeneration in baptism is the implanting of that grace.

2. This conclusion is corroborated by the consideration that the Epistles of the New Testament (except the Pastoral ones) are addressed to Churches of baptized believers, and therefore that the assurances they contain of the gift of life in Christ are predicated upon the baptism of those to whom those assurances are made.

---

[a] John, v. 26.   [b] I. Peter, i. 3.

The Epistles were written to the members of the different Churches, *as* baptized. Those Churches were societies of converts, who had been gathered together into a common brotherhood by the Sacrament of baptism. That they were initiated into those societies by baptism none will deny. Baptism was the act which pledged them as disciples and separated them from the world. Before baptism they were not members of these societies; after it, they were; they were made members by the Sacrament. Hence, when an Apostle wrote to a Church, he wrote to a company of baptized people. That was his idea of the Church to which he was writing; and therefore he addressed to them teachings, exhortations, comfort, warning, assurance, promise, as baptized into the Church of Christ. Their title to take the contents of the Epistle to themselves rested on their baptism. Without that Sacrament, as the door of admission into the visible society, no one had a title to receive, to hear, much less to appropriate the Epistle. It was for the world without, on condition of baptismal entrance into the company for which it was written, but not otherwise. Let the reader, then, refer to the Epistles themselves, or to the quotations from them in the third chapter of this book, for the direct testimony to the fact that Christians are receivers of the life of Christ. Every such text carries with it, as an essential part of itself, that it is written for baptized people, as baptized,—and therefore is implicit testimony that Christians receive this divine gift by virtue of their baptism. Hence, as in our first argument we concluded from the name regeneration to the thing named, so we here conclude from the thing given in baptism to the name so proper for it.

3. A third argument may be founded on the baptismal union of the Redeemer and the members of His Church asserted in Holy Scripture. That union consists in the possession of a common life, derived from Him, the Head, to us the members. It consists not only in being endued with the grace of His Spirit, but also with His grace. The unity of the Church is oneness in Christ, as well as "the unity of the Spirit."[a] The Church is "the temple of the Holy Ghost," but it is "the body of Christ." We are the body, He is the Head, the Spirit is the soul of the Church. We are "members of His body, of His flesh, and of His bones,"[b] is the intensive expression of St. Paul. "The Church, which is His body, the fulness of Him that filleth all in all."[c] "Ye are the body of Christ, and members in particular."[d] Now this union, so intimate, of the body with the head, is declared to be wrought in baptism. "For as the body is one, and hath many members, and all the members of that one body, being many, are one body: so also is Christ. For by one Spirit we are all baptized into one body."[e] And that the foundation of this figure of the body is the life which the Church derives from Christ, the Head, may be inferred most clearly from that passage in Ephesians iv., where St. Paul exhorts us to "grow up into Him in all things, which is the Head, even Christ; from whom," he goes on to say, "the whole body fitly joined together and compacted by that which every joint supplieth, according to the effectual working in the measure of every part,

---

[a] Eph. iv. 3.   [b] Eph. v. 30.   [c] Eph. i. 23.
[d] I. Cor. xii. 27.   [e] I. Cor. xii. 12, 13.

maketh increase of the body unto the edifying of itself in love;" and from Colossians, ii. 19: "Holding the Head, from which all the body, by joints and bands having nourishment ministered, and knit together, increaseth with the increase of God." We reason, therefore, that as we are baptized into the body of Christ, and as we are said to be His body, because of the life derived from Him to us, and as the most proper name for the derivation of that life is Regeneration, therefore the word Regeneration is intended in Scripture to signify the communication of the life-giving grace of Christ to His baptized disciples.

4. A fourth argument for the same conclusion rests on the application of the figure of death and the Resurrection to the baptismal operation, in the well-known passages, Romans, vi. 3–11, and Colossians, ii. 12: "Know ye not that so many of us as were baptized into Jesus Christ, were baptized into His death? Therefore we are buried with Him by baptism into death: that like as Christ was raised up from the dead by the glory of the Father, even so we also should walk in newness of life. . . . Christ being raised from the dead dieth no more; death hath no more dominion over Him. For in that He died, He died unto sin once: but in that He liveth, He liveth unto God. Likewise reckon ye yourselves to be dead indeed unto sin, but alive unto God through Jesus Christ our Lord." So, again, in Colossians, "Buried with Him in baptism, wherein also ye are risen with Him through the faith of the operation of God, who hath raised Him from the dead,"—a passage which has its parallel in Ephesians, ii. 4–6: "God, who is rich

in mercy, for His great love wherewith He loved us, even when we were dead in sins, hath quickened us together with Christ (by grace are ye saved); and hath raised us up together, and made us sit together in heavenly places, in Christ Jesus." The peculiar language used by St. Paul can only be understood as saying in sacred rhetoric, that by the infusion of His grace, making us one with Him, we are made partners of His death and resurrection; buried with Him, and risen with Him, because one with Him; and one with Him because living by His life. And this enables us to see why so much stress is laid upon the resurrection of our Lord in connection with our spiritual benefit, as in that passage of St. Peter before quoted: "Hath begotten us again unto a lively hope, by the resurrection of Jesus Christ from the dead." And again, "The like figure whereunto even baptism doth also now save us . . . by the resurrection of Jesus Christ."[a] And so St. Paul: "Who was delivered for our offences, and was raised again for our justification."[b] For at His resurrection and exaltation He received the power of giving Himself as God and man to His followers, to be their life; and since the possession of Him includes the application to our needs of His merits and atonement, we are "saved," we are "justified," we are "begotten again" by the resurrection of Jesus Christ. Hence, as before, we conclude from the figure employed by the Apostle, that the essential grace of baptism is the life of Christ, and therefore that the communication of it is the regeneration attributed to the Sacrament.

---

[a] I. Peter, iii. 21.   [b] Rom. iv. 25.

With the doctrine thus elicited agree the effects attributed to baptism: remission of sins, salvation, and the gift of the indwelling Spirit, with His heavenly consolations as the earnest of our heavenly inheritance. For,

1. Since Christ gave Himself to be our ransom; since His name is Jesus, because "He shall save His people from their sins," it follows that the bringing His people into union with Himself gives them a title to the remission of the sins He came to take away. His oneness with them in the unity of the body is the meritorious cause of their pardon, transfers to them the virtue of His atonement, and secures their acceptance of God the Father. Hence St. Peter, preaching on the day of Pentecost, said: "Repent and be baptized, every one of you, in the name of Jesus Christ, for the remission of sins, and" (he added) "ye shall receive the gift of the Holy Ghost." And so Ananias to St. Paul: "And now why tarriest thou? Arise and be baptized, and wash away thy sins, calling on the name of the Lord."[a] So, too, baptism is called "the washing of regeneration," and Christ is said to "cleanse the Church with the washing of water by the Word;" showing that the idea of cleansing from sin by the grace applied in the Sacrament is inherent in the scriptural conception of the Sacrament.

2. The baptized are also said to be "saved," or, as the Church Catechism expresses it, "brought into a state of salvation," because by their union with Christ, their membership of His body, their adoption into the

---

[a] Acts, xxii. 16.

family of God, and the forgiveness of their sins, they are brought into that state in which, if they continue therein, they receive now the blessings of God's grace, and shall at last be partakers of the state of glory. For which reason St. Peter declares, "baptism doth also now save us (not the putting away the filth of the flesh, but the answer of a good conscience towards God) by the resurrection of Jesus Christ."

3. Finally, the possession of the grace of Christ brings with it a larger measure of the grace of the Holy Spirit; and this is specially connected with baptism in the passage above produced from St. Peter's sermon on the day of Pentecost. Nor is this the only passage where that connection is implied. In the light which is furnished by what has been said, we can cite here, as bearing upon this point, such passages as II. Cor. i. 21, 22: "Now He which stablisheth us with you in Christ, and hath anointed[a] us, is God; who hath also sealed us, and given the earnest of the Spirit in our hearts;" and v. 5 to the same effect, "Now He that hath wrought us for the selfsame thing is God, who also hath given unto us the earnest of the Spirit." And Eph. i. 13: "In whom (Christ) ye also trusted, after that ye heard the word of truth, the gospel of your salvation: in whom also after that ye believed, ye were sealed[b] with that Holy Spirit of

---

[a] χρισας, from χριω, whence χριστος. The Apostle, by the use of this word, intimates the communication of the grace of Christ, as is evident by his subsequent mention of the grace of the Holy Spirit.

[b] I believe the word "sealed" refers to the apostolic rite of confirmation, which always follows baptism.

promise, which is the earnest of our inheritance until the redemption of the purchased possession, unto the praise of His glory." What that promised grace of the Holy Spirit is, we learn from our Lord Himself: "I will pray the Father, and He shall give you another Comforter, that He may abide with you forever; even the Spirit of truth; whom the world cannot receive, because it seeth Him not, neither knoweth Him: but ye know Him; for He dwelleth with you, and shall be in you."[a] "Peace I leave with you, my peace I give unto you: not as the world giveth, give I unto you."[b] And so St. Paul, declaring the comfort of the regenerate: "Because ye are sons, God hath sent forth the Spirit of His Son into your hearts, crying, Abba, Father."[c] "The Spirit itself beareth witness with our spirit, that we are the children of God: and if children, then heirs; heirs of God, and joint-heirs with Christ; if so be that we suffer with Him, that we may be also glorified together. . . . Ourselves also, which have the first fruits of the Spirit, even we ourselves groan within ourselves, waiting for the adoption, to wit, the redemption of our body. For we are saved by hope. . . . Likewise the Spirit also helpeth our infirmities: for we know not what we should pray for as we ought: but the Spirit itself maketh intercession for us with groanings which cannot be uttered. And He that searcheth the hearts knoweth what is the mind of the Spirit, because He maketh intercession for the saints according to the will of God."[d] It is evident that this grace of the Spirit follows after and is predicated upon

---

[a] John, xiv. 16, 17.
[b] John, xiv. 27.
[c] Gal. iv. 6.
[d] Rom. viii. 16–27.

the baptismal union with the Redeemer, by which the Christian is regenerate; and that this gift is the earnest of his inheritance and the seal of his adoption.

In the chapter upon the grace of the Son, it was said that repentance, faith, and regeneration are the three elements of the Christian's restoration, corresponding to the three faculties of the soul, the heart, the mind, and the will. For simplicity of method, these three words were made to include the whole work of life. Repentance was considered, not simply as the sorrow for sin which leads us to forsake it—it was not merely the beginning, but it was the whole work of the Christian, constantly turning away from sin, and striving after good, continually fighting against temptation, and endeavoring to attain true holiness. It was defined to be the full, entire, and constant allegiance of the heart to God; and therefore it has a place in the regenerate life of the Christian, as well as in preparation for it. Faith was also defined to be the allegiance of the mind to God in Christ, and as such, it also was said to have its two stages, the one preceding regeneration, in which the Son of God is recognized as the Redeemer; the other, in which the Redeemer is known as *our* Redeemer, by personal appropriation of His grace, made over to us at our regeneration into His body. In like manner, Regeneration, in the large meaning required by its use to imply the full communication of the grace of Christ, was not limited to the baptismal act, but was made temporarily to include all the successive operations of that grace in the state of the regenerate, carrying forward the initial act of regeneration to the consummate fruition of the world to come. Here, however, we have arrived at the point where we can limit the word to its proper meaning, the initial communication of the grace of life, and refer elsewhere what relates to growth and continuance. Regeneration thus stands as a middle point in the work of restoration, separating the faith and repentance which precede from the faith and repentance which follow after the administration of the Sacrament. Thus we are furnished with the proper place in the system, of those other words used in the chapter on the grace of the Holy Spirit, conversion and sanctification. Conversion is the operation of grace, producing (the will of man concurring) the faith and repentance that precede regeneration; sanctification is the operation of grace which develops faith and repentance into the holy walk of the regenerate. The three steps of Christian progress are, conversion, regeneration, and renewal or sanctification. The Christian is first converted, then regenerated, then renewed or sanctified.

This statement of the progress of the work of grace in the soul, however, relates only to those who are baptized at mature age and on their own application. Of such persons, the Church is bound to require, before the Sacrament is administered, the profession of that faith, and repentance, and obedience which is the result of conversion. Upon the reality of the fact represented by the profession depends the fact of regeneration in the Sacrament; since unbelief, and sin unrepented of, are a bar to the action of regenerating grace. And it is material to observe that the reality of conversion is evidenced by the result, and not by any real or supposed consciousness of the *mode* in which

Sacraments in the System of Grace. 269

that result is attained by the grace of the Holy Spirit. The modes are infinite in variety—various as the resources of the Spirit and the needs of men; but the result is one—living faith and true repentance. This work, however, can be wrought only in those who have arrived at the age of moral consciousness. In all that has been written hitherto in these pages, the case of the adult has been considered throughout; for, as man fell in his maturity, the parallel was best drawn out between the fall and the restoration, by considering him as mature when he comes to his regeneration.

But it is not to be overlooked that the great majority of those who profess and call themselves Christians are baptized in infancy, before the age of moral consciousness is reached, and therefore when any conscious conversion, any actual repentance and faith is impossible. The question thence arises, Is the baptism of infants valid and operative to their regeneration? or is voluntary acceptance of the initial Sacrament such an absolute law that an advanced age and a conscious conversion are its universal and necessary antecedents?

It is not our purpose, for we have not the space, to go over the whole anabaptist controversy; but simply to indicate those considerations which flow from and bear upon the views here presented. The whole matter resolves itself into this: Regeneration being a free gift of God to man, obtained by no merit of ours, but gratuitously bestowed through the merits and in the body of Christ, conversion, as a condition precedent to regeneration in the adult, operates not to give a claim, but to remove hindrances set in the way of the saving grace of the Sacrament. It removes disabilities from the recipient. Actual sin and unbelief, persisted in, freeze the heart against the precious seed of the Divine life; repentance and faith open the heart to its reception. They follow from the fact that actual sin has been committed, and as antecedents of regeneration they are the removal of a bar. As far as they can, they undo the evil which the preceding years of the adult's life have been heaping up; they seek to drive out the evil, and so make room for the good. Their whole relation to regeneration as antecedent conditions, arises out of precedent actual sin. Now it is admitted, in the case of infants, that, prior to the age of moral consciousness, actual repentance and faith are impossible; but, on the other hand, actual sin is equally impossible. Original sin, indeed, is inherent, and this constitutes the need of regeneration; but original sin is no bar to the operation of the Sacrament, or no one could be made regenerate. Actual sin unrepented of, actual unbelief is the only bar. Hence, from what appears, there is no bar to the gift of regeneration to infants in the Sacrament of baptism.

Nor is there any reason against it in the statement that Sacraments are of voluntary reception. For, although infants, because of their tender age, are incapable of any voluntary activity, and therefore neither of actual sin nor of conscious repentance, yet they may, by the mercy of God, be made recipients of the grace anticipatively and preventively, subject to a subsequent ratification when they arrive at the age of moral responsibility. The grace is thus given to them, that it may, together with the influences of the Holy Spirit and the teachings of the Church, be present in their hearts at the very first opening of the moral consciousness; and thus the question of voluntary ratification of the covenant is presented in a more forcible way than if they were left to grow up outside the pale of the Church. For now, the question put to the person is not simply "Do you accept a grace which you have not had hitherto?" but "Do you ratify, or do you henceforth *reject* the covenant of grace in which you have heretofore been living?" Hence, for the express purpose of this voluntary ratification, the rite of confirmation was established by Apostolic authority,—a rite which obtains its significance among us from its position as the complement of infant baptism, the middle point between an involuntary baptism, and a voluntary communion. For this reason, pledges are put upon parents and sponsors on the child's behalf, bearing witness to the anticipative character of the Sacrament considered as a covenant between God and man, in which God grants the grace before He requires the other part, because of incapacity which does not involve actual sin;— holding man to his side of the covenant as soon as he is able to perform it, and binding, in the mean time, those who have the natural care of children to teach them their obligations within the covenant, that when the time arrives for them to ratify it in their own persons, by coming to confirmation, they may do so, or decline to do so, with a will fully advised of the tremendous consequences which hang upon their decision. Thus, while the voluntary character of the Christian position in the Church is preserved, the Sacrament of initiation and regeneration is granted an anticipative force and efficacy; nor is it to be doubted that those who are rightly baptized in infancy are truly regenerate.

If it be objected to this that infant incapacity for faith, repentance, and voluntary action constitutes an incapacity for receiving the grace of the Sacrament, and therefore for receiving the outward sign, it is replied that, in all consistency, such an objection must be carried further; it is equally an objection against the possibility of the final salvation of deceased infants by the merits of Christ. For infants, lying under the curse of original sin, must, if saved at all, be saved by the application of the grace of Christ. To assert their incapacity of receiving that grace, therefore, is to assert the impossibility of their salvation. But if they can receive it for salvation, they can receive it in that way in which it is appointed to be given, by sacramental communication. The grim and horrible doctrine will hardly be insisted upon, in these days, that infants dying, even unbaptized, will be found among the lost. But if they are saved by the merits of Christ applied in an extraordinary way, surely the argument is all the stronger that those merits and the grace of Christ may be applied to them in the ordinary way, by the use of the appointed means. For the objection to the use of the means rests upon the supposed impossibility of the infant's receiving the gift it conveys; and therefore, when it is shown that they may receive the grace for salvation, the objection falls to the ground, and there is every reason to conclude that they are proper subjects for the means by which that grace is communicated.

Hence, there is no limitation of age in our Saviour's

commission to baptize: "Go ye and make disciples of all nations, baptizing them in the name of the Father, and of the Son, and of the Holy Ghost." The command is to baptize all nations; and it is rightly argued that nations are composed of men, women, and children, that the command is universal in extent, and therefore that children are subjects for baptism as well as grown-up people. It is incumbent upon those who object to infant baptism to show some positive prohibition or limitation by which children are excluded from the Sacrament, and this they can never do. On the contrary, every inference is against such a supposition. In the first place, the Christian was grafted upon the Jewish Church, in which the reception of infants by circumcision was a practice inwoven into all the life and thought of the Jew by express Divine command, so that he could not conceive of a religious privilege of which his child was not the heir as truly as himself. We hear a question respecting the baptism of the heathen Cornelius; but one never could be raised respecting the eligibility of a Jewish child to all the privileges conferred in that Sacrament, when every Hebrew possessed his heritage of "the adoption, and the glory, and the covenants, and the giving of the law, and the service of God, and the promises" solely by the title of his infant circumcision. Hence St. Peter, in his sermon on the day of Pentecost, declares: "The promise is unto you, and *to your children*, and to all that are afar off, even as many as the Lord our God shall call."[a] Moreover, when we are told that Lydia

---

[a] Acts, ii. 39.

"was baptized and her household," that the jailer at Philippi "was baptized, he and all his, straightway," and that St. Paul "baptized the household of Stephanas," it requires something more than mere special pleading to make us believe that no children of tender age were members of the many "households" baptized by the Apostles. Besides, there are many precepts in the Epistles addressed to children as such,—to children of tender age,—commands to implicit obedience and the like, which are based on their membership in the Church,—that is, on their baptism. And though this argument admits that such children were so far advanced that they could understand and receive these precepts; yet it implies that they had been or might have been baptized previously to that development of the understanding. For the command of implicit obedience to parents is not only based upon immaturity, but it is the very first moral commandment under which children come; it enters their understandings at the very budding and opening of that faculty; and therefore implies a baptism preceding all conscious responsibility, as the ground of children's being in the Church to be addressed by the Apostle.

In view of these facts, it can admit of no doubt on the part of those who truly believe the promises of our Lord and the teachings of Holy Scripture, that persons baptized in infancy, as well as others who receive the Sacrament without bar to its efficacy, are regenerate; and it is our duty as believers not to seek to invalidate this conclusion by irrelevant considerations, but reverently to study, with the effort to remedy, those facts which obscure the truth in actual experience. It is matter of deep regret to the truly Christian heart, that the lives of some Christians baptized in infancy do not correspond to the calling of the regenerate; that, in cases altogether too numerous, the falling short, it is to be feared, continues to the end of life; that, in other cases, the soul does not develop a religious life until a comparatively late period. On the other hand, however, the cases are neither few nor hard to discover in which the Christian life goes on from the beginning to its full development, in a continuous course of progressive sanctification. The question is, Can the facts of adverse experience be harmonized with the doctrine of baptismal regeneration as taught in Holy Scripture and held by the Church? It is certainly our duty, if they can, to seek for, until we discover, the principle on which they are accounted for.

1. That very many persons do go on under the full Gospel system to lead the life of the regenerate from the very first opening of consciousness, being trained from their earliest infancy, by the care of pious parents, by the ministrations of the Church, by the leading of the Holy Spirit, to obey the teachings of the Divine word,—the inner life of imparted grace thus receiving its proper culture and all the conditions of its growth —is a happy fact, which proves at once the adaptation of the Divine system to the needs of men, and its efficacy, when operative in all its parts, to work the complete restoration of fallen humanity. These examples of a whole life spent in the service of God convert faith in the Divine word into actual experience of the truth there set forth. We see and know those who thus have calmly and consistently advanced in a true

Christian course,—having their faults, and failings, and lapses, it is true, but on the whole making constant progress, bringing forth in fair abundance the fruits of the Spirit, and giving, in all their lives, the demonstrative example of true piety. Of the baptismal regeneration of such persons there can be no question. And, building upon this foundation, the Divine Spirit works a constant, gradual sanctification, transmuting the earthly nature into the likeness of the heavenly seed, and enabling that seed of life to assimilate to itself, by gradual growth, all the powers and faculties. In this way evil passions and tendencies are nipped in the bud as fast as they appear; and thus *conversion* (which, whether as a sudden crisis or a gradual change, is the condition precedent to the baptismal regeneration of the adult) is entirely absorbed in the process of sanctification. The change which takes place is simply the passage from infantile unconsciousness to mature consciousness, the opening of the sense of responsibility and position, and the apprehension of the fact that the young Christian is and has been a child of God. This is the fact which is represented by confirmation at the proper age, when the child of God takes upon himself publicly the obligations of which he has become conscious, and claims for himself the covenant with God, the benefits of which he has received in anticipation of this his ratification.

2. Others, however, are endowed with regeneration in infant baptism who do not thus use the gift, whose religious life does not proceed forward thus steadily and continuously. A long time elapses before they show any appreciable signs of the influence of Divine

Sacraments in the System of Grace. 277

grace, and it is not, perhaps, until late in life that they are brought to live up to their Christian position. In some cases they never realize this position. Members of Christ, they are diseased; children of God, they are disobedient; inheritors of the kingdom of heaven, they are spendthrift of their heavenly inheritance. The natural heart holds sway over the conduct, and the outward life is a life of sin. This state continues for a longer or a shorter period,—ten, twenty, thirty years from the beginning of consciousness; at length they are converted to the obedience of faith, and finally saved, or, fearful to think, they are cut off in their sins. What is the case with these? Have they ever been really regenerate or not?

Now, having been once baptized, and baptism being the only appointed means of obtaining the gift of regeneration, the fact of their having been baptized precludes the possibility of their ever being regenerate, if they be not so at their baptism. For there is but "one baptism."[a] Nor, however they may have fallen short, if brought to obedience at last, can we think that regenerating grace has been lost and restored in the intervening time. "For it is impossible for those who were once enlightened, and have tasted of the heavenly gift, and were made partakers of the Holy Ghost, and have tasted the good word of God, and the powers of the world to come, if they shall fall away, to renew them again unto repentance." Hence we must understand that other causes are at work which prevent the assimilation of the Divine life, the seed of

---

[a] Eph. iv. 5.

grace remaining, as it were, quiescent, and the mercy of God continuing it in the soul, until the result is at length attained, or until the day of grace is past altogether.

The parable of the barren fig-tree declares to us the dealings of Divine grace with these persons. "A certain man had a fig-tree planted in his vineyard: and he came and sought fruit thereon, and found none. Then said he unto the dresser of his vineyard, Behold, these three years I come seeking fruit on this fig-tree, and find none: cut it down; why cumbereth it the ground? And he answering said unto him, Lord, let it alone this year also, till I shall dig about it, and dung it; and if it bear fruit, well: and if not, then after that thou shalt cut it down." The meaning of this parable is plain. The fig-tree is "planted in the vineyard;" the fruitless man is a member of the Church. He has life in him; it is not yet taken away; but he bears no fruit. The Divine life is inoperative, and meanwhile the natural life bears its fruit of sin (a fact for which, from the nature of the case, there is no parallel in the figure). The owner of the vineyard is God the Father; the vine-dresser is God the Son, whose priestly intercession avails to continue the day of probation, and to defer the final excision. The appliances of husbandry are the external influences and internal grace of the Holy Spirit and the Church, stimulating the sacramental life into activity, even after the lapse of a long time of barrenness; while the implied attributing of moral unfitness to the unfruitful tree points to the true source of failure in the perverseness of the human will.

We learn, therefore, that the grace of regeneration

may remain for a longer or a shorter time, like the seed in frozen ground, quiescent. And yet by the mercy of God, and His long-suffering, it is continued to the individual, and permitted to retain its vitality. So long as it thus remains he is a member of the Church, capable, if he will, of repentance and conversion and sanctification. But in the mean time, as has been said, the natural life brings forth its fruit of sin, and the fearful spectacle is presented of members of Christ, who are actually living the life of the world, engaged in the service of the devil. In the quiescence of the Divine life, rank weeds of a worldly growth fill the whole field of the heart, and require perhaps a bitter experience of severe culture to uproot them, and bring the will into obedience to the holy impulses of the true seed of the word.

The first principle which accounts for the actual life of persons regenerate in infancy is the truth heretofore insisted on, of the dependence of regenerating grace upon the other parts of the Divine system for growth and development. A seed planted within, it requires, besides its own inward vitality, the outward conditions of air, heat, light, moisture, adaptability of soil. It requires the teachings of Holy Scripture, the ministrations of the Church, the training in the law of God, as well as the grace of the Holy Spirit; it requires obedience of the will to these influences to bring forth fruit. By this consideration the whole practical difficulty of believing the truth in the face of apparent experience is met. For in how many cases is it matter of experience that the baptized child is left to itself without careful training and subjection to religious instruction by the negligence of parents and sponsors, exposed to the bad influence of improper company,—the heavenly life thus being cut off from its proper sources of nourishment, and the opposite tendencies of the fallen nature flourishing in full vigor! God has organized His Church for a definite work in bringing forward the individual member on his Christian course. On the principles laid down in the last chapter, He has assigned it a place in the complete system of His economy among all the influences which bear upon the Christian life, and subordinate to this place, He has assigned a place to every member of the Church, an influence of each on all, telling definitely on the result. Parents, sponsors, teachers, associates, as well as clergy, have a part in this influence, the greater while the subject of it is immature; what wonder, then, if these rest in the simple baptism and neglect the baptismal training, that the grace of regeneration is dwarfed and choked, and the heart is overgrown with the thorns, weeds, and nettles of the world, the flesh, and the devil? Add to this, that the total effect of all the influences, internal and external, of Divine grace, is to raise the will of man to a condition of freedom, not to *coerce* him against himself to right; and therefore that it is left in the power of every regenerate Christian, whether baptized in infancy or at adult age, to reject the grace of God and to neglect the duties of his Christian position;—and add further, that amid the diverse characteristics, and peculiar tempers, and various temptations, and the hidden nature of much of the inner spiritual experience of men, a correct judgment of the actual standing of the Christian is not always attainable; and it will be seen that the apparent want of fruit on the part of those persons now under consideration is fully accounted for without the sweeping assertion that they were never regenerate.

It is a part of the meaning of that profound illustration of our Saviour's, of the inscrutable nature and infinite variety of the Holy Spirit's operations, "The wind bloweth where it listeth, and thou hearest the sound thereof, but canst not tell whence it cometh, and whither it goeth," that the Spirit meets such cases of post-baptismal delinquency by special providences of grace. He strives with them in numberless ways; He brings them, sooner or later, if they will follow Him, by a path they have not known, to a realization of Christian privileges and Christian responsibilities. It is in vain, as has been said, to attempt an enumeration or classification of the experiences by which men are thus brought to realize and live up to their position. Suffice it that, whether the way be smooth or rough, the experience calm and gradual, or violent and sudden, the result is a conversion subsequent to regeneration, similar to that which precedes it in persons who are not baptized until adult years; the effect of which is to call forth the baptismal life, hitherto quiescent, into a holy activity, by which the outward conduct is controlled and moulded to the will of God, and the soul made capable of progressive sanctification.

But if this be not the case—if the grace of regeneration, whether imparted in infancy, or at a later period, do not, under the influences of the Spirit and the Church, germinate and fructify; if, by a perverse will, all these influences are resisted to the end, their final excision takes place, the grace of regeneration is withdrawn, and the reprobate Christian becomes, in the fearful figure of St. Jude, "a tree whose fruit withereth, without fruit, twice dead, plucked up by the roots." "If a man abide not in me," says our Saviour, "he is cast forth as a branch, and is withered; and men gather them, and cast them into the fire, and they are burned."

In view of these considerations, we conclude that baptized children are regenerate; since it is easier to believe that man loses his privilege by sin than that the Sacrament of Christ should fail.

"The grace which we have by the Holy Eucharist," says Hooker in the beginning of his thoughtful and profound disquisitions upon that blessed Sacrament, "doth not begin, but continue life. No man, therefore, receiveth this Sacrament before baptism, because no dead thing is capable of nourishment. That which groweth, must of necessity first live. If our bodies did not daily waste, food to restore them were a thing superfluous. And it may be that the grace of baptism would serve to eternal life were it not that the state of our spiritual being is daily so much hindered and impaired after baptism. In that life, therefore, where neither body nor soul can decay, our souls shall as little require the Sacrament as our bodies corporal nourishment; but as long as the days of our warfare last, during the time that we are both subject to diminution and capable of augmentation in grace, the words of our Lord and Saviour Christ will remain forcible, 'Except ye eat the flesh of the Son of Man, and drink His blood, ye have no life in you.'"

Sacraments in the System of Grace. 283

In this paragraph the place of the Holy Communion as a means of grace is stated with a clearness and a fulness which could not be excelled were it expanded into a volume. The Sacrament is ordained for our present life of imperfection and warfare. It is supplementary to Baptism, because the grace of Baptism is subject to loss from our lapses and sins. It was given for the purpose of supplying the waste of the spiritual life, and of carrying it forward to its full growth. It has, besides, other uses, as an act of worship—the highest which the Church on earth can offer to the Father; being (as the name "Eucharist" implies) a sacrifice of thanksgiving for the one great Atonement, and being also a memorial for the confirmation of faith in our Lord Jesus Christ, "until He come." But as this is not intended to be a complete treatise upon the Holy Eucharist, it is sufficient now to consider it under the view presented in the passage quoted from the judicious divine, who never more merited the title than when he wrote that part of the fifth book which treats of this Sacrament.

Now, as we have proved baptism to have relation to the grace of the Son, and as the Holy Eucharist has relation to the same still more clearly, it being, according to St. Paul's phrase, "the communion of the body," "the communion of the blood of Christ," it is necessary first to understand how the Scripture distinguishes the grace of the latter Sacrament from the grace of the former.

Baptism is the Sacrament of the Christian's initiation into life; hence the grace of baptism is called "life" and "regeneration," as well as a "washing" and "cleansing." The Holy Communion is the Sacrament of continuance; and for that reason the grace is represented under the figure of food, as "the eating the body and blood of Christ,"—food being the natural means of nourishment, continuance, and growth. The grace I conceive to be the same in either Sacrament; only that the one Sacrament is appointed by our Saviour to be the means of initial communication, and the other of constant addition, in such manner that the partaking of communion necessarily presupposes antecedent baptism.

What is to be understood of the grace in itself as signified by the name "the body and blood of Christ" it is not necessary to speculate. The whole invisible part of the Sacrament, on its Divine side, is a transcendent mystery, which cannot be reduced to the conceptions of the mere understanding. The truth is revealed to us under the figure of "body and blood;" but at the same time we are informed that these words are not to be carnally understood: "It is the spirit that quickeneth, the flesh profiteth nothing; the words that I speak unto you, they are spirit and they are life." That Christ communicates Himself by means of the Sacrament, as He does in Baptism, by the operation of the Holy Spirit, with saving efficacy to those who receive Him in repentance, and faith, and charity, is all that we know, or can know.

The various theories which have been framed in the attempt to render conceivable *the manner how* this communication is made are equally destitute of authority, and lead to dangerous results. There is no scriptural ground, and no ground in human reason for either the Romish transubstantiation[a] or the Lutheran consubstantiation; the former of which, as is well known, supposes the communication of Christ to the receiver to be made by the miraculous withdrawal of the "substance" of the bread and wine, and the substitution therefor of the "substance" of Christ's body and blood; the latter being divested of its "sensible accidents," and those of the bread and wine remaining as if the substance of bread and wine were present. Consubstantiation is a modification of this doctrine to the effect that the "substance" of the bread and wine remain, and the "substance" of Christ's body and blood is mingled with it, within the local limits of the elements. Nor is there any scriptural evidence, or evidence of any other character beyond the mere ingenuity of theorizing, for the other hypothesis, known to theologians as "impanation," which supposes that Christ assumes to Himself the bread and wine to be parts of His body and blood, so that receiving them we receive Him. These all are but theories, destitute of any ground, and to be shunned by humble, thoughtful Christians.

---

[a] It would be interesting to count up how many different shades of meaning are comprehended in this word as it is understood by the individual members of the Church of Rome—beginning with the gross materialism of the Irish laborer, and going upward to the refined and philosophic realism of such minds as that of John Henry Newman. It raises a shrewd surmise that the Church of Rome favors multitudes of opinions, provided the dry word is retained, in order that she may affirm any for purposes of persecution, and deny any for purposes of defence.

But while theories of the manner how are thus doubtful, it is not at all doubtful, but most certain, that Christ does communicate Himself by means of the Sacrament. And since this communication is a spiritual act, for which there can exist in human language no name, except such as is transferred from matters pertaining to this life, it is named an eating and drinking of the body and blood of Christ,—the mode of speech being taken from the means by which Christ has appointed that the grace shall be received. Thus far we are safe in our understanding of Holy Scripture, which uses singular caution in speaking but very few times of this great mystery. For when our blessed Saviour says: "Take, eat, this is my body;" "Drink ye all of this, this is my blood," His meaning is explained by St. Paul: "The bread which we break, is it not the communion [*i.e.* the partaking, the means by which we partake] of the body of Christ?" "The cup which we bless, is it not the communion of the blood of Christ?" —thus showing that when the bread is called by our Saviour His body, it is called so in the same way in which the spiritual act is called an eating—the visible part of the Sacrament taking a title from the invisible part, and the invisible act being named from the visible.

It has been much disputed whether the sixth chapter of St. John's Gospel refers to the Sacrament or not. That chapter contains our Lord's discourse in the synagogue at Capernaum on the day after He had fed the five thousand with the five loaves and two fishes, one year before the formal institution of the Lord's Supper. In this discourse our Lord holds the following language, rising, by successive assertions, higher and higher in mystery, until He tries to the utmost the faith of those who hear: "Verily, verily, I say unto you, Moses gave you not that bread from heaven; but my Father giveth you the true bread from heaven. For the bread of God is He which cometh down from heaven, and giveth life unto the world." "I am the bread of life: he that cometh to me shall never hunger; and he that believeth on me shall never thirst." "I am that bread of life. Your fathers did eat manna in the wilderness, and are dead. This is the bread which cometh down from heaven, that a man may eat thereof and not die. I am the living bread which came down from heaven: if any man eat of this bread, he shall live forever: and the bread that I will give is my flesh, which I will give for the life of the world." "Verily, verily, I say unto you, except ye eat the flesh of the Son of Man, and drink His blood, ye have no life in you. Whoso eateth my flesh, and drinketh my blood, hath eternal life; and I will raise him up at the last day. For my flesh is meat indeed, and my blood is drink indeed. He that eateth my flesh and drinketh my blood, dwelleth in me, and I in him. As the living Father hath sent me, and I live by the Father: so he that eateth me, even he shall live by me. This is that bread which came down from heaven: not as your fathers did eat manna, and are dead: he that eateth of this bread shall live forever."

The Romish divines argue that these declarations refer to the Sacrament: and thence that the eating the wafer and drinking of the cup are the eating and drinking the flesh and the blood of Christ; and thence, again, that the bread and the wine are transubstantiated into the body and the blood of Christ. Some Protestant writers, on the other hand, deny that they refer to the Sacrament at all, and hold that the exercising faith in Christ, at any and all times, is the eating and drinking of this chapter. The unwary theological student may be misled, if he rely simply upon detached quotations, respecting the position of the best divines of the Church of England. For there is a third and middle ground, which shuns the error of both extremes, and upon which the writers of greatest authority stand. The Roman Church misleads by the ambiguity of the word Sacrament. We might assent to the statement that the chapter refers to the Sacrament, if the word be taken in its widest sense, including the invisible as well as the visible part; but, having beguiled us into this admission, Rome immediately restricts the word to the narrower sense of the visible sign alone; and thence argues that the visible sign is the thing signified—thereby "overthrowing the nature of a Sacrament, and giving occasion to many superstitions."[a] To obviate this confusion of unwary minds, it is to be understood and remembered, that the declarations in question did not, at the time they were uttered, refer indeed to the Sacrament, because that was not yet instituted; *but they referred to that invisible grace and communication of Himself, which our Lord intended to bestow by means of the Holy Communion, having the design to institute the Sacrament at the proper time.* They referred not to the sign, but to the thing

---

[a] Article XXVIII.

Sacraments in the System of Grace. 289

signified by it—to grace which was not then, but which was afterwards connected with the sign, and which therefore is received (not ordinarily by faith at all times, but) by faith determined to that special act of obedience which our Lord imposed by the command, "Do this in remembrance of me."

And in proof of this we need only to consider together the two facts: that the Holy Communion was not yet instituted when our Lord spoke these words; and that, on the other hand, when St. John recorded them, the Eucharist had been established, and of constant weekly[a] celebration in the Christian assemblies for nearly seventy years. From the first fact it is to be inferred that our Lord was not then speaking of the Eucharist, as such, but of the invisible grace of communion with Himself; and this is further corroborated by His express disclaimer of a carnal eating of His flesh and blood, such as would necessarily follow from the Romish hypothesis of transubstantiation: "It is the spirit that quickeneth, the flesh profiteth nothing: the words that I speak unto you, they are spirit and they are life." But from the other fact we are obliged to infer that though the body and blood of Christ are not themselves carnally eaten, yet they are spiritually received by means of, and in connection with, the carnal eating of the bread and wine. It was not for nothing that the record of this conversation was withheld by Divine Inspiration from the earlier Gospels, and so re-

---

[a] See Freeman, "Principles of Divine Service," for the proof that the Eucharist was of weekly and not daily celebration in the Primitive Church.

served until the constant celebration of the Eucharist had moulded the whole Christian thought to the full faith in its mysteries.[a] The men who had for seventy years (like the saintly Polycarp) been weekly recipients of the Sacrament, and who had at every celebration heard the words of institution repeated, could not help but understand St. John, when they read this chapter, to refer to the spiritual grace of the Sacrament. "Here," they would say, "is the requirement, 'Except ye eat the flesh of the Son of Man and drink His blood, ye have no life in you.' By what means can we eat and drink, and so have life? Surely, this sacramental participation of the bread and wine is the means appointed by which we can fulfil the requirement. In this place, He tells us of a benefit; in the other place, of the means by which that benefit is secured." Trained as they had been by constant participation, according to the established custom of the early Church, such would have been their instinctive reasoning, leading them to connect the sixth chapter of St. John with the Sacrament. And this, we are compelled to believe, was St. John's understanding of the import of the chapter. Both writer and reader, and (with all reverence we may add) the Inspiring Spirit also, agreed in this connection; otherwise in St. John's Gospel, the loftiest of all the inspired writings, no allusion is made to this central act of Christian worship and means of Christian grace. On what grounds can we account for the absence of all direct mention of the institution of

---

[a] St. John's Gospel is admitted to have been written near the close of the first century.

the Lord's Supper from the Gospel of "the disciple whom Jesus loved," except this, that the Apostle, knowing when and to whom he is writing, considers it to be sufficiently alluded to in the record of the discourse which declares so fully the nature and the necessity of its grace?

The sixth chapter of St. John, then, with the Evangelical accounts of the Institution, and St. Paul's account of the same, and exhortations founded thereupon in the Epistles to the Corinthians, together with a single sentence in the Epistle to the Hebrews, "We have an altar whereof they have no right to eat, which serve the tabernacle," compose the sacred literature treating directly of this Sacrament. From it we learn, as has been said, that Christ does communicate Himself in a way transcending human understanding to the members of His Church. The gift is a spiritual gift, the food is living food. "The words that I speak unto you, they are spirit and they are life." It is called "His body and His blood." It is therefore a communication of Himself as one who has been dead. "I am He that liveth, and was dead; and behold I am alive for evermore." He communicates Himself also, specially as regards His humanity, to which His body and blood belong. These are necessary inferences from the Scripture statements under consideration. Further than this, our thought upon the mystery is negative; we may be able to define in what it does not consist, as we can say that the infinite is not finite; but we are, with the light afforded in this present life, unable to grasp it in its positive being.

It is more profitable to inquire what are the effects or

benefits of the communication of the body and blood of Christ. From the above analysis of the ideas certainly contained in the Scripture language, we may safely assert that the effect of Christ's communication of Himself to the faithful recipients of His Holy Supper is the transfer to them of all His communicable attributes required by their necessities,—of the virtue of His life, and death, and resurrection, and immortality in the body. These consist in three things: first, the saving and expiatory virtue before the Father of the acts He performed in the body—of His meritorious life and death as an atonement for our sins; secondly, the spiritual powers of His exalted nature, as a risen and living and spiritual perfect nature, so far as they are needed to meet the necessities of our present existence; and thirdly, the seed of our future resurrection and immortality, which we derive from Him, and His indwelling in us.

These effects can be made out directly from Scripture. 1. The phrase "His body and blood," symbolized separately, the one by the bread and the other by the wine, together with St. Paul's teaching, "As often as ye eat this bread and drink this cup, ye do show the Lord's death till He come," connects the reception of the Sacrament with the death of Christ, at which His body and blood were separated, as they cannot be in a living person. Hence He communicates Himself, as bearing with Him the attributes of His death, and if so, especially that attribute of vicariousness which was the very cause and reason of His death; and therefore it follows that He gives the virtue of His death and all His atoning acts as an effect of participation in Himself by means of the Sacrament. 2. The communication of spiritual life and power is contained in the declaration: "As the living Father hath sent me, and I live by the Father: so he that eateth me, even he shall live by me."[a] 3. And so is the power of the Resurrection in the following: "Whoso eateth my flesh, and drinketh my blood, hath eternal life; and I will raise him up at the last day."[b]

Now all these gifts are, in a certain sense, initially bestowed in baptism; but they are more fully and perfectly bestowed in Holy Communion. For in saying that the Eucharist is supplementary to Baptism, we are not to be understood as if it were but a mere addendum to it, but rather its full growth and perfection. It is its supplement, as being greater than it, as filling it out, and, as it were, absorbing it into itself. Baptism is the foundation; Communion is the superstructure. Baptism is as the root; Communion is as the fruitful plant. For the Christian life, which has need of communion after baptism, is a life of growth,—the waste to be repaired is the waste of a developing life,—just as the physical nourishment of the growing child is a supply of the waste of growing limbs, which are *restored* to a greater size and strength. Hence the correspondence between Baptism and Communion, and their mutual relation. As the baptized communicant is penitent, he receives continual assurance of pardon by the atonement; as he is faithful,[c] he is granted power to live

---

[a] John, vi. 57. [b] John, vi. 54.
[c] I would have it constantly remembered, that in speaking thus, the faith spoken of is "faith working by love."

more truly according to his allegiance; as he is regenerate, he is advanced in the possession and power of the life eternal.

The total conception of the Holy Eucharist is threefold, corresponding to the threefold office to which our Saviour was anointed. It is a Memorial, a Sacrifice, and a Feast,—a memorial left us by our Prophet; a sacrifice authorized by our Priest; a feast provided by our King. It is in its entireness the act by which we make good our claim of the Anointed One to be *our* Prophet, *our* Priest, *our* King. We are learners in His school; sinners seeking His intercession and absolution; subjects bound to His rule, and dependent upon Him for subsistence. Each view is full of thought, which here can only be hinted at in passing, as we press forward to the close of this book.

1. It was the office of Christ, our Prophet, to teach the truth of His Father, and to take the most effectual precautions against the quick forgetfulness of mankind. While upon earth, He had few disciples, and they feeble and obscure. When He ascended into heaven, He gave promise of a second Advent to judge the quick and dead. After His ascension, His few disciples became His organized Church by the reception of the informing Spirit; and the term of its present organization is the interval between His first and His second coming. In that interval it is her mission to increase and spread, and carry over the whole earth, her memory of her Redeemer. But in His absence there is danger of forgetfulness which must be guarded against. In the midst of earthly wants and pursuits, the disciples of Christ might become absorbed in en-

grossing cares, choked with the deceitfulness of riches, entangled in the world, and forgetful of the word of life. Christ provided against this loss of His truth. First, by the written word,—the records of His life, and the Apostolic commentaries on His teaching. But this, though invaluable to regulate faith, was not alone sufficient to implant it,—inasmuch as a mere volume might be treated with neglect. It could not search out for converts; it must be sought unto. Hence, secondly, by the ministry, who were set apart to the sole and exclusive work of building up believers in the faith, and urging it upon those who were not yet converted. But even the ministry might be neglected, unless the Christian believer were bound to them, and with them to Christ, by some necessary bond. Hence, thirdly, the Sacrament, instituted as a memorial,—minister and people united thereby in the bonds of faith with the Redeemer, of whom the one is to preach, and in whom both are to believe. "This do in remembrance of me." It is the distinctive worship of the Church, as an act of faith, the constant memorial before God of Christ, our prophet, priest, and king.

2. Correspondent to His office as Priest, it is a Sacrifice. Not as Rome affirms without authority, "a propitiatory sacrifice for the living and the dead;" nor yet, as the direct opposite, the mere commemoration of a sacrifice once made; but a true Eucharistic sacrifice,—a "*sacrifice of thanksgiving*" for an atonement fully made, and a propitiation perfect and sufficient. The propitiatory sacrifices of the Law, needful as types before the oblation of the Cross, are now and forever abolished. "The blood of bulls and goats which could

never take away sin," is no more to be sprinkled upon the altar of burnt offering; because "Christ being come, an high priest of good things to come, by a greater and more perfect tabernacle, not made with hands; neither by the blood of goats and calves, but by His own blood, has entered in once into the Holy Place, having obtained eternal redemption for us." But the sacrifice of thanksgiving, the Eucharistic sacrifice, is not so abolished; it is still offered up a true sacrifice, the memorial of a completed redemption. The priestly act of the minister in the church on earth, the broken bread and the outpoured wine, offered up upon that "altar whereof they have no right to eat which serve the tabernacle," unite with the priesthood of our Lord and the sacrifice of His body and blood on Mount Calvary; the merits of which enable us, as "a royal priesthood," to "offer ourselves, our souls and bodies, a reasonable, holy, and living sacrifice unto God," the prayers and thanksgivings of devout worshippers being mingled with the incense of His intercession, who "hath an unchangeable priesthood." Thus, as the Eucharistic memorial confirms our faith, the Eucharistic sacrifice strengthens our hope, through the assurance it gives of an all-sufficient ransom.

3. In its relation to the Kingly office of our Saviour, it is a Feast. In this view, it is more especially connected with the subject of these pages. What has already been said respecting the communication, by means of the Sacrament, of the Body and Blood of Christ, belongs to this part of the transaction. This appeals to our charity, as the others to our faith and hope—the memorial, to faith; the sacrifice, to hope;

the feast, to charity;—and all to earnest Christian work for our own salvation, and the salvation of the world.

Now the Feast of the Holy Eucharist enters as a factor into our religious life in a twofold way. It is the reparation of a loss; it is also the monitor of Christian progress. We are continually losing, little by little, by our voluntary and involuntary slips and failings, our baptismal grace,—and that, notwithstanding the great help afforded by the grace of the Holy Spirit; even though the Christian may be actually making progress in sanctification, and in the ability to bring his actions more and more near to the Divine standard of duty. This may seem a paradox; but, theoretically, it is strictly true, and lies at the foundation of a correct, practical view of the relation of the Eucharist to our spiritual needs. The illustration before used may help the reader to comprehend the fact the more readily. The Christian in the present life may be likened to a growing youth, whose frame enlarges by daily increase, while his system constantly wastes by the wear of muscle and destruction of tissue. Were the waste permitted to go on unchecked, notwithstanding the growth,—nay, because of it,—death would soon supervene. So in the spiritual life. Every act, inasmuch as it partakes of imperfection through the still remaining "concupiscence" of the regenerate nature, is an element of waste of the baptismal life; because it taints the soul with sin by reason of its imperfection; while yet, since it is done through grace more perfectly than the last, it marks growth in grace; just as bodily exercise promotes the waste and the growth together. Hence, it will at once be seen, the Eucharistic participation bears the same relation to the soul that the natural food does to the body.

Life and death are the two terms of spiritual existence. Death is not annihilation. It is not for us to conceive the fearful ultimate reality of eternal death; and our prayer to God is that we may never know the meaning of those awful words; but we know that it is not annihilation. The soul is immortal, and yet it may die,—nay, without Christ, it is dead. "Dead in trespasses and sins," it is out of God's favor, cut off from the influences of the Holy Ghost, out of the harmony of all the world, corrupt with all manner of sin, and subject to the vengeance of the Divine wrath. The death of the soul, then, is a state of total sin, with all its terrible consequences. On the other hand, the state of life is the state of righteousness communicated by regeneration in Christ, and preserved in continual and progressive sanctification. Between these two points, *total* death and *perfect* life, lies the interval of Christian being; and this may be traversed from life to death, by imperceptible steps, as well as by bold leaps. When a person becomes regenerate, the change from condemnation to pardon is instantaneous,—it is God's act of a moment; but it would be strange indeed if persons fell entirely from the grace of regeneration in opposition to the strivings of the Spirit, as quickly as it was wrought in them by His power. When one sins after regeneration, so as to die forever, that death is the sum total of all his sins unrepented of. One sin might have been repented of and forgiven; but sins persisted in and repeated bar the heart at length against repentance and against mercy. A course of sin, then, is the downward road from life to death. The great and deadly sins are the acute diseases which lead immediately to the catastrophe; the waste of the soul is the sum of the imperceptible, involuntary sins of ignorance, of omission, of commission, of nature, of carelessness, which each of us, day by day, commits. Now, were it not for our Lord's provision of Divine food and nourishment of our regenerate life, by the grace of the Holy Eucharist, this waste would go on without any repair until the soul died of inanition, the baptismal life being (as it were) entirely expended or withdrawn.

This constant waste, or tendency to death, is inherent in our fallen nature, though regenerate, and therefore it is, in a way, mixed up with our progressive advance in holiness of outward life. For, to recur to our illustration, the youth, if he were in a consumption, would continue growing in size of frame, while yet he was wasting of the disease; so the Christian, without the constant nourishment of the grace ordinarily given in the Holy Communion, might, so far as his acts of obedience and endeavors after holiness of walk would avail, be really growing in personal sanctification; while yet the lapses and imperfections attending even his best efforts would have a reflex action upon his baptismal life, which can only be adequately represented by that figure of waste. It is true that to attempt to state this, formally and scientifically, may provoke a demurrer; but when we come practically to verify our experience as it exists in our own consciousness, we accept these two apparently contradictory facts as the ground of our religious thought and conversation. We speak, as prompted by experience, on the one hand, of our many faults, and failings, and lapses, we confess them as sins, and sorrow for, and repent of them; but, on the other hand, we hope that we are growing in grace, that we are gaining in sanctification, and living daily more and more as it becometh the children of our Father in heaven. We find, *practically*, no contradiction in these statements; they cohere perfectly in our experience; and therefore they may be accepted when stated scientifically as well as popularly.

The explanation of the apparent contradiction consists in the distinction between grace given and grace (so to say) assimilated. We have shown that grace may remain, as it were, quiescent, as, for example, in baptized infants, before they have reached the age of moral consciousness. It is necessary, in order that the Divine life may assimilate to itself the nature and being of man, that he should act under its impulses; the acts of the Christian life are, as it were, the kneading and compounding into one mass of the Divine and natural life of the soul. By this means the Divine life grows into the full-formed plant of Christian virtue. But, in the process of the assimilation, there are, as it were, counter-currents in the circulation; the perfection of the Divine life flows into the soul's natural life, purifying and sanctifying it under the auxiliary influence of the Holy Spirit; but, on the other hand, the faults and imperfections of the actions of man react upon the inflowing current, mingling with it the corruption of our sins, and thus, to that extent, absorbing and destroying it, so that new supplies must be drawn from the fountain of life by the Sacrament of Communion.

It is not intended to assert that when baptized Chris-

Sacraments in the System of Grace. 301

tians are placed, by the Providence of God, in such situations that they cannot receive the Holy Communion, their life of regeneration is subject to total decay, and themselves to eternal loss, while yet they are endeavoring to grow in the grace of sanctification. It is distinctly laid down that the Sacrament and the grace of the Sacrament are different; and, therefore, in such cases, where the want of the Sacrament is providential, and beyond the control of the person himself, God will convey the grace by other and invisible means, nourishing and replenishing the baptismal life. But the ordinary means of this spiritual nourishment, for the great mass of Christians who are not in exceptional situations, is the Sacrament of Holy Communion. By this means, received in repentance and faith and charity, the members of the Church of Christ are fed with His body and blood, they receive constant renewals of the baptismal life, they are cemented more firmly, "as living stones" into the "temple of His body," they are united more closely with Him, as their Redeemer, and obtain the gift of all the communicable attributes which are implied in the partaking of His body and blood.

The benefit of the Holy Communion, therefore, as a means of grace, is twofold: firstly, the replenishing of the baptismal life, thus repairing our spiritual losses; and secondly, the carrying forward our sanctification to a higher point; aiding in the growth, as well as restoring the waste of the soul's life. For sanctification is, as has been already shown, the assimilation of the conduct and the active powers of the Christian to the Divine life, under the influence of the grace of the Holy

Spirit, which is to the Divine seed, as air, light, heat, and moisture are to natural plants. Hence, unless the Divine life be replenished, as oil in a burning lamp, it cannot advance the work of sanctification. There will be a point where the loss in one direction will balance the gain in the other; and then, as the waste will continue without any correspondent gain, the life cannot be stationary at that point, but must recede on both lines. Hence, though sanctification is the work of the Holy Spirit, which does not depend on Sacraments for its exhibition, it cannot advance, except on the condition that the baptismal life is fed with Eucharistic nourishment. The baptismal life must be kept up to its original vigor; and the active life must advance beyond its former attainments, as the condition of worthily partaking of the Lord's Supper.

By this course of remark, we arrive at the qualifications set down by the Church as requisite, in those who come to Communion, and the reasons for them. "What is required," it is asked in the Catechism, "of those who come to the Lord's Supper?" The answer is: "To examine themselves, whether they repent them truly of their former sins, steadfastly purposing to lead a new life; have a lively faith in God's mercy through Christ, with a thankful remembrance of His death; and be in charity with all men." It has been made matter of objection to the Church, that she makes Christian effort, by the doctrine of baptismal regeneration, to be the effort to regain a lost innocence.[a] The

---

[a] E.g. Robertson's Sermons, vol. ii. p. 81. In that sermon, it is true, he calls it the Romish view; but he does so to discredit it by misnaming as well as misstating it.

representation is not a true one. It is the attempt to replenish the baptismal graces, but it is also the endeavor to advance in active holiness beyond all that we have reached hitherto. The two are inseparable. Hence the required qualifications: firstly, repentance for the sins which have caused the loss; secondly, faith and charity, the fruits of precedent sanctification, and the ground of further advancement. For unless there had been sin, and therefore loss, there would have been no need of repentance; and unless there had been a measure of sanctification, by the grace of the Spirit, there would be no possibility of faith and charity.

The Holy Communion, therefore, is the keystone of the arch of Divine grace, which binds in its place all the parts of the system. It is the means of the Christian's perfection, and has its place in the Church on earth, as the representative of that reward which is reserved for the saints in the heaven above. For that reward will consist in the cleansing body and soul from all the last remains of sin; in perfecting sanctification; and in giving the soul to feast forever on the glorious vision of God. The Holy Communion is in each particular the representative of the end. It follows, therefore, that as the object of life, as a whole, is the attainment of final blessedness, that object will be accomplished if every part of life be lived in the endeavor to be the worthy recipient of each successive Holy Communion.

And thus we are brought to the last thing necessary to be noticed in this treatise: that the grace of the Holy Spirit is auxiliary to the grace of the Son in this respect also.

It is made sufficiently plain that the prevenient grace of the Spirit is auxiliary to the grace of the Son, in converting the sinner to the right frame of mind and heart for the reception of Holy Baptism. The aiding and sanctifying grace of the Spirit, in like manner, has for its object the making the Christian a worthy recipient of the Holy Communion. For without that grace, moulding and controlling the active life, and enabling the baptismal grace to take root in the soil of the heart, neither the repentance nor the faith, nor the charity required is a possible thing. And inasmuch as the communication of the life of Christ, in its highest degree, is the gift of the title to heaven, and the power which reconciles us to God the Father, the grace of the Spirit has wrought its full effect when it has sanctified the believer for the reception of the body and blood of our crucified Lord, by which "He dwelleth in us and we in Him."

The threefold grace of the Holy Trinity is the pardoning, justifying grace of the Father, the redeeming grace of the Son, and the sanctifying grace of the Spirit. And the relation of each to the other is that the grace of the Spirit prepares us to receive the grace of the Son, and the grace of the Son admits us to the grace of the Father; having attained which, we have joy and happiness forever. The grace of the Father enables us to *become*, the grace of the Son enables us to *be*, and the grace of the Holy Spirit enables us to *live* as the children of God.

THE END.

www.ingramcontent.com/pod-product-compliance
Lightning Source LLC
Chambersburg PA
CBHW022111230426
43672CB00008B/1346